WISDOM'S DAUGHTERS

Conversations with
Women Elders
of Native America

Written and Photographed by

STEVE WALL

Editor and Advisory Consultant ▾ Harvey Arden

■ HarperCollins*Publishers*

HarperCollins books may be purchased for educational,
business, or sales promotional use. ▼ For information
please write: Special Markets Department, HarperCollins
Publishers, Inc., 10 East 53rd Street, New York, NY
10022.

FIRST EDITION

Designed by Principia Graphica

Library of Congress Cataloging-in-Publication Data
Wall, Steve.
     Wisdom's daughters : conversations with women
    elders of Native America / written and photographed by
    Steve Wall; editor and advisory consultant, Harvey
    Arden.—1st ed.
       p.   cm.
    ISBN 0-06-016892-7
     1. Indians of North America—Women. 2. Indians of
    North America—Religion and mythology. I. Arden,
    Harvey. II. Title.
    E98.W8W27   1993   92-54753
    299'.7'082—dc20

93 94 95 96 97 ▼ / CW 10 9 8 7 6 5 4 3 2 1

To B. J.

She taught me
the meaning
of love

CONTENTS

ACKNOWLEDGMENTS

Some time ago an elder told me, "We are a part of you." Over time I have come to realize how true her statement to be. So I give thanks to all the women in my life. Had it not been for some I would literally not be here today. Through their sharing, patience, tenderness, frankness and absolute honesty my eyes have been opened and I can truly say that I know real love.

One person cannot accomplish anything alone. We are all interconnected and it takes many to make anything a reality. This book is no exception.

Credit must go first of all to my family. B. J. put up with me, edited the first drafts and shared her wisdom during the entire process. Lisa and Chris were always there with love and encouragement and never minded being used as sounding boards.

Others contributed to this book as well. Chief Leon Shenandoah, Tadodaho of the Iroquois Six Nations Confederacy, sustained me with his friendship and continuous encouragement. Guy Crowe trusted me before he really knew me and continued trusting me afterward. Carl Bergman, a master artist in photography, put aside his own work to take the time to skillfully print and help expertly edit my photographs for this book.

My heartfelt appreciation goes to Hugh Van Dusen, Executive Editor of HarperPerennial. I have never met a person of such stature. His spirituality and sincerity radiate.

Gathering the material and working on this book has made me more mindful that we are, indeed, a part of each other. I am most thankful for all of those who have contributed to and enriched my life.

FOREWORD: THE TIME OF THE WOMAN

"I know what you're doing. Word gets around."

I didn't even notice when she sat down beside me. With a smile permanently etched across her face, she appeared much younger than her years. Her eyes sparkled with a hint of mischief, yet clearly reflected a distance of miles a lifetime of experiences has a way of revealing. There was just a knowing about her, even a little intrigue. She was the type of person you could swear you had always known.

Being the straightforward person she was, it was obvious she had something on her mind. With her there was no superficial exchanging of pleasantries, although we had met earlier at the traditional gathering we were both attending.

"There are forces at work most of us do not want to acknowledge," she started. "Only now do you understand enough to be given these things. I come to you on the feminine side, because *this is the time of the woman,* time of the feminine. We have our prophecies, and these things must come out.

"Spiritual communications come through the feminine side. Oh, there is nothing wrong with the masculine side. Action is masculine. Producing is masculine. But, there must be balance. When one listens to that gentle voice within, there is balance. But! Be careful. There are two voices; that's just the way it is. Always listen to the good voice, the one that speaks softer. The other voice is dark and tries to rule, make you do things that raises the temper, makes you selfish, feel hurt.

"Everyone comes into this world with a work to do, and there are special forces to guide in accomplishing that work. To truly do this work with the purest expression, you must be with the spirit, mentally and physically," and she put her two index fingers side by side, raised them up to her eye, and pointed them outward right at me.

Then she continued, "That's what we as traditional Indian people try to live by, what our ceremonies are all about.

"Most never really touch the spirit, because they cannot get past the physical." Then she paused, clapping the palms of her hands together.

In a split second, in a flash, I was aroused, sexually. There was no controlling the surge rushing through my body. It felt as if six pair of hands were fondling my body and leaving me in a quandary to understand where this stimulation had come from.

She laughed out loud. "Like I said, you can have a connection, and it can be stimulating but not be physical. You don't even have to want me, and yet I can get through. There are forces!" she said, raising an eyebrow and giving me a quick, piercing glance and whispering, "Most never really touch the spirit, though. That's too bad.

"Others can't get past the mental … the logic of things.

"So, the spirit goes wanting, but it's there. Women know it's there. Some are starting to recognize and acknowledge it. Men better, too!

"Until everyone acknowledges the spirit, there will be much unhappiness, wars, all kinds of drug abuse, want, desires, hunger, unfulfilled love. There will be all kinds of violence against each other, against animals, against the earth and all of creation. These problems all produce hurt in the long run.

"Everyone has a path. Everyone! To be on your path you must understand the connections, have love and respect. To be off of that path, there will be pain and confusion no matter what else you do. That goes for a country as a whole, and the world. That is where we are today. See what is happening all around.

"Things are changing. This is the time of the woman. She's here whether she can be seen or not, you can count on it. We are in the age of receiving and that's feminine. Receiving inspiration through creativity is feminine.

"We as Indian people have never forgotten the status of women. Those who have gotten away from the traditions may act as if they don't remember, but all of us know inside. Our memories are long, as long as the line of the generations. The elders have always passed on this knowledge. We have been told to never forget. So we remember and pass it on, too. With us there is no past, everything is now, and the only future is the generations to come.

"So we continue the ceremonies. To participate in them is to participate in the circle of life ... the whole circle—seen and unseen. They remind us to maintain balance, to live in peace with each other, to honor the Creator, the earth, and to acknowledge and show respect for those forces I told you about.

"Some people have no ceremony anymore. To have no ceremony is to fail to remember just where human beings are in the creation."

Nodding fondly in leaving, she added, "I know what you are doing. No need for my name. This has come from the elders, and I can't accept any of the credit."

And she was gone, leaving behind only the lingering warmth of her presence and the echo of her chuckle.

For a long time now I have continued to hear the words of that powerful yet gentle woman. They keep coming back no matter where I am or what I'm doing. They are more than just a part of the memory of that October encounter. I hear *her* words in *her* voice, especially what she said barely above the din of the gathering as she walked away: "You have heard the words of the elders, now all you have to do is take them to heart and pass them on."

PREFACE

I am a journeyer, a crosser of boundaries. For nearly a decade I journeyed behind the Buckskin Curtain with writer Harvey Arden, meeting with scores of Native American spiritual elders, recording their words of wisdom and ancient philosophies, photographing their families and communities.

After completing what would become the book *Wisdomkeepers* with Arden, I stumbled, seemingly my path disappearing before my eyes. Searching for direction, I remembered the gentle words of an elder long ago appealing, "We have to find our own path. The Creator only gave each of us one. So that's the only path we got. Sometimes it's hard to see. But it's there, always there right before us. Look closely and thank the Creator in advance for making it clear."

Soon, even without my knowing why, I once again found my path leading back to the Wisdomkeepers. This time the trail would guide me to the Indian women, the clan mothers, faithkeepers, mothers, and grandmothers—the matriarchs of Native America. They are the carriers of life, transmitters of sacred knowledge, the keepers of ancient ways, the hearts of the nations. Through them the generations pass and the wisdom of the ages flow. Highly venerated in their culture as the conduit connecting the worlds of the past with the now, they are revered for giving life, both physically and spiritually, to the world to come.

Within moments of entering the world of *Wisdom's Daughters* and starting the process of closing the door on the theater of my misconceptions, I realized I was at the deepest level of human discourse. Like others before me, I thought I was looking for secrets, but secrets are dull—the open, freely given truth is transforming.

In my crossing of two boundaries at once, the gulf between man and woman and the boundary from white to red, I have finally traversed frontiers from which there is no return, for I have learned, much to my surprise, more about being male than being female and more of what it means to be white than Indian.

By going to the women—call it a spirit-journey into my own soul—I have been to the well that boils with life. I have walked with them as they shared their inmost feelings, listened as they passed along the words of the elders who have gone before them, sat with them as they took me seven generations into the future, and participated, by invitation, alongside them in numerous ceremonies. I am convinced that the Indian prophecies are true. It is, indeed, the time of the rising of the feminine.

Now the work continues. I find myself off to the Andes seeking the way to the condor among the indigenous people of South America. More journeys to make, more boundaries to cross.

We give thanks to Mother Earth because she still fulfills her original instructions, providing for the health and welfare of the people and other life forms in the world.

So, right up to this time Mother Earth never failed us. And so we continue to be thankful to her.

Then, in the nighttime we see, sometimes, our grandmother, the Moon. She, also, is given a duty to regulate the cycles of the female life forms all over the world. Also, she directs all the waters in their movement.

And she has never neglected this duty. And so we are especially thankful to our grandmother, the Moon, for working with the female cycle of the earth.

Excerpt from the
Hotinonshonni Thanksgiving Address,
recited by Tekaronianekon
(Two Skies Together),
Mohawk Nation

The women emerging are the hearts of the nations.

Megisi
Turtle Mountain
Ojibway Nation

WISDOM'S DAUGHTERS

TEWA ▾ TESUQUE PUEBLO

Vickie Downey

IN THE BEGINNING were the Instructions. We were to have compassion for one another, to live and work together, to depend on each other for support. We were told we were all related and interconnected with each other.

Now people call our Instructions legends because they were given as stories. But to the Indian people, that was like a reality at some point in history. So most of the Indian nations that we know of, they have their own story of where they began. Some will tell you they came from the sky, from the stars. Some will say they emerged from the earth or they emerged from a lake as a people. In that emerging, it's almost like they were choosing their language, choosing dress style, songs, their dances.

So that was the beginning.

The Instructions during that time, at the beginning, were to love and respect one another even with all the differences, different cultures, different languages.

We were told we were all from the same source. We were coming from the same mother, same parents.

The Instructions was to live in a good way and be respectful to everybody and everything. We were told if the Instructions were lost, then harm would come to the people.

In the beginning we were given our Instructions of how to live. So that's been handed down from generations to generations until now. "This is how to live."

We were told to be good to one another. Respect one another. Take care of each other, as well as ourself. These are some of our Instructions. As long as we do what we're supposed to do, these are the basic important things, then we have no problems. Once we start hating our neighbor and start stealing from our neighbor and start lying to them and not growing our food but depending on somebody else to grow the food, that's when we unbalance ourself. That's what the legends, our stories, tell us.

At some point the stories tell how we made a mistake somewheres. Like Coyote, in the stories, always is the trickster, and he's the reminder to our people not to go in that same direction. That's why we have those stories so that we can pass it to the children so they can understand their own mistakes.

Now, in some parts, we're not doing our stories, because there's the television, and it's taking the place of the storyteller. So the Instructions aren't being passed down.

PIECING TOGETHER OUR GRANDPARENTS' WORDS

Now we have more books, more television, we have more communications, and we have more transportation to get from one place to the next, and, yes, in my generation, we can see this now. In my generation we have to piece together what our grandparents told us. Not particularly telling us, well, this is what's going to happen in 1992, 1991, or the year 2000, just telling us, "If you don't do these things, you're going to run into problems."

We didn't foresee the problems, but as we grow up we know; we recognize what the problems are.

THE ANSWER IS PRAYER

The base of all things is just love, respect.

Everything's so simple, and we make everything so complicated. That's why we're confused.

All we have to do is be simple again and things will work out for us.

The answer is prayer. Keep praying.

The important message for the world right now is for everyone to pray for the earth now. We, especially the female, can feel her because of the situation she's in, the struggle she's in, and what she has to do to heal herself; we can help her and we can also help ourselves. Think about her and ask for assistance for her, because whatever she goes through we will go through.

The women are feeling it now, and the pain is getting intense. Tears are coming down. The feelings and the constant struggle in our individual communities adds to her tears. It just feeds that struggle. It gets very hard to carry that. It's like a load that we have to carry.

WE HAVE TO TAKE RESPONSIBILITY

We want people to take responsibility and not put blame. As Indian people we're not blaming white people. We have to take responsibility.

I have to say, "Yes, I'm responsible."

We must forgive and forget, and at the same time we have to acknowledge the elders. They're poor, but they're still fighting for land, and they're fighting to preserve the earth. They're struggling. People have to acknowledge what is happening and ask, "How do we change?"

People carry selfishness; they carry greed. The environmentalists ask Indian people for their philosophies, for ideas, for help, but then they go out and do it on their own. They never bring the Indian people in. The mentality that Indians can't be trusted is still there.

RELYING ON THE SPIRITS

We rely on the spiritual world for our protection. We listen. The spirits, they're our guidance. They tell us it's time. It's time to speak out.

SEEKING THE VISION

During the time when Jesus was around, he went out and fasted for forty days and forty nights, and he had his vision. It's like that in the Indian culture. We fast. Abstain from food.

We abstain, don't give anything to the physical. We have our body, then we have our spirit, and then we have our mind. Those three things connect.

So in order to reach the spirit, we have to abstain from food and water. Then we'll get to our spirit. That's our prayer.

The prayer is just reaching a state of mind where you acknowledge your spirit. Prayer is coming into a frame of mind or into that spirit, your own spirit. When you come there, you feel that compassion, or you feel that love which is the base, the source where you came from.

GIVING THANKS TO THE CREATOR

You give thanks before you even receive your gifts from the Creator. When you ask, you give thanks. Your prayers are thanksgivings for everything—the sun, the moon, the snow, the water, the fire, the rocks. You see them as being alive, having a life of their own. A tree has its own life, but look how many trees are massacred at Christmas.

ACHIEVING AWARENESS

In our language we have a word that means two things. It means to listen and then it almost means to behave. So when we're behaving, we're listening, and that's the awareness. We're aware of things happening around us. We're training ourself to do that. By listening all the time, not just listening with our ears, but listening with our eyes, we're observing things. Our mind must stay aware of what's going on. It takes practice.

People have to practice that awareness to come to that place in their mind, in their thinking, in their lives. If we can teach our children while they're still young to be alert and be listening all the time, then they can avoid some of the confrontations that can come to them.

Trying to teach our children, it's hard now because we have to compete with the television. We have to compete with the radio and the fashions, the sports, and everything that's out there for them. The video arcades, the movies. It makes it hard to make them aware. Whereas before we didn't have that. Then the kids knew they had to, like, bring in the wood, or they had to go hunting, had to clean the snow when it came into the house. They were part of that working, working together, doing things together. But now we don't have that. So we have to deal with that.

HOME AND THE CHANGE WITHIN

For me to change, I guess, it was experiencing what it's like outside of my own community and going back and remembering my grandmother, the kind of life

she lived. It was seeing like how New York City is, the fast-paced life out there, the coldness that's there with people arguing. There's no Good Mornings, Good Afternoon. All people are rushing around and there's anger. You can see the anger.

You get in a taxi and you're going so fast, people just rushing somewheres. And the crime that's out there.

I'm trying to understand why people stay there, and yet people tell me that they love that city, that's their home. So I respect that.

When I was young I was confused and wanted to get away from what my grandparents were telling me about tradition. I didn't want to deal with that. So I would get away, and I would learn so much. Then I appreciated what I had at home. But when I came back home, I would want to change things here. People weren't ready for that. So I would get really frustrated, and I would leave again. Then I'd come back. It was like that for the longest time. Until finally, now, I'm home and I feel good. I feel happy. I feel safe. And I deal with whatever problems we have here. I work with it.

Now when I go somewheres, I'm not really looking forward to it. Yet, I always tell myself I'm home wherever I go, because that's part of the earth. When I go someplace, I take whatever from here and try to share it with that place, give them something. Then, I come back and, also, deal with whatever I brought back here.

When you come back home you just feel the peacefulness.

AIDS AND THE INSTRUCTIONS

Right now, the AIDS disease is affecting everybody. It's here, and what it's showing us, the reason it's here, is to show us how to love. So out of loving each other, we'll cure that disease. Love is the answer to everything.

If there's a person with the AIDS disease, you give him that love to let him know that he's, he's being loved no matter what he's got and no matter how much the disease is threatening to you. You still love that person so that he can, in order to heal himself, have that love. He has to have that love to get rid of that disease.

If you give him fear, if you're afraid that you're going to contact and get his disease, then you're just instilling in that person that fear for his own life. If you feel sorry for him, then he's feeling sorry for himself, and he doesn't need that. You just give him love.

In the Beginning, We Were All Related

At the beginning of time we came from love. We were all related. There was a time in our legends where they say that we could talk with the animals, and they would understand us, and we could relate to each other. Somewhere in time we disobeyed the Instructions, the universal law, so we couldn't communicate anymore. So we came away from love.

Now we're at the point where we don't respect each other, we don't love each other. There's racism, prejudice, injustice. When we come back to love, it will make that whole circle again. Only love for each other can save mankind.

Love is being open and being able to accept the other person as a part of you. Everybody and everything. It goes back to the feeling; you feel for that person.

It's easy when we get angry to strike out at somebody, but it's very hard to love somebody that is hurting us. That's what it takes, though, is that love to change that person we don't like.

I mentioned AIDS, but there's natural disasters like that earthquake in California caused the bridge to fall on those people. It brought people out to help. All over, people just came and helped. Sometimes it takes that to bring people together to help each other, to take care of each other. Unfortunately, after the tragedy is over, we go back to struggling for ourself and earning money for ourself. Maybe it'll take some big disaster for people to understand and say, "Oh, that's what the Indians were talking about."

OVERCOMING HATE

When I was younger, I would read the history books about what happened to Indian people. What it did to me was it hurt me so much, and it made me so angry, and because I was so young, that anger was towards all white people. I hated them because of what they did to the Indian people. But growing up and learning, I learned to accept that, and then I learned to love that race or that nation, even though it's still going on. I send love to them no matter what is still going on. It's hard; it's hard to do that.

We can fight prejudice, injustice, and hate with love and respect. These are our weapons.

It's harder to love than to hate. Yet, nothing can stop love. There is no weapon that can stand up against love.

Love is the medicine for all the ailments that we have. That is the medicine. That's the cure for the earth, also.

The lack of love for each other is what's hurting the people, hurting the society, hurting the nations, and that's where all the wars and all the disease comes from. The thing that is doing that is ignorance.

A PLACE OF PEACE FOR ALL PEOPLE

Just because we're Indians don't mean we are on the bottom of the ladder. We're equal to all races of people. Why can't people understand that?

We must work together, side by side, to create a world of peace for all people, all children of the world. Then there will be that love, that unity, and compassion, and sharing, but as long as we have that ignorance we'll be unbalanced. We'll have all these things to worry about forever. That forever can go into lives after this one, because when we die, when our physical body dies, our spirit continues to go on. We continue and will have turmoil in that life. Then there's no peace there. We're creating trouble forever just because we don't have that love.

PROBLEMS BETWEEN MEN AND WOMEN

One problem many have to deal with is between men and women in relationships, in marriage. Sometimes there's abuse, both emotional and physical. They're both harmful. Lots of times, whoever, they don't want to get out because of the fear of what's outside. There's insecurity. So fear and ignorance are the big problems, but in abuse you don't stay and take it. Sometimes there's no alternative but to separate, to get out. That takes courage, but you have to do it. When you get on the other side of the problem, you look back and see you did it, and you know you are stronger.

Some stay in the relationship and say it's because of the children. Really, that is not the best reason to stay. You have to really look at it hard. It may be better for everybody that you separate. Everybody has to deal with these things and do the best they can, but each experience is to learn from and grow from.

RELATIVES IN THE STARS

In the Indian's thinking, the earth is the mother and the sun's the father, and we have all our relatives in the stars in between, our brothers and sisters.

The earth, she's sick because of the corporations going in with their machines, cutting down trees or digging the minerals out of the earth. Those are the bones of Mother Earth, the lifeline. The minerals are like organs of the human body. The earth has been torn apart. It's like somebody going and doing surgery on a person. So she, like, she's very sick and she's very tired. She's upset. And she will heal herself, in her way. She will have to heal herself, because her children are not paying attention to her.

We see what's happening. She's healing herself right now. That's what we see in the changes. A lot of water coming. A lot of wind. A lot of the earth moving, eruptions of volcanoes. So she's healing herself.

As people we have to do the same thing. We have to acknowledge, either as individuals or as groups of people, that we did do wrong to the Indian people and to the earth.

TIME OF THE FEMININE

It's the time of the feminine. With a woman it's what we feel. When I look around at different women, I see sadness and a heaviness in themselves. What they're experiencing is what the earth is experiencing—her sadness and her heaviness because of the way her children are living today. Women, they have that; the feeling is there in their hearts more so than the male people, 'cause the male is always doing things. The male also has to realize that he has a female part to him, and he has to start feeling that same feeling.

Women have to be recognized. The words of women have to be recognized.

The women will come out. It might be prophesied or doesn't have to be prophesied, but the feeling is so strong that the women will come out and voice their feelings. Whether people want to hear it or not, it's going to come because it's meant to be. It's that time.

Most women can't comprehend what it is. They feel it. It's like a depression, so they go to psychiatrists, therapists, trying to figure it out. Or it turns into physical ailments. Feelings into physical ailments. So they don't know. They know something's going on, but they can't pinpoint exactly what it is.

As a people, as native people, we're trying to do our best to tell the world this is what's happening to you. This is what's happening to us. This is what's happening to the earth. No matter how many words we give them, how many books we give them, how much information we give them, it won't help them until they finally decide, "Well, I'm going to accept this. I am sick. I am a sick society. I am a sick world. I am a sick person."

When we do that, then we can heal. Then we turn around and we help each other. Then we won't have homelessness. Then we won't have hunger. We won't have wars. But until that time, and if that time doesn't come, then there's that handful of people that will be saved because of what they know. And the rest of the world will just go with the wind, with the water, in the fires, whatever.

GIFT OF THE INDIAN PEOPLE

We Indian people, our mentality is: we give and it'll come back. It'll come back in a different form, but it'll come back. It might not be material, we might get it in a spiritual form, but it'll come back. It'll make that circle.

In the non-Indian mentality, you're … I guess it's that fear, maybe, that fear that you protect yourself and you don't worry about the others. You're looking out just for yourself. That's what you run into when you don't have the elders, 'cause people are always moving. There's no time.

Also, with the non-Indian world it's like a question mark. You question everything because, I guess, you have to have an answer for everything—a logic, thinking in that logic. Whereas we, sometimes, we don't question, but we rely that there is something that will take care of us. It is in the back of our minds, it's there, that knowledge that things will work out. We might be struggling with man or something or we might be struggling with financial difficulties, but yet we know it'll get clear. We just rely on prayers to do that for us.

The non-Indian, he thinks with his mind. The Indian thinks with the heart.

If you look at it that way, also, the female is closer to the heart. The male is more toward the mental. He can put the mental into the physical.

It's easy for women to relate to the spirit, because they can feel directly.

MEN WITH SPECIAL TRAITS

In every person there is the male and the female. In some males, the female is more dominating the male part of themselves. That is where the characteristic comes in with some males wanting to do women's work or talk like a woman or walk or act or whatever it is.

Long time ago that was looked at as something special, a gift. So we accepted that person as a part of whatever else was going on. If he wanted to stay at home and work instead of go hunting, we respected that because that's how he felt. So there was no discrimination in that way. But in this time that we're at, people always put labels on things. So there's another label. If you're that way, you're different. You're considered sometimes bad.

CHILDREN OF THE TURMOIL

With the young kids, they are feeling the turmoil. They don't understand it, and we can't tell them what is really happening. If we do, they'll think about suicide or they'll try to run away. They'll have to deal with it. The world will have to deal with the seriousness we're in. It can't be gotten away from. It's like a wound in a person; we have to clean it. We have to clean it and heal it.

Right now what people are doing, they have a wound and they're just putting a bandage on it. That's not going to help, 'cause that infection is still there. So we have to acknowledge that infection. We have to acknowledge that pain and then we start healing from the inside out.

THE SPANISH BROUGHT THE PRIESTS WITH THE SOLDIERS

About our religion, yes, we've kept that alive even with exploitation that came in and tried to wipe out our religion. We've maintained that. Among the Pueblos there's a church in each pueblo. With the Spanish they brought the priests along with the soldiers. Together they tried to exterminate our communities, our villages, our spirit. But we've maintained our way to this time. It's been a struggle, but we've maintained it. A lot of the other Indian reservations, they've also maintained it.

With some Indian nations the religion was completely taken from them. So now the only religion they have is the church religion or the Christian religion— Baptist, Protestant, Catholic, whatever. They practice that, and they practice it with a spirit in there that it puts to shame the religion that the non-Indian people have, the churches that the non-Indian people have. Go to an Indian community that has a church, and they go practice in that church. Those poor people have the spirit in that church, whereas a lot of the other ministries don't have that spirit. It's all for that monetary reason that they create these churches.

INDIANS RELATE TO GOD

We can relate to God; it's not something long time ago. It's like now. Also, we can relate to Jesus. He's like real. He's not from a thousand years ago. He's now. Since he was once alive, his spirit still lives. To us, we call them spirits. It's an unseen force. That's what we believe in. The spirits, to us, are just as real as flesh and blood. Why can't everybody else believe that?

It's not the church itself that's wrong. It's the people in it. If the people are willing, you can bring that spirit into any building, any church, any structure.

We don't have many participating in the church anymore. And a lot of them disagree with the way things are going in that church. We do have some people that are completely saying they want nothing to do with the church. We have that group. Then, we have some that will only participate on special days like Christmas, Easter, and then, we have some that are loyal to that every Sunday. Some of the elders are in that group, loyal; they're there all the time.

My sister is completely out of it. Her family will have nothing to do with it, even though she was baptized. I'm like, ah, I would say I'm in between, where I go when I can, and not just Christmas or Easter.

The way I see it is that I see the spirit in it. I know there's a spirit present there in that building. The priest we have is not a very good one. He still has ideas that are very kind of like obsolete. He judges people. In order to change that, I have to be there to help him see. I can understand all sides, because I was part of saying that I didn't want to have anything to do with the church. I stepped out of it for a long time. At that time, which was only like in the early seventies, the majority of the people were in church. So there was a few of us that were stepping out.

Now that I'm back in there, I see that the majority of the people are out of the church.

NON-INDIANS COME LOOKING

Many non-Indians come looking for something, while some are like tourists. You collect those people that are sincere and you work from there. Like when you're going to plant a seed, you put that seed in there and then you take care of it. You water it and nurture it, give it love and everything. Then it grows into a plant. That's what we have to do, whether it's in education or government or our own families. We have to plant those seeds and start over.

INDIANS AS ELDERS TO THE WORLD

The Indian people are the elders of the non-Indian. They haven't been respected in that way. Now some people are realizing that and they want to learn· We have non-Indian people coming to an Indian elder and asking him for directions, and the Indian elder is willing to give those non-Indian people directions. But as soon as the non-Indian people receive those instructions, they think they are qualified to do a sweat lodge. So they go ahead and do it without really understanding the process of how the spirits come in.

In our ceremonies we know spirits do come in. So, we're afraid for people. They can bring in spirits, too. Sometimes it's not good spirits that come in. Bad spirits can come in, and harm can come to the people in there. That's the danger of that unbalance, whereas we're aware and try to balance it out. That's the harm in instant medicine people or non-Indian people wanting and looking for religion, because some have that power to bring in those spirits.

Remember, we're spirit, we're body, and we are mind. As a people we try to be as spiritual, we try to be with our spirit as much as we can every second of our lives. With the non-Indian people it's more a physical thing, take care of the physical body. They don't really think about the spirit as being part of that.

INDIAN RELIGION, GOD IS YOU

You may say the non-Indian's religion came from outside, like God being out in the sky somewheres with His kingdom and the people being down here trying to work their way up to heaven. Whereas

in the Indian sense, God is you, in you, part of you.

And that's our beginning, our Creation when we first were created. So we carry that with us, and we teach our little ones while they're still little how to pray. We have our ways of teaching them how to pray and so they see that.

When we do a dance, it's a part of our prayer. We're dancing, but we're also praying at the same time. Or, even when we have stick games, lacrosse games, games, you call them games, and you're having fun, but it's also part of a prayer. Your spirit, your physical, and your mind are all in there together. It's not separated. You're not just doing something physical. Your mind is praying and your spirit is there and it's all connected. It's not separated.

The way the American society is, is that you separate and you label everything. You've got to have a term for this, and you create these words that are really big words when what it means is something very simple and very short.

BEING AN EXAMPLE BY THE WAY WE LIVE

It's very difficult to help our children. It's very difficult because it's like two cultures clashing and there's no connections between the two. The best we can do is instill in the children the pride of who they are and what they have and where they came from. We give them that; we continue through legends, through love, and through food, and just being an example by the way we live. Be an example so they can see with their eyes, when they hear songs, when they feel feelings of love.

So when they have to go to school and deal with math and English, science and social studies, they still have that in the background, and that will carry them through in their lives to whatever experiences they have; it will be reinforcement. Something will come into their lives, and they will say, "Oh, yeah, my grandmother used to do that," or, "My grandmother used to say that." It reinforces.

When I was a young child, some of the elders used to say, "You have to go to school. You have to learn what they're teaching you."

I didn't want to go to school. I didn't want to learn what they were giving me, but in the back of my mind, I said, "The elders are saying it, so there must be a reason why they want us to learn." The elders could already see, they could foresee that we were going to need to be able to read books. We were going to need that information for a certain time in the future. So now, I can see why, because now we have to deal with the society we live in. We have to think like that society in order to continue to survive.

PEOPLE HAVE A NEED TO FIND THEIR HOME

The real problem today is that people have a need to find their home. That's what they're searching for, but actually home is just right within themselves.

To get there you have to work on yourself, then with your immediate family, a wife and children, if you have them. That's who you work with. That's where you start your education process—teaching each other, respecting and loving, sharing.

LOOKING AT CHILDREN AS TEACHERS

Most people look to the elders as teachers. They are. But we also look at the children, look at them as teachers.

We study life. Our life is studying. We study everything, everybody, even the tiniest insect.

Like the other day, we noticed that the ants went into the house early. So what does that mean? We study that. We watch the ants or the bees or the trees.

Every second of our life we're studying everything around us. The sounds. The music. Outside our culture people don't have that awareness. We have to bring that awareness back. It's just being in tune with the spirit. So what people have to do now is be in that awareness.

RETURN OF THE WHITE BROTHERS

We have questioned among ourselves, Why did all these things happen? Why did the colonizers come? What we are beginning to understand is that we have to go through these experiences. In the long run, like the prophecies where they say our two white brothers are going to come back, well, we're seeing that.

Our white brothers are coming back. As long as we keep the Instructions till when they come back, we will be able to guide them. When the hippie movement came in the sixties, that was part of that coming back of the white brothers.

Some say that the hippie movement was crushed by the drugs. But you have to ask, Where did the drugs come from? Were the drugs put there to divert the energy? Who was in the background on that? Maybe they feared the movement.

There is good and evil, a battle. So the evil continuously tries to disrupt or do things to divide. But in the end, evil can never crush the good. We have to all follow the Instructions and use that power in the prayer.

CHUMASH

Juanita Centeno

TEARS FLOODED HER EYES and rolled uncontrollably down her cheeks. Trying to talk about the valley, she found great difficulty getting the words to come out right. Even with my face buried in my hands and my heart racing, moved by her emotions, I could still see the sculptured majesty of the golden California hills rising from the gently sloping floor of the valley. The lazily meandering river, twisting and turning in broad sweeping curves, had nurtured the land for centuries, creating a veritable inland sea of wildflowers the imagination could not even measure.

I listened as Juanita led me along a narrow path through this indescribable paradise of fragrances and colors, frozen momentarily in time and space by the pink-oranges of the setting sun. Somewhere along the way an elderly man, carefully watching his steps, feebly rushed along trying to keep his happy, playful little granddaughter in sight.

"Gone! Gone!" The words, "Gone! Gone!" came again, echoing off my euphoria and clouding my view of the vision unfolding before me. As if from a dream, I was being forcefully pulled by Juanita's waves of sobs from a place I did not want to leave. I dropped my cupped hands from my face, and suddenly, I was at the kitchen table I had never left. I was back to reality, back on the Santa Ynez Chumash Indian Reservation near Solvang, maybe twenty-five miles from Santa Barbara, back in Juanita's tiny government-financed modular home in a neighborhood of concentration-camp–style modular homes built not fifteen feet apart and crammed together on a clay bank under the shadow of former President Ronald Reagan's Rancho del Cielo or Ranch of the Sky.

My shock at her reality didn't faze Juanita. The vision was playing on, still flickering in her water-filled, bloodshot eyes. She had been telling me about the valley, about the flowers, her grandfather, herself. Then, she looked right through me and said, "The Valley of the Flowers. Now there's no more, there's no more flowers."

Wiping away more tears, Juanita added through sobs, "We had our flower festival here last year, in June or July; people didn't come. Why should they come?

In the fields that we used to have of flowers, just condominiums all over now. There's no room for the flowers anymore. It's just a sad situation. It's a mess.

"And people should pay attention. Today there's murders, kids shooting each other, kidnaps, everything is happening. Destroy nature and you destroy yourself."

The Valley of the Flowers is gone, never to be again, and few are left who can remember. For Juanita it's not a matter of remembering, however. She lives it. The valley permeates her life, and she walks among the flowers and smells their fragrances today as she still races ahead of her grandfather on that narrow footpath. I count myself among the privileged, because although mine was only a dream journey, I, too, have been to that valley, experienced the exhilaration of the fragrances, and marveled at the river of flowers seemingly flowing to the sea.

In a valiant attempt to revive the essence of that valley of the ever-present long ago, Juanita works the grounds within her little fenced-in yard. Plants and flowers abound, yet few flourish. Many have withered. The soil just cannot support them. Still she shows them off, pride flashing across her face as her hands lightly caress the stalks and her fingers gently stroke the dried leaves. Tending her treasures with tender loving care, Juanita struggles along with her plants to survive, bloom, and brighten the landscape—a U.S.-government-provided speck of what was once a vast domain running along the California coast. Beginning with the Spanish colonization in 1769 by Franciscan priests, Chumash lands have slowly been eroded away ever since.

Although they were the original inhabitants of the land, the Chumash were pushed further and further away from their traditional lands with each new influx of outsiders. There were the Spanish, the Dutch, the Easterners, the opportunists, wealthy ranchers, sun-seekers, and on the list goes to include today's multimillionaire movie stars. With each wave or onslaught, the Chumash were relegated to the lowest positions on an ever-rising socioeconomic pyramid. Even the complex of coastal Chumash villages, including Notcho and Hondo, still vivid in Juanita's memory, were overrun and bulldozed to make way for the 100,000-acre Vandenberg Air Force Base.

Juanita, however, stands tall as a reminder and a warning that not only is she still here, but her people are here as well, and they are going to be here tomorrow and all the tomorrows of the future. She is doing her part to insure a Chumash future down to the seventh generation. Not only is she preserving and teaching the culture, she *is* the culture, and every fiber of her being shouts that culture. Even her home—with every inch of wall and floor space taken up with artifacts, art, and items relating to the Chumash way of life—is a virtual living museum testifying to the continuing existence of the Chumash as a viable people.

No one speaks for Juanita Centeno, but when she speaks from her culturally cluttered kitchen, she speaks to the heart of all humanity.

LIVING IN PARADISE

This was a paradise. It was when I was growing up. It was. My grandfather went to the store every fifteen days just to get the necessary things. We had our coffee berry. Today we make it a conversational piece for the kids when I'm teaching the kids. We make them into necklaces. Back then we made coffee, and it's a medicinal. It's sacred bark, they called it, but it's a coffee berry, coffee bush.

A lot of people don't realize it; we still use those things. We get our mustard greens way up in the mountains, but we have to boil them two or three times because of the pollution and poisons.

The watercress, you can't eat the watercress 'cause the cows and streams are polluted, like they cut the veins of the springs. They are smelly; you can't use them anymore.

I call the hills and valleys my shopping centers of a long time ago; the hills and the mountains were our shopping centers where we gathered the cattails, the tule, the berries, the bullrush for our shoes, our skirts, for eating. You can eat the root of the cattail. You can make like a casserole. And the wild tomatoes, we had *every*thing you could think of. The flour from the acorns, then the cherry pits. The Catalina cherries. The pit, we'd use it for medicinal ... coughs and stuff. The willow tree, we made cradles. The homes were of the willow. And it was good for headaches, for chewing the bark. Straighten your teeth with oak tree bark. A lot of things my grandfather taught me how to use.

Today, the doctor gives you a pill to calm your nerves, to calm whatever ... gee.

THE GIFT OF SIGHT

I was born during the influenza when people were dying by the housefuls. Then, I developed whooping cough, and I coughed my eye right out of the socket. My eye dried up. They took me to the county hospital in Santa Barbara. They couldn't do anything. I lived there two years. My sister stayed with me. One day she was wheeling me in a wheelchair down the corridor and this little old man called me, "Hey, Buckaroo, come here!"

I don't know why he called me Buckaroo, but I had little boots. I was always dressed as western. And I said, "OK."

I said to my sister, "Let's go see what he wants."

Well, he was laying in bed there and he said, "Hey, Buckaroo, I hear you lost your eye." He says, "Would you like to see again, Buckaroo?" He says, "Tell the doctor to come."

So we got the doctor. Doctor Lovern. I remember that name, but he was really Doctor Love for me that Doctor Lovern. And the little old man, I think his name was McKenzie, Mr. McKenzie, he tells the doctor, "I'm an old man. I'm ready to die any minute. I'd like to donate my eye, if I can help Buckaroo here get her sight back. I'd like to donate whatever she needs for her eye."

And he told me, "When I'm gone, Buckaroo, please keep me with you all the time." And I do. I have him with me. He donated his nerve and he died the next day. They had me asleep when they were cutting him to be able to connect the nerve to the eye. But I am able to see. They livened the eye up again. It was closed and my eyelid was like leather; you could pound on it like a drum. It had dried up. Then, the doctor livened my eye up again with the nerve of this little old man. I was eight or nine years old.

LOSS OF THE VALLEY OF FLOWERS

They took our food away. We can't even get our mustard greens or mushrooms. We can't even hunt cottontail rabbit. There isn't any more. Deers are extinct. All our animals are extinct. Our fish is gone. Our streams of water is gone. We're drinking their poison water. Why can't they leave us alone? Why can't they send us back to the hills? They think by giving us a chair or piece of furniture or cracker box like this, they think we're living in luxury, but ... at nighttime, we have to get up because the house creaks. It opened up. When we moved here, they had to patch it. It opened up. These are modular homes, two trailers put together. The house tilted. They say, "Who cares! They're Indians. They don't know the difference."

Look how much I worked over there for the government, even volunteer work. I was only getting five dollars an hour. I did my job to protect what my ancestors left behind. I wanted to save the plants because we still use them. I'm a basket weaver.

The valley of the flowers. Now there's no more flowers. We had our flower festival here last year, in June or July, people didn't come. Why should they come? In the fields that we used to have of flowers, just condominiums all over now. There's no room for the flowers anymore.

I used to gather at Squirrel's Nest. I fought and fought to save it. It was beautiful. Here comes the PetroTech, the oil companies, and railroad—bulldozed it. It doesn't exist anymore. Isn't that something? These are the things that I have tried to protect. They're gone. And if we go gather our material, it's brittle, it's no good. We're sick, but we keep going. We're like robots, I tell you. If we eat anything from the stores, we get sick. We can't go fishing, but they can do it. They go hunting at the Vandenberg base, the air force. They have the food we should be having. We can't go get our abalone; we can't go fishing. We have to get a permit. We have to have air force security with us there so we won't steal the ocean or I don't know what they think we're going to take. I wouldn't want a missile. And that was our land. Where our village was. They took it.

WE CALL THE GREAT SPIRIT EVERY DAY

We pray to the Great Spirit. We call the Great Spirit every day for togetherness,
for going back to where we were—not living out in the open, because we couldn't survive now. Everything is so polluted. Our animals have been driven away or are extinct. The oil companies have cut the veins from our springs. They killed the springs, poisoned the water. Now you can't find any water and they ration us our water; they ration everything. Even the bathroom; we pay from thirty to forty dollars a month for our sewer.

I used to cry when I'd see them cutting the earth. My grandfather walked here. They'd even steal his footsteps ... God only knows they'd bulldoze them now. They left us nothing, not even my grandfather's footsteps.

THE DIAPER THAT WON'T GO AWAY

All the pollution. Our roads ... all the Pampers you find. All the beer cans
on the highways, and they want us to keep America clean. There was a lady driving
by in a car out here; she threw a Pamper out the window down on the Harris grade
and it's been about eight months, the Pamper is still there. The cars have run over it.
They don't deteriorate, those Pampers. The cars run over it and over it, and I have
run over that Pamper and it's still there. It is flat, really flat and like part of the road
now.

We go over Harris grade to get our elderberry. We go gather acorns over
there and whatever we can gather. We see that Pamper, still. There was a guitar by
the road, too, an old broken guitar; somebody must have had a fight there. The

guitar is gone. The guitar is gone, all the wood of the guitar is gone, but that Pamper is still there. They make that Pamper out of the cattail that we use for the cradle boards and that's from Mother Earth and I think that Mother Earth is trying to tell us something.

I have been called barbarian for shooting the cottontail rabbits for breakfast. But, we didn't destroy. From that rabbit, the skin was our leggings. The meat we ate. The bones were needles for my grandmother to sew baskets. Every single thing we used. But today they don't. They eat just what they want and throw it in our backyard.

TRUCKLOAD OF WATERMELONS, BOXES OF BANANAS

We get things brought to the reservation. I've got boxes of raisins. I don't know what to do with them; I can't eat them. They're full of worms, but if I throw them out, people will think I am throwing out food and being ungrateful.

A truckload of watermelons came in. They were so soft you couldn't eat them. Then, in came a load of bananas. Boxes of bananas. They were half-rotten. And there were bananas all over the reservation. In the parking lot, boxes of bananas. Old clothes that they bring in … why don't they see if we have a decent bed to sleep on, food, good food, and money to pay our rent? Those are the things we could use, not discarded stuff.

LIVING ON CLAY

See, we're living here. We don't own this land. It's federal land. And we have to pay forty-five thousand for this junky stuff. The floor … we're going to sink in one of these days. The sink just deteriorated. Bugs fly in. We have snakes and tarantulas and everything in here.

We can't go out when it rains; it's just clay out there. We have to put our cars over in that street because we can't drive our cars out. We get stuck. Then, they get vandalized, stolen, and broken into. We can't sit and guard our stuff all our lives.

This reservation is cursed. We have white people, white trash I call them, 'cause there is good people in the white people. I was raised in with the white people. I have daughters-in-law that are white and they are very wonderful. They're just like daughters. We have this trash in here. People, the white people, they come here. Smoke pot and teaching others to do it. That's what our people are learning from these trashy people that come and squat in our reservation. We can't get them out. We have some people that like to smoke pot and they let them in, because they want part of it. But you should see the trashy part of the reservation. Old trailers, old cars. It's a trashy place.

We're not living. We're robots. We don't know if we're going to come home, because we're surrounded with the big white ranchers, big rich people surrounded here. We don't know if we're going to come home or they're going to find us dead somewhere. That's a fear we have. Oh, it happens. It's happening every day.

Long time ago my people traded. Today we have to sell what we make to survive. I don't even call this place a home. This is a house. We don't have a tree or anything around here. Good thing we're not living where they have those tornadoes and whirlwinds. We'd be gone. These things, these modular homes, they're the first to go. We don't even light the heater; we're afraid it's not even wired right.

MY ANCESTORS WERE FREE

We are worse off today than our ancestors. At least they were free. There were no boundaries like we have boundaries today.

There's a fence here and there's a no-trespassing sign. You can't go in there, and if you do find a rancher that let's you in, you are in fear because the other ranchers that see you might shoot you thinking you're going to go rob him. We're in danger every minute of the day and we're teachers. We're teachers of the culture. Still we have to ask permission for everything that we do.

I read a lot. I study a lot. And I got my education from people; that's why I

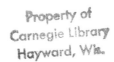

am able to keep going and to keep my health and myself in physical condition. I'll be seventy-three this month; Thanksgiving was my birthday. I study a lot, researching more of the culture. It's there. We were here.

Chumash people were the most peaceful, the best basket weavers, but they erased a lot of our culture. I don't know what happened along the way. Sometimes I blame my parents, because they tried to take things away from us, the Indian ways. They thought they were doing us good by saying, "Don't even mention you're an Indian. If you go and ask for a job, say you're Spanish or Italian or Portuguese or something else. Don't say you're Indian. If you say you're an Indian, you're not going to get the job."

Sure enough! We'd forget. We'd say, "Well, we're Indian."

"Well, we'll call you. If we need you, we'll call you."

Never called us.

WALK IN OUR SHOES

Only when you are in our shoes can you know how hard it is to, to walk out that door.

When we go to the store, to the drugstore, to the grocery store, people around here say, "I wish those damn Indians would get out of that reservation. It looks awful." I feel that pain; I pretend that I'm even, not even an Indian. I buy things quick and get out of there.

We were at the mission. They only give us a barbecue for all we work, which I don't care. I don't care what they have. But, we were coming out. We had our regalia on, buckskin dresses, and we all were coming out with our plates. I was the first one out. A lady comes up, she says, "Oh, you like barbecue," she says. And I said, "Yes, and it smells good."

She says, "I thought Indians just ate lizards and snakes."

And I got so angry, and I said, "Well, I, I eat people, too. So you better get out of my way." She took off, you know. I say, "We eat people." I don't know why people are like that. It doesn't stop there; it's always poking remarks. I don't know. And we respect. They don't even respect the flag. I fight for our flag. We were born under the red, white, and blue. I see it on tennis shoes. I see it on garbage cans. I see it in curtains and vans.

I can't understand why people do all these things. What has happened?

WHAT IS WHITE?

I go to prisons. I go to hospitals. I go to colleges. I go to television stations and say, "What is white? Why do they push us around like, like kickballs, like basketball? Why do they dribble us like basketballs?"

We know who we are. We know we're Indians. We know we're trash in their eyes; but who are they? What is white?

They can adopt our kids. They can adopt black kids. They can adopt; if they want a kid that bad, they'll grab it. They'll pay money for a kid; they'll pay money to an Indian or to a black person to have a surrogate baby and to do many things that are illegal. But, let us stand out there in front of a white man's house, they'll call the cops. How can we let them see that we're human? Shall we cut ourselves and bleed in front of them?

There are so many impersonators. Why are these white people coming to teach our kids the culture? What do they know of the culture? What do they know of the materials of what our people used? What can they tell us? We have teachers that come here and try to teach the kids the plants, the clothing, but they're mixing the cultures from other tribes into our tribe. And here I am trying to get to the real, my culture.

There was a man. We were going to Lompoc and he was in front of us in an old station wagon. All of a sudden we saw this station wagon going all over the place and down an embankment. We went down and got him out. Brought him up the bank. I'm a nurse; I was able to do it. I have a certificate from nursing. So, I went, Jose and I went and brought him out. I took my vest off and I told Jose to go get a jacket from the car. I put it under his head and I stopped the bleeding. I got a weed, I don't know what it was, it stopped the bleeding. Made him comfortable. A passing car went and called an ambulance. And the doctor said that we did a good job in getting him out. If you don't have a certificate, you can't touch them. You've got to leave them there, but I had my certificate in nursing.

The fire department came and the ambulance. Then, when he woke up and they had him in the hospital, we went to see him. He says, "Well, I want a complete examination if this Indian touched my body." Can you imagine? And, "Get out of my room. Get out." That's the way he approached us. He wanted to be disinfected. "If that Indian touched me, I want a complete examination to see if I got any of her diseases."

Long time ago I had an uncle that was very ill in Santa Barbara, and my mother didn't have the money to go see him and be with him. The house we lived in was paid for. The neighbor came over, and she knew I had pneumonia and my little brother had pneumonia. So, she saw that my mother was very anxious to go to her brother in Santa Barbara. He was dying of pleurisy.

So the lady said she would lend the money. My mother said, "Well, could you lend me enough to go see my brother?"

She said, "Whatever you want. A hundred, two hundred . . ."

"Lend me two hundred," my mother said, "'cause I'll have to stay over there and I have my kids sick here."

"Oh, I'll give you three hundred if you want."

My mother said, "No, two hundred is enough."

So my mother, being anxious to go see her brother and us sick with pneumonia, well, she signed the IOU. The lady said, "Will you sign here?" My mother signed it.

My grandfather took my mother in the buckboard to Santa Barbara. When they came back, my little brother had died.

Well, it was our fault. We got up from bed and, you know how the ice forms on the ground, the frost from washing, and we went and ate the ice from that. And my little brother died. And I got double pneumonia.

They had the funeral for him, and they wouldn't tell my mother my little brother had died. So my uncle died a week later. My mother was all broken up. My grandfather said, "I'm going to pick up your mother." So he hitched up the buckboard and went after her. But, when he got there she had already buried my uncle.

When she came home, she found out about my brother, and on top of that we had an eviction. The lady who loaned the money took the house. We tried to get whatever we could. They couldn't bring everything we owned. Came back to the reservation to live.

When they took our house away, they said, "You better go now before I call the sheriff." So that's all we could do. The place is still in Lompoc. We were born there; my mother was born here on the reservation. I managed to get a picture of the house.

And here we are again. We came back. I don't know why.

THAT RANCH OF RONALD REAGAN'S WAS OUR WORLD

I have walked many, many of these mountains. I go over there and stand on the highest peak of the mountains to look down. There isn't a place that these white people haven't destroyed. The ravines are full of old dead cows they haul and throw there, and the garbage, and old fences. There's always some kind of old pump, like an oil pump that they raped Mother Earth with is dumped there.

There's no sacred place for the Indian now. There are no places sacred to the white man. They never had a sacred place to call their own. They had to take somebody else's.

That ranch of Ronald Reagan's was our world. That was our White House there. The big cattle ranchers came in and took it. We ended up working for them. Then Reagan got it and started tearing up the trees and everything else and even the burial ground. We had a regular burial ground with the monuments and crosses and all that, and he bulldozed all that. And then, the rock paintings of our ancestors, he just ruined them. He wanted the land cleared for his parties and gatherings and for whatever they do up there.

I was a Native American Indian specialist observer and monitor at Vandenberg Air Force Base. I worked there. I was raised there at Vandenberg. Our original village was there before Vandenberg was built. All this pipeline came in. Even our own people have sold us out. The pipelines pay them $18.75 an hour. I was watching tractors, bulldozers. Not all the Indians care about what is happening. They just gave up and they just don't want to hear about it. I'm getting that way, too. I just don't want to hear what is happening.

There's no solution. We stand on the outside watching them destroy the earth. We watch them. If they would only let us go to the hills and the mountains just to hear the echoes of our ancestors, of our grandparents, and let us gather at least a leaf that we use to soothe our nerves. I roamed these hills in my youth. Why can't I go to those hills? Why can't I go to the river and be safe?

Just walking that ground would make us feel better, just by letting us walk in our ancestors' footsteps. There's still some remains of our people up there. There's still some rock painting. And who can go up there? Just white people can go to the painting. Now they have the painted rock fence, and we have to ask permission to go and see our own ancestors' painting.

It will never happen that we can walk in peace. I see the four corners of the earth. There's no way to go. There's no trail for us to take anymore. We're stuck here right where others want us to be.

FILLING THE OCEAN WITH TEARS

I have kept that ocean filled with my tears, standing in those hills, watching.

When that pipeline came in and I saw the burials and everything being bulldozed, I said the heck with it. But, I just couldn't. I couldn't. I'd come home and cry. We go over there all day long in the sun and the rain and the wind and half-starved because we can't get down in the hills.

When the archaeologists wanted me to work with them, I thought I was protecting the wetlands; I was protecting the plants because we use the plants. But it never happened. It was very different, very different than what I thought. I thought I was going to be like with my grandfather, protecting. No, it's for themselves. They get these grants and they use our names to get the grants. See?

The archaeologists had a lot of fun. "Well, these are human. We've got to have them analyzed." I said, "You're not supposed to do that. You just leave those bones alone." See, they create jobs for themselves to make money with our dead people, our burials.

What right do these people have to go dig? Why don't they ask us? To me, they're, they're ...

When I worked at Vandenberg, there were seventeen scrapers and eight tractors, and here I was in the middle going round and round and round trying to protect. How could I see what they were pushing? And they had me there just 'cause it's required to have an Indian in any excavations.

My grandfather had said, "Never, never tamper with any remains or any skeleton that you find, because they're going to the ocean. They're traveling to the ocean. They want to go home. That's their home, the ocean." And those bones traveled, traveled till they bulldozed the road, and God only knows what happened to those bones I was taking care of.

When I'd find a whole burial, I'd have them put wire on it. But hunters broke the wire and dug. Nothing's sacred.

PEOPLE WILL NEVER UNDERSTAND AN INDIAN

We were raised to protect. We weren't raised to destroy. People will never understand an Indian.

We're never included, not even in voting. When they send us our voting papers, there's Vietnamese and there's all kinds of languages, but is there an Indian language that we can vote in our own language?

When I was young, work and recreation was the same. We made the work recreation by seeing who could work the fastest or who could run the fastest or who could milk the cow the fastest or get more milk in the bucket. It was work and recreation at the same time. There was no dull moment. To tell you the truth, there was always something to do. It was also early to bed early to rise.

Anything I'm teaching, anything I'm saying may keep the culture alive. Maybe somebody will remember us sometime.

We Are Mission Indians

But, we are mission Indians. My ancestors were digger Indians 'cause they dug for their food. They were digger Indians 'cause they were digging. But they became mission Indians because of the missionaries. And that's what we are. We're Chumash. What is Chumash? I'm a mission Indian. That's what I call myself. A mission Indian.

How does it feel to be an Indian? I feel myself like a trapped animal. Can you imagine what a trapped animal feels like? Because he can't talk! He can't tell you, "Please get me out of this trap," or "Please take this bullet out of my ribs," or "Please help me." That's the way we feel. Like trapped animals! We can't tell anybody that, that we hurt. They laugh. They think an Indian has no feelings. Why? Why is it that people can't understand us?

I want to be free, not to be gawked at or just looked at because I know how to make a basket. I'm a human being. I'm not a machine. I want to be noticed that I'm a human being, not just because I'm an Indian.

I'm not different. I speak their language. I can speak six languages—Japanese, Chinese, Filipino, Spanish, English, my own language. Now what do they want me to do?

Anything I make has a sad meaning. It reminds me of the life my ancestors had. Anything you buy in the store don't mean a thing. It breaks. Even these damn chairs. They don't last. At least the villages are still up where my people were— rocks, paintings. They're vandalized, but they're still there from so long ago. Nothing lasts now.

The Great Spirit Has Helped Us

The Great Spirit has helped us. We're never broke. We're never without. We have our cupboard full of food.

America is going to go through hard times. Remember the Noah's Ark. Water. This time it's going to be by fire.

We used to ride our horses to Ronald Reagan's ranch and then go on top of the mountain and down to my grandmother's house in Santa Barbara. Now there are houses and fences. Now the archaeologists want to find the boundary of the Indian sites. The Indians didn't have a boundary. They were free.

I'd rather have the stars for my roof and the dirt for my floor, living under a tree and weaving a basket or do what I used to do. All I wish is that we could be more free to go to the hills and the mountains, to spend a day in the hills. Just to bring back memories of when we were there.

I could walk in the Rattlesnake Canyon and not get bit by a rattlesnake. Today there's no snakes anymore. They don't even survive, and they want us to survive on what the people are doing to us—the contractors, the earth movers, and all these tractors that are our enemies, and bulldozers.

What is freedom? We simply were free. We didn't need a word for it. We didn't have progress in our vocabulary. We lived free and progress was the everyday life.

ALL YOU OWN IS YOUR BIRTH AND YOUR DEATH

I used to watch butterflies. I used to watch the snakes. My grandmother would say, "Get me that snake over there so I can get the bladder for my basket," or "Get me that leaf," or "Get me that spider web." It was just a beautiful life that I lived. And today it's just a ... We don't have a heart. We're just empty. We're just like a robot. We're not even alive. We can't go out there and pick our herbs.

My grandfather was right. "All you own," he said, "is your birth and your death. That's all you have. Just think of that," he says. "You don't have nothing. You can have millions of dollars, you have millions of diamonds, millions, what good is it going to do you?"

That's why I don't want nothing. My people lived so happy having just what they ate, what they did.

I don't know what they expect out of us.

The old people could see gifts in the children. It would be coming down from the parents or the grandparents or whoever raised you. You have to follow their footsteps. That's why I follow my grandfather's footsteps in protecting. I can cure. That's all we use is the wild plants for curing ourselves and eating.

Every one of us has something that's not just right. If someone is insulting you, laugh, laugh right along with them. Make them look like fools. I do that and I laugh about myself. I tell stories about myself. How I used to trip my grandfather and laugh, and I could have broken his neck at times. Sometimes he would just stay there, and he had this rattle belt on me so he could hear me where I was. I would always want to go far away and walk in the bushes and go all over. I would tie a rope. He was getting old, poor old grandpa, and he would trip. And I would laugh at him instead of helping him. But he would come and hug me. Then, I'd tell, "Did you get hurt? When you fell?"

He'd say, "No. With your laugh I got well. I broke my leg, but it healed with your laughing."

I had a lot of fun. I had a good life. A good bringing up, which I'd like to pass on. I wish I was Xeroxed; I wish there were five of me that I could send to different parts of the world to teach. It'll never happen, I know that.

THIS LAND WAS HEAVEN

My grandfather raised me. He brought me into this world. I couldn't forget him. He taught me everything I know.

I used to lay at nighttime and I could see him. It was just like television watching myself with him in the hills. I could see the places I had been with him. It was just something that you couldn't describe. My grandfather helped me through. I used to scream and holler, and he was right there. Sometimes I could feel him. It was in the hills when I saw him more 'cause I was with him in the hills.

My friend, she says, "What's the matter with you? I hear you talking to yourself all the time." She says, "You made me feel like you were a little bit off."

And I told her the story and then she says, "It's time that you forget. Let him go. Let him rest. You haven't let him rest all this time."

My grandfather had such love for the land, such love for the animals, such love for the people that surrounded him. He helped anybody, and I think that's in every Indian.

I think they had such a beautiful life. It was just, it was just heaven. You lived in heaven.

My grandfather used to say, "When you're with a white man, never laugh, never smile. An Indian never smiles." But they do smile. When we work together we would laugh like they were tickling us.

I dreamed about my grandfather, too. He was horseback riding and he ran into a tree and he was hanging from the chest in a tree. I heard him hollering. So I got up and I was going to go help him, but I couldn't get by. There were snakes all over. I was just walking. I could feel them. I was stepping on them all the way. And I woke up sweating. It was just a dream, but I didn't get to my grandfather.

My grandfather never called me by my name. He'd always call me Rawhide or Redwing. My father wanted a boy and was going to name him John. Well, I was a girl, so he named me Juanita. Then, when I was baptized my grandfather put that name Barbara on there, too.

PEOPLE WANT TO ADOPT US

Why are we telling the white people of our trouble? They have troubles of their own, and they're not guilty of what happened to our ancestors.

People, teachers from all over, they want to adopt us. We're not kids, we're not orphans. We're not just an old mushroom that they can come and pick. Why?

There's people that tell, "Oh, we're guilty of what our people did to you people."

Why talk like that? Why don't they say, "We'll come over and help, or we want to learn what you're doing. We can help you. You need anything?" No! Take! Take what they can.

LIVING TO HELP, TO HEAL

I wanted an education so bad. I wanted to have a ranch. I wanted to just teach what my grandfather had taught me. I managed to go to school. Horses and the animals and the ranch, that was going to be my life where I could help everybody. It's not happened.

You can tell a lot about people by watching them. That's how I got my education. Then, I went to Berkeley, to the university, to get the psychology to be able to cope with the people. I'm able to talk now. Before, I was afraid. I'd cry. But my boss said for me to get out there with all the intelligence I have.

I go to school to teach; my grandchildren are in school. I say, "That's my little Indian boy over there." They look ashamed and say, "Grandma, I told you I was only an Indian at home. I'm not an Indian outside."

I'm sorry ... I'm sorry ... I can't help crying. ...

That hurts when my own blood has to hide who they are.

I decided I was going to have classes for just teachers to teach them how to teach the kids in school. How to approach an Indian. How to go to visit a museum. How to visit a hospital. What questions to ask from these sick people. How to ask. And how to answer the kids. How to teach the kids. What we're doing is teaching teachers now.

I was a nurse. I passed my test of nurses in eight hours. I got my certificate to help people, to heal people. I wanted to live in a world that I could help.

I WORE THE DUNCE CAP ALL THE TIME

When we started to school we didn't have Filipinos, we didn't have blacks, we didn't have no other kinds, just white people and the Indians. And we lived here on the reservation and went to school. Well, the white kids would beat us up because they thought we didn't have a feeling; we were animals from the hills. My grandfather never taught me to fight. "Don't fight. You be the dumb one; let the other guy be the smart one." That was his philosophy. "You be the dumb one, let the other guy be the smart ..." Well, when he died, I said, What the heck am I doing letting these people hit me over the head? I have cracks on my head where they'd hit me, and I couldn't fight.

They put an outside toilet for us. They didn't let us use the white kids' bathroom. They put a trough for us to wash our hands. They put a faucet outside for us.

We were the monitors for the school. Let the Indians do the cleaning. Let the Indians take the baskets to the incinerator. Let the Indians clean the yard. Let the Indians do this. That's the way we were treated in school when we started. But I kept going. I got my education.

We learned who we were in school. They taught us about Indians scalping and all that. We tell my grandfather and he said, "That! No, no, don't even listen." But we had to. We had to be in school or we would be punished.

So, I wore the dunce cap all the time. At school talking about scalping, I told the teacher, "I didn't hear you." He says, "Well, you're going to hear." He'd get my ear and put the dunce cap on and take me to the corner.

What Goes Around Comes Around

The nuns washed our mouths out with soap. You feel sorry for them because what goes around comes around. That goes for the white people. What goes around comes around. The day is coming. I've seen a lot, but I've held it to myself. These people have done us wrong; they don't pay us sometimes. They think we have to do our things for nothing, that we don't have feelings, that we don't eat. They think we're living like pigs or something, that we don't need anything, we can eat garbage, we can go without eating.

Teach the Children, It Is Later than We Think

If anyone has children, they better teach their children to follow the traditions that we're leaving behind because it is later than we think with all that's going on.

Today there's no respect. The children do not want to come to grandmother's house because there's nothing for them to do. But, there's no more grandmothers either. The grandmothers want to be teenagers.

We never put our elders in nursing homes. We always had turns taking care of them or brought them home. Today, they abandon them. People don't have time for the elders. Look how the elders are abused; I've seen it done.

The kids today are so damned spoiled that they won't go out to work. Today there's murders, kids shooting each other, kidnaps, everything is happening. Destroy nature and you destroy yourself.

You Can Judge Me

Maybe I'm doing my part. I don't know. You can judge me. I work all the time. I'm doing things for people. I'm trying to protect the vegetation which we still use, the wetlands which we still use for cradleboards, skirts, sandals. It's a big job. Not even the police could protect it. That's why it's so hard for me, one person, to protect all these wetlands.

People say there's no rain, that it's a dry season. God, if they would collect my tears, it wouldn't be a dry season.

I shed so many tears that I could have the Santa Ynez River flowing, trying to bring back the world my grandfather knew.

NORTHERN CHEYENNE

Lena Sooktis

AS THE AFTERNOON WORE DOWN and dusk approached, Herman rounded us up and headed for the hills to cut firewood for the sweat he intended to hold after nightfall. About five or six miles out of Lame Deer, Montana, heading east, we left the main state road and cut across the field, careful to follow the ruts of previous vehicles carrying woodcutters, probably Herman. As far as the eye could see were hills covered with the surrealistic charred skeletons of trees devastated by last year's horrendous forest fire. Thousands and thousands of areas had been burned, the trees ruined for timber but just right for sweat-lodge fires.

Herman Bear Comes Out, the Northern Cheyenne traditionalist and spiritual leader, was a technician with his chain saw. With surgical precision he felled those blackened remains and cut them into lengths we could carry. His sense of humor got the best of him, and gradually we carriers of the logs realized something was amiss. The logs were getting heavier and more unwieldy without our understanding why. Then, it dawned on us. He was doing it on purpose. His cuts were not as short.

We began to murmur to each other about the weight. So one of us, I don't remember just who, said something about the length. We looked at each other. Then at Herman. He was all over himself laughing. He had been laughing behind our backs all the time. Now he roared.

Laughing and trying to talk, Herman said, "The last time I had a white guy out here, I asked him if he wanted to cut or carry. He said he had never used a chain saw, so he would carry.

"By the time we finished he said he would take the saw the next time, even if he sawed himself up trying to learn how to use it.

"I guess my logs just got too heavy and long for him," and Herman bent over laughing. "Yep, said he'd take the saw, even if it killed him. Well, I gave him the choice; his decision."

As I trekked across the forbidding landscape, carrying the last of the logs, I glanced about, feeling the former forest alive. The trees were somehow like elongated figures creeping about in search of their former existence. It reminded me of the Ute stories of the "Stick People" sorcerers supposedly send out when they do their medicine to influence events and the Hoh's "Stick Indians" bound in the spirit to the rain forests of the Olympic Peninsula.

The darkening sky silhouetting the wooden corpses and cold night air watering the eyes heightened the eeriness. I was relieved when the last of the logs had been loaded and Herman finally got the truck out of the mud and back into the ruts leading to the highway.

By the time the logs were split and stacked under and around the rocks, everyone was smudged black from the fire-ravaged trees. With a strike of a match, a blaze was set and within minutes a bonfire raged, lighting the small backyard and casting shadow giants from the figures of those guarding the fire.

To heat the sweat rocks, in order for them to reach the intensity needed, the fire must be made properly. First two sticks of wood are laid parallel to each other but about two feet apart. Next comes a foundation of paper, the ignitor. This is followed by a row of wood on which the sweat rocks are placed in a pyramid formation. Rows of wood circle the pyramid of rocks leaning into the center. More wood is added on top. Just the flame of a match sets this structure on fire and the shape creates a chimneylike effect. Within minutes the night sky is lit. Herman knows how to build the fires to perfection, for he is the master of sweats.

As the wood is consumed and turns to embers, the rocks begin to glow with such yellow-red heat they appear to be translucent. It is as if one could actually see right through them.

Herman gives the cue, motioning with his outstretched hand and his husky voice bellowing, "Let's go, all you sweathogs." And he laughs out loud, but there is seriousness in his intent as he lumbers out the back door sporting only his bathing trunks and a towel. "We're all going in," he beckons to me.

There is no color when it comes to Herman's invitations to sweat. They are open to everyone who is at his home when it is time for the sweats to begin.

One by one, and in no apparent order or rush, men, in swimming trunks, and women, modestly attired and wrapped in blankets, make their way out the door and into the freezing Montana night.

Off to one corner of the tiny yard, secluded by a high wooden fence from the next house only feet away, a dark canvas-covered dome rises seemingly right up out of the earth. The sweat lodge.

Almost kissing the ground, the five or six men and women, including Herman's wife, Sharon, and two-year-old daughter, Lindi, bend low with knees tucked up to the chest and inch their way through the canvas doorway and into the structure. Lindi is the only one who can walk upright, tilting her head slightly. While holding the flap up, Herman instructs, "Go to your left, go around the pit to your left. In a circle."

Now crawling, I make my way along with the others, and sit. Waiting. And shivering, teeth hitting teeth that I can't stop. In front of us, cut into the earth in a circle, is the pit.

When everyone is in, Herman sits at the end of the circle—or is it the beginning?—closest to the door. But Herman's brother is still out. Within minutes the reason becomes clear. Mike, this night, will be the firekeeper and participant.

With only swimming trunks on, braving the cold, Mike begins bringing in the glowing rocks with a pitchfork. Two or three rocks a trip. By the third trip, Mike's face is as bright red-orange-yellow as the rocks he is carrying. Herman motions "enough" and Mike scoots in on the right side of the doorway.

Closing the flap, Herman shuts out the cold and seals in the heat. Darkness, not just darkness but blackness, envelops the enclosure. Immediately it feels better. Sighs are heard around the circle. Teeth stop chattering. Relief.

Starting the ceremony, Herman speaks in solemn, reverential tones. He asks if this is anyone's first time to sweat, then he says, "If the heat is too much, put your face close to the earth. It will be cool and breathing will be easier. Put your hands behind you and outside where the canvas touches the ground. If it is still too hot, lay down. Then, if you think you cannot take it any longer, anyone may leave. Just slip out from under the canvas from where you are sitting," then he quips, "or laying."

A deafening silence rises as Herman pauses and waits as if getting instructions from some unseen source. The glow of the rocks dies back. We sit, each in our own thoughts. Then, cedar is sprinkled over the rocks and the aroma fills the stilled air.

"Reach out and take a handful and cover yourself with it," Herman shocks the silence. "Breathe it."

The cedar had a soothing, healing feeling. Earthy. "This is for purification," he added as the cedar filled our lungs. Then, quiet again, and each escaped into one's own thoughts.

Water hitting the rocks jolted our senses back to the here and now. Steam instantly rose, rolling in great waves of unbearable heat. My body was surrounded, overpowered, engulfed. My nostrils flared and my lungs struggled to keep from bursting. My head swirled. Every pore of my skin screamed. Within seconds water flooded my body from the top of my head to the bottom of my feet and soaked my swimming trunks on its way to the ground I was sitting on.

Get out, escape, flee, my mind roared. But I sat still, calming myself as I took on a more embryonic position. As I silently talked myself into a more peaceful, accepting mind frame, I realized a higher power was coming into focus. I sensed the cool earth, felt the closeness of those around me, realized the connectedness of the circle, and was drawn even more to the heat of the pit.

As I pondered thoughts racing through my mind, the drumbeats began. Amazingly the thumps of the drum and the rhythm of my own heart seemed to merge and become one. I was back in the womb, I thought. I knew it couldn't be so, but the thought flew through my mind. I was comforted, at one with those around me. I had heard that the sweat is like being in the womb of Mother Earth. Now I was experiencing the effect myself.

When the drumbeats slowed to an end, Herman said after each one of us had prayed, "These prayers are not new. The prayers were started thousands of years ago by someone else for us today. They had us in mind even then. They are still the

same. It has just become our turn to say them. One day it will be someone else's turn to carry them on. I am thankful someone started them, and I am grateful to take my turn to carry them on for those coming behind us."

As I flew through this darkened womb of my thoughts, feeling as if I was at the spiritual center of the earth, in the very heart of the mother, the flap of the doorway was flung open and the temperature of the lodge plummeted. Our watery bodies were not prepared for the night's freezing breath. We sat motionless, unable to move for fear of arousing the wrath of the cold even more by fanning the air.

Mike raced to get his task completed as firekeeper and return to the sanctuary of the sweat. Although visibly shaking from the chill, he hurriedly brought more rocks from the dying fire and carefully placed them into the pit. Then, the flap was dropped again and soon the heat was beating our bodies with renewed vigor. A new round began.

Four times the rocks were brought in. Four times the flap was opened. Four times the shock of steam filled our lungs, and four times the freezing air ravaged our bodies.

When the flap was opened for the last time, everyone made for the house as fast as was possible. Even in the haste to get out of the cold and into the confines of the warmth, I knew I had been renewed, reborn.

After soothing showers, we came together again, the circle begun in the sweat reunited around the central gathering place of traditional families—the kitchen table. Before us, without one inch of space left, was fry bread, potatoes, salad, deer, and elk. Laughter, wedged in between the talking and eating, lifted the rafters. A bond, a kind of kinship, had developed and been brought together by the spirit of the circle.

For the spiritually sensitive traditional families such as the descendants of the famed Chief Braided Locks, ancestor to both Herman Bear Comes Out and his cousin Lena Sooktis, there is little time for rest. Their counsel and leadership is sought almost daily. Working closely in spiritual matters, they complement and help each other. Herman says of Lena, "I couldn't do my work without her. She is always there without my even having to ask. She supports me in the work." And he does work. He is always available.

The cold arose with the sun as the day dawned Saturday morning over the sparkling Montana hills. Puffs of clouds drifted by and occasionally snow fell from some of those fluffy whiffs, creating a strangely beautiful blue sky filled with white threadlike streaks. Word has come that a distant family member is very ill and in the hospital. A request for a healing ceremony has been made. Plans are in the works for the ceremony to be held that very night. Herman drops any other arrangements previously made for that evening; he is needed and Lena will be there, too. The decision is quickly made that it will be held in the old cabin on the backside of the property, the usual place established decades ago by Lena's father for such events.

By the time Herman and his family arrive at nine, many who will be participating have already arrived. The main house is filled with people, most of them eating and talking around the kitchen table. After an hour or so, a slow and intermittent procession of men and women, many carrying wool blankets and pillows, makes its way along a weaving path to the old cabin across the dip and up the gently sloping hill. Three or four horses nosily prance up to the fence at a curve of the footpath and snort brazenly, eager to discover what has unsettled their usually peaceful domain.

A fire has been started earlier in the tiny wood stove in the center of the small, uninsulated one-room structure to ward off some of the cold. Still the chill remains, but it is bearable. In front of the stove is a large wooden frame filled with sand. In the middle of the square is a sand-molded crescent moon. Medicine jars sit to one side. Cedar has been placed at one corner. Men and women, in no apparent order, sit on the floor around the walls. Conversations, none above whispers, are carried on around the circle.

Soon a drummer begins striking the drum and a singer begins the prayers. After four rounds of the song, the drum is passed to the next person and another singer begins four rounds. From one to the other the drum is passed and another picks up the singing as the jars of medicine are passed around. Everyone drinks and passes them on. Around and around the drum is passed.

Occasionally someone will enter or leave the cabin; there are no restrictions, although reverence is always maintained and the central focus is never shifted from the purpose of the ceremony. All night long the prayers continue, never stopping. Over and over drumbeats and singing circle the room.

As darkness gives way to dawn, the blurry-eyed intercessors move from the whitewashed cabin to a sweat already prepared and in waiting to seal the incantations. The speed of the healing process is now in the hands of the Creator and the afflicted.

By noon a feast has been spread, with food—elk, deer, buffalo, chicken, salads, vegetables, and of course, blueberry pudding—covering two long, banquet-sized tables. At the starting end of the tables the traditional bucket of water reminds those gathered to be thankful and mindful of the essentials of life. Each in turn—elders always honored by being at the head of the line—takes the long, thin-handled metal dipper, drinks heartily to the last drop, and hands it to the next in line.

At the corner of the table Lena talked and laughed with those crowding patiently for their turn, but she was carefully watching for the toddlers edging up to the cloth-draped tabletop taller than them. Quickly she turned, caught their attention, and with hand outstretched, interrupted the passing of the dipper. She took a scoop of water with the utensil and lowered it to the children. Having taken their drink, they were now ready to receive their share of the abundant food.

Minutes later, sitting with her daughters lined up shoulder to shoulder behind her, Lena said, "We can talk in the morning at eight. I'll meet you at Herman's house," and then resumed her laughter-sprinkled conversation with relatives surrounding her.

Lena Sooktis ▼ My great grandfather was a chief. I come from chief's family and the Elk Horn Scraper Society.

We don't really have clans here. My uncle always tells that since my father belongs to that society, then his kids can belong to that society. Actually our men are to be the ones to fulfill that society.

Today, nowadays, they say there should be a woman's sweat. But, a long time ago, my grandfather used to tell me that there was never a woman's sweat. Always men and women together. Men are the ones that take care of the sweat; they take care of that for the woman. Woman is the one that prepares the meal for the sweat and all that.

TEACHING ROLES TO DAUGHTERS

There's roles for men and roles for women in our Northern Cheyenne culture. A woman is supposed to be able to stay home, take care of their kids, and take care of the household, and to be able to carry on what they learned from their mother. A woman is supposed to be able to sit down and talk to their girls and that's what I do to my girls. I tell them who to respect, what to respect.

A woman is supposed to correct her daughter, what she's doing wrong. Recently I talked to my girls about when you go in sweat. You supposed to be able to have a good feeling when you go in, good feelings about sweating. When you go in you wear dress. That's what my mother used to tell me. You put on a nice dress to go in and sweat.

Talk about lot of things that help, help these young woman to understand, show 'em a road that you are a lady.

WOMAN'S POWER WEAKENS MEN

A woman has a lot of powers when it's her time of the month. She's supposed to stay in her bedroom at least four, five days until it's over. She's not supposed to participate in ceremonies during that time. What happens is that you weaken the lives of a man. During that time a woman has powers. I always stress that to my girls even in Sun Dance, even into peyote meetings. It's probably the scent of the flow, you know, woman's blood, that weakens them. I always stress to my kids that whenever you have like, you know, your period, don't be around men, don't hang around them because they going to know you have it. You're going to make that man or that guy weak.

So, it's really hard for some of these young generation that was never brought up the traditional way that they don't really, really know what, what's the meaning of that. They always say that, "Why it's nothing. It's normal life for a woman." But in here, if you're brought up in traditional way that God had made, you know, made us, the Creator made us to have that for a purpose to respect our men.

The woman's flow kinda weakens the men's, men's, ah, men's body. They turn like weak, I guess. My dad used to tell me that the scent of the blood is what makes the men weak. They don't want to go out and work. They just want to lay around. That's how it works.

WOMAN'S POWER WEAKENS MEDICINE

It affects the medicine, too. My dad used to tell me and my mother used to tell me that if a medicine is in the house, in the house and you, if some woman has their period, it poisons the medicine. That medicine will not work if exposed to that woman in her period.

My mother used to tell us that if you have your monthly menstruation, if you know that there is some doctoring inside the house, then we don't want you to come in because that person that is being doctored is going to turn worse. Is really going to get sick, because the one that is doctoring, it's not going to work anymore

because you're the one that is blocking what that medicine man is doing. You're poisoning the medicine that person is using.

These old people used to tell me just to be aware of it. A woman has a lot of powers and control in ceremonial life. We have to pass it on. That way no one don't hurt themselves in their own lives.

We as Indians still have to follow that tradition, that traditional law that our great-grandfathers and our mothers passed on to us, pass on all that they have taught us.

From that menstruation that power happens to every woman on this earth. It happens whether you realize it, whether you understand it or not.

If a woman didn't have that, you know, then how would we be able to know these things like my mother used to tell.

The Creator put spiritual powers in a woman.

Going back to ceremonies, just like this last Sun Dance we had, right across where we stay, one of my girls had her time of the month. She came over and she said, "Mother," she said, "I don't think I can make it to the Sun Dance, to be able to come over and help you."

I was fasting at that time. I went to Sun Dance. She said, "I'm really sorry that I won't be able to make it there. It's the time of the month for me. I don't want to make you sick, or I don't want to make any of those men sick. So I'm going to prepare a meal for you, but what I'm going to do is that I'm going to have my husband cedar it and then bring it over to your camp. So that way, it'll be purified, and I won't get you sick.

"'Cause you always tell me never to prepare a meal unless it is purified. I try to do that so that way I won't weaken my husband or weaken anybody that is eating my food."

I said, "I'm glad you know that. If you do come to the Sun Dance, I want you to stand on the east side or either on the south side because the wind goes this way. The Sun Dance lodge is … if you stand on this side, you going to get all them guys sick. When you do come around, you stand on this side, that way you can stand a good distance away."

She said, "Well, better yet, maybe I'll just stay away."

So I always stress to my girls about that. They always want to know why. Why does a woman have their monthly, you know, period? Why do they … why does it affect men? That's a real good question to me. I have questioned my mother on lot of these things, too. It's one of the beliefs that a woman has to obey, they have to … like in men, there's certain things that a woman can't do, and there's certain things that's a woman's role that men can't do. Having the period is a time for us woman to think about the moon, how we're so close to the moon. We follow the moon.

WOMEN FOLLOW THE MOON

Long time ago, when woman were going to have their babies, they used to follow the moon. They never counted by the months. Woman and the moon is connected. The woman would say, "This is the time of the moon for me and that's the, when that moon comes, if it's like half moon, full moon, well that's when I'm going to have my baby."

Even in peyote meetings men are the ones that are just taking care of moon for us. We're the ones that own the moon because we're, we have to be the ones to, ah, be connected with the moon in our ceremonies. How men take care of that moon is that they're ... it's just like taking care of their mother.

If they destroyed that moon, it would be like beating up their wife and that's how they would take care of their mother or their sister or their daughter. So we have to learn how to protect ourselves and watch the men how they take care of that moon when we go into peyote meetings.

In the peyote ceremonies the moon is part of the altar. The moon is in the sand. Men are supposed to be able to take care of that moon for us. Be able to put things on there that will protect us woman. Even when it's time, it refers back to our monthly period. So woman are supposed to be able to follow that moon. That's how close connections we are with the moon ... with woman.

First thing I do every day is that I look up at the moon. Nobody never tells me that; I just go look at the moon to see how it is. That's how close connections, you know, you are with the moon.

I try to pass this on to my girls. So a woman's role is supposed to be able to pass on what a woman knows from her mother.

WOMAN RESPECTING HERSELF

I always tell my girls a woman's supposed to be able to respect her sanity towards men. When you go into a sweat, when you sweating with men, you're supposed to be able to respect men. Not be spreading your legs out in front of men.

Not be moving your body towards men. A woman has a lot of power this way.

Long time ago, my mother used to tell me that if you do these things, you don't have any respect in men. A man is going to be able to think that you're, you know, you're a prostitute in Cheyenne. Men is going to be able to take advantage of you, advantage of your body, because you don't respect your body. I always tell my girls that. I say you respect a man and a man will respect you.

I always stress to my girls about having respect in themselves and be able to do lot of things that a woman is supposed to carry on in their life and in their home.

Once when you become a motherhood, you're supposed to be able to fulfill that you are a woman ... that the Creator has put you on this earth and He made you a woman to fulfill these things. Do lot of things for the Creator.

DUTIES BEFORE MARRIAGE

My parents used to tell me, "Before you can speak out loud, you do a lot of things a woman can do. You learn how to bead. You learn how to cook. Learn how to make fry bread. Learn how to make pudding. That's one of the things you have to learn how to do before you can accept a man."

My mother, she said your mother-in-law's going to test you out. She's going to test you. If you ever get married, your mother-in-law's going to test you to see if you are woman enough to get married, to accept a man.

And so, there are things that you going to have to learn as a woman. Your mother-in-law's going to ask, have requirements. If you don't fulfill them, then you will never be accepted in that family.

Your in-laws, they going to test you out, see if you can fulfill that. I always try to teach my daughters things so that way they won't be caught off guard from another woman. When you accept married life, you are being tested, tested all the time.

WOMEN CARRY HEAVY BURDENS

There's a big role for woman that lot of these men don't understand. It's just like carrying a big load from day to day, from the morning when you get up.

The day you come from the wedding is the day your family comes home. You prepare a meal for them. There's never, never a time that a woman is supposed to be able to give up once when you accept, you know, you chose to get married.

My girls always tell me that, "Geez, it never dawns on us that this is true." Just like my oldest girl, she now knows that a woman has a big role in a household. Men don't know how to do exactly the same things that a woman does. Without the woman, eventually a man is going to give up.

It's like my girls. I told my girl, why did you chose to have a man? If you have chose your man to do everything for you, then, God made a mistake on you, I said. You have to understand God made you a woman. You supposed to be able to do a lot of things in your role as a woman.

These things a woman is supposed to be able to carry on to their kids, to have them understand what it is all about.

FEMALE POWER IN CEREMONIES

A woman has a lot of power in ceremonies. If it wasn't for a woman, lot of these ceremonies wouldn't ever be carried on. Men would never, never go through them 'cause even in peyote meetings and Sun Dance and other ceremonies, a woman does everything. In peyote meetings when a woman carries in water for the life, they say it's the life of the newborns. A woman carries that in. Even in childbirth, a baby is surrounded by water. That's the reason why they say that a woman carries life. If it wasn't for a woman, how would a child be born? How would that child ... even in birth, if you have a dry birth, a woman has difficulty. A baby is in the womb and it's surrounded by water. That's the reason why they say a woman carries life and it's water.

In peyote meetings a woman carries in water. They're bringing in life into the altar to have everybody share, share the water. If a woman never brought water in, the men would have to stay for days and days. They would never be able to fulfill what they're praying for.

Even in Sun Dance, a woman carries the buffalo skull. If it wasn't for this woman to fulfill this, a man would never go through the ceremony. There's always a woman involved in everything. So, in Sun Dance woman is the one that brings the skull into the Sun Dance, then the men they're the ones that paint the skull. They take care of that skull for that woman. A woman is the one that brings in the earth into the Sun Dance. That woman is supposed to be able to carry that earth, put it in the center. So, that way a woman can fulfill everybody's wishes, kids, and everybody that lives on this earth.

Other words, if that woman stumbles and drops that whole earth, then there would be no … everybody would be suffering. Everybody would be dying. That man that's trying to put on that Sun Dance would be having problems down the

road. So a woman has to be really careful, think about all the kids, all the people that are living.

It's really important for that woman to have to take care of the Mother Earth that we live on today. The Mother Earth and the moon, it's so powerful. Your mother might die, but you still live on this earth. You call it Mother Earth. Your mother's the one that takes care of you.

Your mother's the one that does everything for you. This Mother Earth does the same thing.

Your Mother Earth brings in berries for you. Your Mother Earth does everything for you to live.

IT'S SPECIAL TO BE A WOMAN

These are the things that I know. It makes me special to be a woman that I can be able to control men sometimes, that I can tell them. I'm the one that has to make decisions for lot of things. So, makes me feel proud that I can be able to control anything in the house, can control a man.

I've watched lot of young girls that are lost, that never were told what a woman's role is. It makes me feel sad for some woman to not tell, relate to their girls. You supposed to be able to have close connections with your girls, females, by telling them these things. This is one of the reasons I relate these messages to my girls. Someday my girls will be able to use these workings, all the things that I talk about that nobody ain't going to come and share these things with my girls. I tell my girls that way they can carry on and pass these on to their kids. They can say, "My mother used to teach us these things."

My mother used to tell me, "Your grandmother used to tell me these things." These things, what I tell my girls, they carry those on to their kids. I want them, my girls, to know these ... it's an honor to be a woman, to have respect in yourself, feel honor of all the things that we do. It makes me feel really good when, like, men ask me to pray. I feel honored so that way I can fulfill lot of prayers to help lot of these young girls that are growing up.

When they ask me lot of things, even in cooking, I'm really, always really happy to teach a young girl in cooking 'cause it was a gift to me that I've learned how to cook, satisfy lot of young girls.

It's a privilege to carry on my great-great-grandmother's tradition how it was passed down to me. Like today, my mother's gone, but I use her words to teach these young girls what I know. It's an honor for me.

MEN JUST HAVE NO CONTROL

My mother used to tell that men just have no control of themselves. When a woman comes in, a man can lose control of themselves towards woman. For instance, like, she used to stress to me that never wear tight clothes, never wear sexy clothes, or don't expose yourself to a man because that man doesn't have no control over themselves.

Once when they see a woman, first thing comes to a man's mind is that, "I'm going to get hold of that woman, somehow I'm going to butter up that woman and say lot of good things about that woman and see how I can cheer up that woman or I'm going to give her money to buy her something so that way that woman can come towards me."

That's what comes to a man, but some woman they buy those things. You, yourself, have to put a distance towards that man to have that man respect you. That's when the insanity comes in, when a woman exposes themselves towards a man.

There's a lot of things that a woman is supposed to be able to do. Protecting herself is one thing. She should comb her hair good but never just throw your hair away 'cause some men, they use their spiritual powers to get that dirt off the hair, and they might take that hair and do something to you.

Lot of these woman, they sell themselves. Expose themselves. They say that later on down the years when you sell yourselves like that as a woman, you end up paying for it. Men can continue to go on, can go on and say, "Well, I've used her." But to have a woman to have men respect her, she's supposed to be able to keep her sanity, to have respect for herself.

Like my mother used to tell me when I used to clean myself up, she said, "If a man likes you, that man is going to look at you how you are, how you conduct yourself. He's not going to say, 'Well, that woman dresses really sexy; I'm going to go for that woman.'"

You're supposed to be able to show that man that you can do lot of things. My mother used to tell me, "If a man likes you, and where you come from, too, what kind of a home you come from, that's the way he's going to get you."

Like my husband, he knew that I come from a traditional family. In Sun Dance I usually participate, cook, and all that. He knew that I can do lot of things to keep our marriage together, and we been married for twenty-three years now and never broke up, never. We have our ups and downs, but we raised all our kids, our grandkids.

A WOMAN HAS A CHOICE

A woman really has a choice. Like, I always tell my girls, if you're ready to settle down, if you really think that you're ready to have this big responsibility, then accept this married life. If you're not, if you're not ready to choose what you see in this household, what I go through, then don't choose a man yet. If you choose a man and don't want to take this responsibility, down the road your marriage ain't going to ever last long. You have to think, Well, I'm going to try to make a good, happy life for my family. When you and your companion chose to get married, down the road you bear kids, and a kid never asks to be born if it wasn't for you and the man. You supposed to look out for that child, protect that child, teach that child.

I always tell my girls, you chose this life to marry, marry this guy. Along the line, while you're married, you don't turn around and try to accept another man, flirt with another man. You only cheating on your kids and yourself. You hurt yourself that way. You make your life short.

If you lead a good life for your family, then your married life is going to go long ways and you're going to be repaid at the end. A reward at the end.

Someday I might grow old and my girls will be able to know where I came from. Hopefully they will say, "My mother taught me; it still stays up here. I'll never forget it."

SEMINOLE

Jeannette Cypress
Agnes Cypress
Susie Billie

THE SKY CHANGED COLORS. Fluffy, cottonball-sized clouds began to roll. In the distance a violent wind raced across the glades. None of the mourners noticed, only inched closer to the grave as the Indian Baptist preacher ended his sermon by saying, "He's flying with Jesus in heaven now. Best dead instead of at fifteen out doing what these kids today are doing in this evil world."

On cue the undertaker clutched the tiny white fiberglass coffin under his arm, stepped down into the shallow pit, and placed the capsule into the grave.

Barely had the dust settled from the last shovel of dirt filling the wounded earth when lightning flashed to the ground just beyond the tree line and ricocheted in giant bolts heavenward. Thunder cracked low, tumbling over and over. A single menacing thunderhead stalled overhead, blocking out the sun and casting its shadowy black cape over those left tearfully embracing. Suddenly the raging monster

lost its power and, as if only a whisper with a cool breath, blew across the freshly mowed Seminole burial grounds. Then, just as the rains, still packing a punch, came in horizontal bursts, it was over. Silence rose where minutes before the noise, like a thousand voices from another world, reigned. The dark veil lifted, the sun returned, and again clouds lazed in an endless blue, summer-still sky. Blaze Kowakuce Tommie, born June 25, 1991 and died June 25, 1991, had been laid to rest.

A lingering cloud of apprehension had shadowed my drive out Alligator Alley that previous Monday morning as I sped toward the Big Cypress Seminole Reservation in Florida's Everglades to meet with Jeannette Cypress, a friend from years back. I'd talked with her the night before and she was concerned. She had started dilating but the baby wasn't moving and she wasn't feeling well. I knew something was terribly amiss. Hoping for the best, I feared the worst.

A week or so earlier, I had talked with Jeannette, and she was so excited because this was to be her's and Danny's first baby together. She and he, both, had children from previous marriages, but she said this baby would seal their relationship and draw their bond closer.

When I entered the tribal offices, few said much. Everyone was pleasant but not talkative as I waited for Jeannette to arrive. Finally, Mabel Jim, a relative, said she thought Jeannette had gone to the doctor in Fort Myers and that Danny would be coming by soon to talk with me. Something wasn't right. When Danny arrived, he asked me to step outside, to be more private, and told me that Jeannette was in the hospital and that the baby was dead.

My purpose for rushing to Big Cypress had been to document the grand occasion of a new generation coming into the world. I guess I hoped that it would be a girl, for it was the female world I had come looking for. Instead of a girl, it was to be a boy child. Instead of the joy of new life, boy or girl, it was to be the sadness of death.

Now, as the rains pounded and I gazed through the fogged windows, I remembered the undertaker putting the little coffin in the hole, Jeannette's nineteen-year-old daughter placing Blaze's unused diaper bag in alongside the casket, the sounds of the shovel scooping up the loose dirt, and the dirt falling into the grave. In my mind I again heard the wind and saw the little black cloud. Then, the rain ... the rain!

WEEKS LATER, returning to Big Cypress, I spent several days with Jeannette, her mother Agnes, and her 102-year-old grandmother Susie Billie. They spoke of the baby's death and of the larger Seminole world view, as seen from women's perspective.

THE HARDEST PART

Jeannette ▼ At the funeral everybody kept asking me if I was all right. The hardest part was not the funeral, it was waiting to have the child, because I knew it was already dead. But yet, when I had it … I don't know how to explain it. It was when it finally came out 'cause I had to admit to myself it was not alive when he … when I finally delivered. While I still carried it, it was like there was still hope even though he was not moving. That's why I think I had a hard dilating because I kept trying to hang on to whatever. It was like my body was trying to say, "If you have it, it's not any … no longer there." Even though, really, he wasn't really there anymore as far as life goes.

I wouldn't, I think, I wouldn't have it any other way. I mean, I don't wish that on anybody and I … I hope it never happens if I have … decide to have another one. But, I think, I'm glad I didn't have a C-section and I was awake and I had the child and I saw it. Because now, at least, I feel like there was life in me all that time, and then, when I worked for it and delivered it, I still, at least, had time with it.

Whereas, if I didn't see him at all, I think it would have bothered me more.

I went to the funeral home to make the arrangements. They said for an infant death like that, people didn't really know the child, we just have a small little ceremony and we don't really make a really big thing out of it. Now I looked at that guy and I said, "It is a big thing for me. And I want everything you would do for a normal funeral. I even want the sign-in thing you do for everybody else."

He looked at me; he knew I was serious. So he made all those up for me.

I wanted my baby's funeral to be handled just like it would be for anyone else who had actually been alive and lived for a while. Used to be funerals were handled differently. Customs change some. The way of burial is different, but medicines are still used afterward. My mother remembers how it was. . . .

BURYING IN THE OLD DAYS

Agnes Cypress ▼ In the old days we didn't do like we're doing now . . . for the funeral. We didn't go out and buy flowers. We didn't go spend money. We were told to just like drop everything. No activity. Just stay in the camp till the four days were over, when the spirit was gone, and all the medicine and everything was over with. They said if you start spending money and getting into the material things, that would continue with us. So we would just go ahead and settle down and pay our respects and not do anything. And they didn't have a bunch of people that come to the camp, 'cause way back they lived in camps, and like eat and then take off. If people came, they stayed with that family and ate of the same thing and stayed till the four days were up and then they left. But they didn't eat and then turn around and go home. They had to go through this whole different process like, I guess, what we're doing today probably is . . . it's like we've still got the old way 'cause we're doing the sending off spirit and all that, but yet we've lost some because now we have people from all over coming that's just eating and leaving. They don't stay for the four days.

Now, after come back from the funeral, they supposed to take a shower before going home and eat. We used to. They don't even do that part now.

We always tried to bury the person, anyway, before four days 'cause if we don't … they always say that if you don't bury the person before the four days, then it's going to take another spirit with them and there'll be another death soon right after that one.

Lately it's been where one right after another's been dying. My mother says that lately people have been burying people after the four days. Remember all these ones buried after four days. Maybe the old saying's right.

We used to never want to bury people in the ground 'cause they always said Indian people weren't supposed to be buried. We left them above the ground, and they always said if we start burying our people, then our people will start dying out. Now they say that's why we have so many deaths.

People are starting to follow more the white ways; we're doing the burial services like them.

GRANDMA'S MEDICINE

Jeannette ▾ When the baby died, my grandmother wanted to hurry up and do what I was supposed to do. So she start medicine on me. The older ones usually want a dead person buried before the fourth day, and then they want you to go through like a cleansing process. She wanted me to hurry up and have all that done. She thought they were going to do a C-section on me and they wouldn't. So that really upset her because I laid there for two days with the child still in me. Elders have this thing about death anyway, and she was saying the baby's already dead and it needs to be out of there.

I couldn't sleep at nights after I got home for quite a while, and I think, to me, part of it was because the baby used to be more active in the evenings. So I think my body was still like waiting for the movement, and with her she explained to me, since you carried the child for so long after it was already dead, 'cause I must have carried it what about four days, 'cause it was already dead by the time I went to the hospital, I might have even carried it for five days after it had already died. I don't really know if it died Saturday or Sunday. Monday was when they discovered it dead and it took two more days to deliver. So she told me I needed another medicine done because the reason why I'm not sleeping was because the baby's spirit, even though we had the funeral, it hadn't really left because I carried it so long. She wanted me to have like another medicine done to help me get over, 'cause at nights, I told her, was the time I had trouble. She said, "Usually spirits"—I guess non-Indians would call them ghosts but we call them spirits, not really a ghost— "they sleep in the daytime and they're out at night. Since you carried it for a while it's probably around you at night and it makes you uneasy."

My grandmother always told us,

> *"Sometime when they're leaving, the dead'll come and tell certain ones that they cared for they love 'em, or their last good-bye,*

which will be like maybe it'll appear to you in some form or you might feel something touch you. Don't be scared."

I had those feelings twice, no three times, with three people I was really close to. So I believe in a lot of that. Some people probably think, "Oh God, that's a big joke," but you know when something happens to you and . . .

My mother can explain better than I can. . . .

SENDING OFF THE SPIRIT

Agnes Cypress ▼ With Indian people, like, we do, ah, we always do like the sending off of the spirit every time there's a death. So that it doesn't hang around, whereas with white people they don't have a ritual, or whatever you want to call it, they go through so that's why they always talk about reincarnation 'cause it's probably possible because the spirit never leaves. With us, we're taught . . . I guess it leads back to ... you don't see it on us now but, like a lot of the older people, they have scars on their hands and stuff. They used to even burn like leaf ashes to leave marks on them, and when they die and when their spirit leaves, it's supposed to be like a guiding light to help them cross this pathway to fend off the evil part. Supposedly when you die they light up. When you die they're supposed to be a light that comes from where you burned before. Like a stick, it's a certain little ... it's out of one of the medicine plants we use. It's a little piece of it we take out, like a little piece of stalk. They stand it on the arm or hand and they burn it. It has to go through the skin.

'Cause they believe that if we don't use the medicine for the sending off of the spirit like we're supposed to so they can go to where they're supposed to go, then they'll make you sick. They'll hang around till you join them.

There's a place like a Spirit Town ... the place for spirits. When we do die we're supposed to go where the rest of them are. We'll see, when we join up with, like, say the baby.

When you're going to the spirit land, there's a certain path you will have to go and if you don't have that to shine because it's dark ... there's not really a creature, but there's another ... something that's evil that's there that you have to pass and if you don't have that thing, then it will get you. But that's what scares it off ... the light.

Also, we're supposed to always burn like four sticks and put them out wherever the belongings are left out in the woods. We used to leave them by the body but now we bury it with the body. Before, it used to be up on top of the ground. There's a ... cypress wood, like put it together and lay on top so it's not on the ground. It's covered up. They left the bodies on top; they didn't bury them back then. They just left them. Before, it was forbidden to bury people, but now we do it.

There are places out here—Grandma knows where a lot of them are—where they had left the bodies or the belongings out on the trail. When someone died, got struck by lightning, they laid him to rest with like a canvas, them old type dark canvases, and for a long time some people would see the spirit still around with that dark canvas around him.

THE DEAD STAY AROUND

Jeannette ▼ So that's why they just used medicine on everything, in the yards, and they would hang some bay leaves up. Then they would have to stay in the chickee, and out of the house, for about four months. Somebody would have to sleep in the house, though. It can't be left abandoned, 'cause if it is, the spirit will stay there, 'cause you left it.

Grandma told me I could keep my uncle's little blue house. But she said I had to stay in it. Nobody wanted to sleep in there, but I had to sleep in it. Left a little light on. The kids wouldn't stay there. OK, I slept in it.

Grandma told us, "Don't be scared 'cause there's worse things to be scared of. You could get raped or runned over or mugged or something. This is your own relative. Maybe he'll come back looking for something, but he'll go 'way. Don't you be scared of it."

One time when I was staying in that little blue house, I was looking for her social security card and I couldn't find it anywhere after my uncle died. And the very first night, I felt, that was the same night he died, I felt like somebody sat on me. I was asleep and I ... it was ... it had to be him. I think he came home and was going to sit on the bed. Didn't know I was laying in the bed. All of a sudden, you know how if a person sits on you, you kinda get out of breath. I did. It was like I was asleep but yet I wasn't. I started talking. I remember telling him, "Hey, it's me." And then I was laying there and all of a sudden the weight came up, and I just laid there. Then he went behind me. I couldn't see nothing, and there was a book or something, and I felt him going through the pages. After that, it disappeared. I looked up and I thought, I could have sworn I saw him looking at me through the window.

When I told Grandma the next day, she said he was only saying good-bye. He came over and was trying to sit down and accidently probably sat on me. He was just saying good-bye and was probably just looking his last look and left.

So I went and it was an old book sitting there. I started going through it. The social security card was in the book. I found it. He was telling me there's my card.

That time he sat on me was before the medicine. After four days they're supposed to leave. If it's not four days, he's probably hanging around.

Palmer, that was different. He kept hanging around me. Grandma said, "When they don't leave like they're supposed to and they constantly stay, that's 'cause they want to take you with them." With Palmer that lasted about two months. He kept hanging around 'cause I was getting kinda sick.

When Palmer laid in the bed, and I took care of him, he had this certain breath. It was a certain ... I don't know how to describe it. It wasn't bad breath, but it was a certain breath that he would always breathe on me. I could sense it. He was kinda going like ... having a hard breathing all the time. So when he was gone, I felt like it was inside *my* mouth. I could taste it and feel it. I found myself feeling like I

was doing what he was doing. Every time I'd go in the car I could feel him back in the backseat.

I wasn't scared of him, but it was just like everywhere I went, he was there. I stayed at a friend's house in another city, and he must have rode with me there or something, 'cause he was there at that house.

My son was little at the time, and he got really sick with some kind of fever. He started hallucinating or something, telling Grandma that something was there. Next morning she says, "We need to do some medicine for you."

"Why?"

"I saw him."

I said, "You did?"

She goes, "Remember the Indian jacket you made for Palmer for the funeral? He was wearing that. When you left the house, I was looking out the window. You went into the chickee and he followed you. He's been with you ever since he's died. That's why you've had these feelings."

So they put me through the medicine. When they did that to me, he started on my son. My son got sick and screamed like somebody was standing there in the room. There was nobody there. Grandma said it was Palmer again. He couldn't have me so he chose the next thing that was closest to me. My son got really ill, so we did medicine on him, too.

We always do the medicine after the funeral is done. We smoke the bay leaves and all that. But still some spirits sometimes … he was determined; he didn't leave for a long time. Then he finally left.

OF DYING AND THE SOUL

Susie Billie ▼ People have to accept that it just wasn't meant to be. That person or life just wasn't meant to be, so they pass on. You just kinda accept that.

At birth everyone has some kind of death date and certain number of days. When you get to that point, that's it. There's no way to go around it. Some people just never, they never have a chance at the beginning.

The body dies. The body is just what the soul possesses or what the soul was in. The soul lives on.

It goes to the place where all the rest of them are. There they continue their lives the way they did, because they join the rest of the people that's there. They'll see the other family members that's passed on. When they get there their spirit or whatever just does what everyone else is doing.

Jeannette ▼ I've noticed a lot of older people; they're not really as upset over dying. They are, but yet they have this peace within them that even though we're not going to see them anymore, they're still going to where they're supposed to go. Like, in their mind, they know it couldn't be avoided. That's it. They accept it and don't try to drag it out.

Sometimes, many days, I've wondered why I had to lose the baby. Why did this have to happen to me?

My mother told me she thought the reason it happened the way it did was maybe to spare me. She felt that the person upstairs felt like it was best to take the child and maybe it wasn't my time.

She said, "You just have to accept what happens because there's reasons for it. It was best for that time."

You start thinking to yourself. I know I ate right. I watched what I did. I didn't use drugs. I didn't drink alcohol. And then you start thinking, golly, all these other girls, they don't take care of themselves, they drink, they use drugs, but yet they have healthy babies. It's not a big deal to them. Some of them don't even want their babies.

The nurse looked for the heartbeat and she couldn't find it. Already I was in tears. She said, "Don't cry 'cause sometimes they lay in a different position." But I could see in her face something was wrong as she walked out and said, "Well, I need to go get the doctor."

They put me on that monitor. I could see the baby; his head was just like this. Couldn't hear nothing. He'd died.

They induced labor. It took me two days to deliver. I just couldn't dilate no further. I think my body was fighting against it. They wanted me to take medication for the pain, it was hurting so bad, but I wouldn't take nothing.

I asked, "Is it possible for me not to dilate 'cause down inside I know the child is dead and if I let go, that's it? You know, once the baby comes out, that's it, but even though it's dead and I'm still carrying it, it still feels like it's part of me? The other way it's going to be gone."

All that time it was like I was trying to punish myself, too, if that makes sense. I don't know if deep down I was like, "Well, the baby's died, so I'm going to suffer." You think of all sorts of things.

When he came out, he was perfect. That's what made it so hard. He was perfectly, ah, happy looking. He just looked asleep. I checked his fingers, his toes, his hands, everything. He looked like a normal kid. Eight pounds.

I even took clothes for it. I treated it like a regular birth. They took it out and they laid him right there when they delivered the baby so I could see him. Then they wrapped him up just like any normal child and they said, "You want to hold the baby?"

And I said, yes I did.

They gave it to me and I held him. They asked if I wanted to spend time alone with him. I said, "Yes." So they left the room and I got to spend time with him. Then they asked if I wanted the father to come in 'cause he had gotten back. So, he came and he … I gave him to him like a regular child and I had him hold it. It was harder on him, I think, 'cause he didn't know whether to take the child or not.

BORN IN SILENCE

It was so strange for the baby to be born in silence. I was so used to have a child and right after the birth to hear the baby cry. So here there was no noise, only silence, but yet I had the same feeling. It was kind of weird. It was like … I was happy I had a baby even though he was, ah, he was dead, if that makes any sense?

GRANDMA HAD NAMED HIM BEFORE HE WAS BORN

He already had a name. Grandma had named him before he was born. That was unusual. Name givings usually come later, about a month after birth. Some people never got a name when they were born. Some ask Grandma after they are older and she gives them a name. She will sometimes take from how the father acted or stuff like that for naming the child. Sometimes they pick something from a medicine chant.

Grandma chose the name earlier in my pregnancy. She was staying with us 'cause her son had got ill. She was sitting there on the couch like something was wrong when we came home and we were asking her, "Are you sick?"

And she said, "No."

But she didn't act normal. She acted like she was thinking about something. So, I figured maybe if something's wrong, she will tell me later. So I left it alone. She went on to bed and we're sitting there still watching TV and it was about midnight, I guess. She comes out of that bedroom, her hair was like standing, her hair was all over the place. And she goes, "I thought of the baby's Indian name."

So I asked her, "What is it?"

She told us what it was and that it came from one of the medicine songs. And she goes, "And don't forget it." Then she went back to bed. All that time she had been thinking about what to name it.

NAMING THE UNBORN BABY FROM A SONG

Susie Billie ▼ It was from a song for the medicine to taming snakes. This would be a poisonous snake that could do harm to you. At the end of that song, that's where the name comes from. That's why I had chosen that name. Like medicine song to tame snakes. But since the baby was named before he was born, you can use that same name for another child because he actually didn't receive it.

They don't receive it till they're born. So if Jeannette decided to have another
baby, she could use the same name.

MEN WERE TAUGHT MORE THAN WOMEN

Agnes Cypress ▼ In the old days they had the rituals where they would go
out and do a fast. It was all for men. Men were taught more than the women, but

the women sat around and listened to the uncles, or whoever, and picked it up. Now that a lot of the men are dying out that knew it, the women are carrying it on. If it wasn't for them learning it, kind of sneaking, it probably would be totally gone … plus you figure the menstruation comes in, too. During that time woman wasn't allowed to hear nothing. She couldn't even listen to the songs during menstruation.

Most of the medicine work was done by men. If a woman knew it, she not supposed to do it until older. There's certain medicine that has something to do with aches and pains. There's a certain thing they do to it and to the individual. That one, women can't do it, men can, unless you're real old, like an elderly woman that's been through your cycle for a long time. Then you can do that one. The illness is associated with blood, and I guess they relate menstruation to blood and all that ties in with it somehow.

A lot of the girls don't follow it anymore, but way back you couldn't even eat off the table, eat out of the same utensils. I think they just associate that it's not, not being clean.

Your body's cleaning itself at that time. They consider it dirty; you're dirty at that time. It's something handed down. With us it's always been a cultural thing where you're taught that when you're on your period, this is just what you don't do. You wait till everything is over with and you wash yourself, take a shower or bath. Then you can eat at the regular table. When you go through childbirth, you don't even sleep with your husband for four months. You got to go through medicine.

With us, if you follow it the way it's supposed to be, it's always supposed to be four months. If you follow it.

THERE IS GOOD AND BAD MEDICINE

There is good medicine and bad medicine. It's not a sex, male or female, thing. It's just what the person chooses to learn. They can learn them both, the bad and good medicine. Some choose never to learn the bad side; they just learn the good. Then, some choose never to learn the good side and want to learn how to do something bad to somebody.

> *Good medicine is for healing. To do it, a lot of it is belief in it. If you don't believe in something, if your heart's not in it, it'll be hard to heal.*

AS SOON AS CENTENARIAN SUSIE BILLIE learned of the baby's death, she immediately began preparations for making the medicines she knew Jeannette would be needing. Exercising her position as elder, she dispatched her daughter, Agnes, to the Medicine Fields. I was invited along.

Out from the village, long past the water tower, beyond the community center and the cemetery, Agnes turned right onto still another shell-white two-lane, this one without the double orange strips. Less than a quarter of a mile down, she abruptly stopped her van by a very nondescript field. Climbing out with a butcher

knife in hand and rivers of sweat already rolling down her face, she was ready to dig and cut medicines. With grandson in tow, Agnes streaked knowingly across the field.

FINDING THE RIGHT MEDICINES

Agnes Cypress ▼ This one they use it for woman's afterbirth. This they use for sores on your leg or on your body and it will heal up. They use it for what they call snake disease.

My mother fixed medicine for me when I got it. The sore would get worse and get deeper inside, make a big hole, and a lot of pus. Worse than a rash. Started off like a little rash and you scratch it and it get bigger and goes inside. Every year it keeps coming back. Same month, every year. If you see somebody like that, it's caused by snake disease. You take the medicine and don't eat certain things for four months. If you go by it, you get well. If you don't listen, you don't get better. They tell you not to eat things. That's what I did, so I got well. I used to have them bad on my leg.

Fast for four days when you're using medicine. You finish all the medicine up. You have to use it for four times, finish the whole thing. That's what you do and then you don't eat food with salt on it.

When you put medicine on your body, you have to stand that way the sun comes up. Don't face that way or any way else. Every time you touch the medicine, you have to face that way all the time.

That purple flower, we use it for vomiting, for people drinking or like separated or going through divorce, they want to forget about the other person. Or they want their face clean … they have been kissing … so that's what they use for like cleaning out from that person. Clean the body; they have to throw up or something. They take a whole bunch and you have to vomit it up four times. You start it up in the morning. Sometimes medicine person make you lay down, not do anything, just stay inside.

This one, this plant, it's for bleeding. If the lady's bleeding a lot, if she keeps on bleeding, this one is all you have to do.

Bay leaves, now, they're good for a lot of things. What you call it? Like hallucination. Like the people see something … scared. Bay leaves for them. Like bad dreams, like they seeing dead people. If you got ghost, you can drink it. Sometimes you have to burn it and let the smoke blow on yourself, smoke it around yourself. If the ghost goes in the house, in the building, and you hear it all the time or you see it sometimes, that'll make him go away, too. That's why they fix it for you, to protect you. But you have to carry it with you all the time. You keep it in your car; they protect you. Just break the leaves and put it on your body. You scared or sometime you feel ghost or something goes by you, close to you. You can feel it, so that way you can just break it. You feel that way, just crumble it and put it on your body, rub it on yourself.

ON HEALING

For healing part, you have chants that have to go with the herbs. There's a certain plant out of all the ones you collect; there's one that you have to know a little song or chant you have to say before you even get it out of the ground. Some people think that if, if let's say someone tells you that branch over there or that leaf over there will make you feel well, I think a lot of people think you just go and pick it and do something and take a bath in them, but it's not. It's other songs and stuff that go with it. And then you also have to know how to use it.

It's hard learning a lot of the plant names and stuff. I kind of know plants. I've learned some but I can't hardly pick up the songs too good. You have to practice and practice. The songs are hard to learn. It's not in our language. It's a different language. It's like an old language. They're handed down from a long time ago, so the songs have not changed. The language is still like the old Miccosukee words. They probably sound like Creek, even the ones that speak Creek, they hard for them to learn. We thought it was easy for them to learn, but they're not.

Like for my mother, since she can't get around too good anymore, she'll tell us what kind of plants to get. We go dig the plants and bring them back, but she's the one that has to sing. So when she passes on, if other people don't learn the songs, it's going to go with her.

I'm trying but I can't learn the songs. I got, I don't know what I got, a nervous breakdown or something that blocks my memory, that's why. Nothing stays that goes into my head. Nothing. So my mother gets real mad at me.

LATE ONE AFTERNOON, as gentle breezes shook the heat from the Everglades' swaying reeds, Jeannette and I sat and talked with her mother Agnes and revered grandmother Susie Billie under a thatched-roofed chickee—much as generations before them had done down through Seminole history.

ON LEARNING

Jeannette Cypress ▼ It's hard to learn all we need to learn, but then if you don't give up and you keep trying … I guess with me sometimes, I'm like "Oh God, how can she learn that stuff." But then sometimes I think, well, if I keep trying, maybe I'll at least pick up something that'll be part of her that'll still be here even though she's long gone.

I think Grandma herself don't realize all the other things with modern technology that we deal with, like working. She gets aggravated. But, yet, it makes her feel good to at least know we try. Some don't even try at all. My best friend and I went out a couple of times, brought back the wrong plant; Grandma just laughed her head off. And then she sent us back out again.

One time we were laughing at her 'cause she kept saying there was one man out here that, ah, went to get a certain plant and there's another plant that looks just like it. It's a baby oak tree. When it's young it looks like this other plant. You got to really look at the colors. So she said, this older man, he should know better. He picked the wrong kind. She was laughing about it. We took her to the woods one day, she picked exactly the same thing he picked up before and put it in there. And we told her, "Here you are telling somebody they should know better and you go pick the same thing!"

We all laughed, but she acted like she didn't hear. She has a great sense of humor. She can really joke.

Big Cypress was really isolated until a few years ago. Grandma lived a different life than we are living. It was not like nowadays where these teenagers are getting married or having children. Back then they waited till later and had to know what to do, like how to take care of the kids. Not like today, where it's little kids marrying each other.

She was telling me before that, like a lot of her brothers, the reason why they don't want kids or they never married was because they waited till way late in their years, and they decided they didn't want any kids.

For Grandma, only the last one was born in hospital. Pilot. Her other kids were born when she was by herself. She said she could usually tell like about a week before the baby was going to be delivered. She would already start making plans and moving away from the rest of the family, and then she would have it.

ON HAVING A BABY

Susie Billie ▼ The worse one, the worse delivery I had was in the hospital. My outside deliveries were way better than the hospital 'cause I squatted; the baby

91
▼

was in a natural position. It seemed to turn, and everything was better and easier. In the hospital they had you kinda laying down working against yourself, and the baby kinda kept staying up in there. Outside you're kinda squatting and have something to hang onto. They put a pole or branch for you to hang onto. You have to hang onto something. Every time you got pain, feeling it coming, just lift yourself up with the pole. If you don't have any pain, you can set yourself down.

When the baby starts coming, you know not to sit on it 'cause you know it's going to come out and you kinda ease yourself down. It'll just slide out. You just take the baby, put it to the side, and you wait for the afterbirth. Then you just clean up your baby.

I would be prepared ahead of time. I would already have my bucket of water there, the fire started, and some clothes, and string to tie the cord with. I would be prepared, so I would have everything right there where I was going to have the baby. I would heat the water a little bit and bathe my baby in it, put the clothes on, and that's it.

About four days would be the longest I could stay in the woods because that would give me just a little bit to rest. I still had other children to come back to. I had to feed them and cook and care for my family. My newborn would be right there with me.

I had eight children. Six have died. Two are left, Pilot and Agnes.

Didn't have birth control. There was really nothing you could take by mouth or anything, 'cause if a woman started having kids too close together, too many of them, they would take the afterbirth and bury it in the ground, like deep into the ground. All the other births they would just bury it shallow. But when you don't want a child for a long time, or to space it out, they would bury it real deep.

One lady out here that buried hers real deep, she never had any more children. She had put a rock on top, then buried it. She never had kids again after that time. She had four before doing that. No more after.

Where the World Is Going

They disciplined their children more back then. They didn't have so much crime like it is now. In a way, it was kinda better back then. You didn't have this burglary, mischief, and everything else. Before, we all worked together and we all tried to teach each other.

We were always told that it would get to this point in this world, and I think that's where it's going.

We were always taught to try to keep the heritage and the traditions and keep it going because that was the strength of the land or the earth.

Now the younger people go to school. They mix in with a lot of people and different nationalities. Different people have come to this area. Now it's gotten to where they're not learning anything. They always said that when things like that start falling apart, that we were going to destroy ourselves, too, as well as the earth or the land. I think it's gotten to that point already.

OJIBWAY

Betty Laverdure

TWILIGHT IS THE TIME the dead look back. Reflecting on that ancient Ojibway philosophy of the dead's journeying into the afterlife, I walked among the spirit houses covering the graves in the old Indian cemetery. As the sun slipped closer to the horizon, shadows began dancing with the cooling breeze. I had been told cemeteries are sacred places and envoys from the spirit world guard them. Here, within these hallowed grounds, many medicine people were buried beneath the spirit houses—actual houses several feet high with wooden shingled roofs and openings on the west side for food and tobacco offerings to those in the otherworld.

Without waiting to be caught by the encroaching darkness, I made my way back to the Midewiwin lodge for the night of the Ghost Feast—a meal held in remembrance of the dead during annual fall ceremonies of the Three Fires Society.

Having been invited to attend the four-day event by the grand chief of the

society, I detoured to Lac Court Oreilles Reservation in Wisconsin on my way to South Dakota for my meeting with Turtle Mountain Ojibway elder Betty Laverdure. This gathering would be a hands-on experience of building the lodges by those who chose to come and participate.

All day long the supplicants worked building the longhouse, the Midewiwin lodge. They had come from all over the land of the Three Fires—the territories of the Ojibway, the Ottawa, and the Potawatomi (today's Michigan, Wisconsin, Minnesota and parts of Canada)—for their fall doings.

Just yesterday the weather was in the sixties and seventies with clear blue October skies and crisp autumn sunshine. Then, a front passed through last night, bringing rain and lower temperatures. Today, here on the southern edge of the Hemingway-made-famous North Woods, the slow drenching mist and bone-chilling forties lasted all day. Shivering from the cold, but without complaint, men, women, and children worked steadily and quietly, almost reverently, constructing their ancient nature-born, earthen-floored cathedral in which they would pray, sing, and dance for the next four days.

Slowly, like a half-moon rising up out of the earth, trimmed birch trees and canvas tarpaulin came together to form a structure some fifty feet long with a pit for the fire at its center and a door opening east and west at either end. A flap sealed the western door; entering and exiting would only be done through the eastern door.

It was said that we enter the world through the eastern door—birth—and leave through the western—death. The experiences between east and west are a road, the road of life. At the center—the very heart of traditional Ojibway life—is the Longhouse, the Midewiwin lodge.

At the starting of the first fire, it was said, "The spirits are pleased. They have told me that they are pleased with the people. They see their children gathering around the fire.

"We thank the spirit of the fire and the firekeeper, who must keep the fire going around the clock until the ceremonies are completed.

"It has been work and it has gone slower putting up the lodge, but our people have worked well together as it has always been.

"It has taken effort to put up the lodge, but nothing has been accomplished without effort."

With the burning of tobacco, the ceremonies began.

Now, on the second day of the doings, anticipation for the night of the Ghost Feast was building. After my day among the spirit houses, my own anxiety was peaking.

As thin fogs rose and night fell with gentle mists, people moved through the damp quiet, bringing special foods in memory of dead loved ones into the smoky, dimly lit spiritual refuge. As the Longhouse filled to capacity, with blankets covering every square inch of the dirt floor and people packed tightly around the central fire, teachings were handed down as the feast began with tobacco burning. No one was to cry. "Don't shake hands with the spirit world by crying," because crying would cause the loved one on the other side to weep, too, and attach to the mourner. The dead were to be remembered only in love and just the good times recalled so that they could go on, continuing their journey in the spirit world and not be held to this one.

Young and old stood to call the name of a friend or relative. When the tears rolled, as inevitably they would, an appointed elder immediately rushed with a bowl of burning tobacco to fan the person with an eagle feather to help them release and move the spirit of the dead one.

With the food spread on the altar for the feeding of the dead, everyone in attendance was invited to eat. Instructions were given that all the food had to be eaten, nothing was to be saved or thrown away.

On the last day of Thanksgiving ceremonies, a healing rite was held for the release of problems and troubles that cause pain and disease. With songs and drums, Otherworld spiritual helpers, with duties just for healing, were called in to aid each one in looking within himself. At just the right time on an unseen spiritual clock, the sick and those seeking cleansing were told to dance backward with eyes covered—an acknowledging of the turning of the back on the illness and not being able to see where the illness goes. Certain individuals assisted the dancers by guiding them around the fire. Then, at the command of the elder, everyone released.

A din of silence rushed the tight confines of the Three Fires' cultural womb in anticipation of the announced arrival of "a very special guest representing the Creator." As many meditated, others waited in reverence. Minutes seemed eternal. Hearing became acute. Only now did the sacred fire seem to crack and pop. The breathing of those assembled rose and fell in unison. Heartbeats became drums pounding in orchestrated rhythm. Heads turned in slow motion to the slightest movement that might indicate the guest's entrance.

Suddenly, without warning, the shrill, soul-piercing eagle bone whistle was blown. Once, twice, thrice, four times its call reverberated around the circle and shook the stillness away. Immediately the flap of the eastern door was thrown open wide and the leather-hooded "guest" was brought in. After the smoking of the medicine pipe, the pouch was removed from its head and the tobacco smoke was fanned over the magnificent bird.

A warning was issued. No one should move. Children must be quiet.

Then, with its eyes blazing, the immense bald eagle was carried about the lodge. Hauntingly it stared at one then another, searching souls and connecting with the spirits. Awestruck, no one could move, and at that elevated moment, it was gone—back out the eastern door—and the ceremonies ended. The western door was opened for the first time. Drums began beating in rhythm. One section of the lodge after another rose to dance around the fire for one last time, and when nearing the door, each turned backward to exit.

The next day, with the drums still beating in my mind and the eagle's stare arousing my soul, I raced over the chocolate Wisconsin landscape just ahead of a severe winter storm on my way to meeting with Betty in Aberdeen, South Dakota. Little did I know when my journey began, but I would soon learn that my participation in the fall ceremonies would actually be preparation for the education I was about to receive from the powerful woman and judge from Turtle Mountain.

Betty Laverdure ▼ I'm Ojibway. My clan is the bear, Bear Clan. I have been recognized as an elder since I was about forty-five. I was called Grandmother at that age. Grandmother, that wonderful name, has always meant teacher in all of our society. That's a good distinction and I'm proud of it.

I was a judge at Turtle Mountain. My own tribe, Turtle Mountain Ojibway in North Dakota on the Canadian border. I became a judge there before coming to work among the Sioux here in South Dakota. Traditionally my people have been in that capacity. My ancestors. Judges. There used to be three people, three elders, who determined all issues. So I followed the tradition of my family.

As a judge you are never a really popular person. It's kind of an odd job. You never get any compliments or Christmas presents. I had to develop a thick skin.

DESIGNING GOVERNMENTS, CONSTITUTIONS, AND COURTS

I design governments and constitutions and courts. I wrote the codes for my tribe at Turtle Mountain. We had to reassume jurisdiction. We were under state jurisdiction and everyone was tried in white man's court. Suddenly, states had no jurisdiction. The tribes were sovereign, and we had to take jurisdiction and establish a court.

TELL THIS COURT WHERE THIS HAPPENED

I helped set up courts for tribes. So I had spent several weeks at this place. This one day I was going to survey my handiwork, and I thought I would see the court. Well, the judge, he impressed me. I sat in there with the policemen and witness in a rape case. Here was this young lady who was about to get married. She was dressed in nondescript clothes, hair hanging down. She had charged two guys with rape. He dismissed one; I never knew why. The social workers were there. The police. All sitting there.

So the judge read the charges of rape, then he says, "Tell this court where this happened."

She pulled her dress up and pointed between her legs and says, "Here. Here."

Everybody looked at each other. I was just going to die. I didn't know whether to laugh or do something. I had to brace myself.

He said, "No! I mean, did it happen in the reservation?"

We were just choking. He acted like we'd imagined it.

And he was speaking in Lakota and English.

I just collapsed in my car after I got outside. I couldn't even drive.

That's why he impressed me. He was determining jurisdiction, personal and territorial.

I HAVE A SOLEMN PLEDGE

In my job presently, working in discrimination rights, I have a case that involves leave, religious leave.

There's this man who's at an agency and his superior almost didn't let him go for the Sun Dance ceremonies. Our superintendents are Indians. By and large, we don't have any non-Indians. One non-Indian superintendent out of twelve in the twin states. The superintendent told this man he could go for five days like everybody else, not realizing twelve days are needed for solemn pledging. He just made it very tough for this man.

The man said, "I have to go. I have a solemn pledge. So whether you sign my leave or not, I'm leaving at 12:30."

The superintendent signed it, but he signed it for annual leave. Not for religious leave. He would not give him religious leave. So when he came back in June, he filed a complaint under religious discrimination.

When the man went to the Sun Dance, there was a police officer there that was supposed to be dancing. Two days before they Sun Danced, the superintendent decided he wouldn't let him go. He, too, was going to walk off the job. That would have made it a class action—more than one agency and more than one person with similar issues. But the acting superintendent changed her mind and allowed this policeman to dance, but he went through all that nerve-racking stuff. He had been coming in his off-hours, and he was just taking like four days of the Sun Dance, and actually it's twelve days. There's four days purification, four days of dancing, four days afterward for ceremonies and things. So actually the first man couldn't stay that long because of too much stuff to do at his office. Then, he got a performance appraisal, which is reprisal. The superintendent called the man a "shithead." Because the man had filed a complaint, the superintendent was calling the man a shitty employee, and it will affect the man's entire career. The man is brilliant and he was rising in his job. But he wants to get out because of the duplicity of our own people. That's what is happening. We become our own oppressors now.

I don't think you should question anybody's going into the Indian ceremony any more than you question somebody that's going to another religious ceremony. They all have different requirements. I think one church had the requirement of ten days of church services a year. Those people have to go. I say the same thing with the Sun Dance. Says it's twelve days that's required.

The whole work week is based on Saturday and Sunday to accommodate the other religions, the Catholics and Jews, and the other religious denominations. Then, you have Good Friday; nobody's going to ask you on Good Friday. You have

Christmas. That's automatic; that's a religious holiday.

There's no enforcement of that religious freedom act. It's there, it's beautiful, but you can't enforce it. There's a movement in the works to amend that act to give it some force and to deal with religious sites, too.

MANY CHURCHES, MANY GODS

When white people first came in here, the old people said they had so-o-o many gods; that's why they had so many churches. When the churches came in here, they were vying for members, but they were being subsidized by the government.

I don't have any conflict with the church, but I think what I'm doing is a more intense way of praying. I feel that I am reaching the Creator.

I went to church here a couple of times. They pay so much attention to whether you look right. I knew that everybody was looking at me because I was new to see what kind of clothes I had on.

It was really sad it's like that. I feel really emotional about the whole thing because they are people, too.

Some Indians are still torn between the two ways because negative things are said at church about traditional ways and the Indians say things about the church. It's hard.

THE INDOCTRINATION WAS TOO MUCH

The way we were colonized, the indoctrination was so great. At home, Turtle Mountain, everybody's Catholic there. The indoctrination was too much. In my family, on my mother's side, we had the Jesuits because they were across the Canadian border, and French was the language. They were something like the Mormons as if they were carrying on the Crusades and Christianization of the natives. They had different philosophies than the English or the Spanish.

Until 1934, Christians were subsidized to civilize us. The United States government did that. When the churches got land grants, they established churches, and they were subsidized to educate each child. In fact, the parochial schools, until the late seventies, were given money to educate us. Government giving money to civilize Indians.

It was openly that they'd give a slice of pie to some religious denomination, Catholics over here and whoever, Lutherans or whoever, on this side and over here. They subsidized them to civilize Indians.

THERE'S MORE POWER IN THE RELIGIOUS LEADERS

Americans never truly understand spirituality or religious beliefs from politics of other peoples. They don't believe there's more power in the religious leaders than in the political leaders.

They killed our leaders; you couldn't at that point separate the political from the spiritual. They couldn't understand that. Couldn't separate the traditional leaders from the spiritual leaders.

WITH THE ENGLISH, THE WOMEN WERE CHATTEL

We talk about the colonization. The English came in. Their women were chattel and their children had no rights. They had to pass acts to protect children—child labor laws and all that kind of stuff. They're the people that colonized the Sioux nations. And you will find those are patriarchal. The men we know, that's where they get that idea of women walking two steps behind.

TRYING TO CHANGE INDIANS

Our culture, it's matriarchal. Go to Turtle Mountain, all the churches are St. Anne's, grandmother of Christ. See! All the names are the grandmother. All the churches. Psychology. The spirituality was there; they just had to tap it some way. That's how they did it.

The Mormon church, they're trying to say bring your pipes and things like this. They want you to give up all that and become the true Lost Tribe. The true Lost Tribe. But if we go there, we have to give up all the traditions. They're not bringing us in as an Indian people ... they're submerging what we have. Again, like the Catholics did. All the churches did it. It is just insidious because those people believe.

There are good Christian people, really good Christian people. But they say we're worshiping false gods. We're not. Like they used to say we worshiped the totem, and actually they were clan designations so we wouldn't have incest or marry first or second cousins. You couldn't marry within the same clan. They said those kind of things were pagan. I think they feel sorry now. I think some of them truly believe that they destroyed so many beautiful things.

For example, they're all going to the priest and have reconciliation with God, but what about with your fellow man? They're not thinking about how beautiful to reconcile with your fellow man before reconciling with God. They destroyed that.

CEREMONIES OF INDIANS WERE OUTLAWED

Certain ceremonies of Indians were outlawed by the government; you went to jail for having them. In the past, if you went to those ceremonies, you were denied your rations for fifteen days. They imposed their religious beliefs on us, the European beliefs, because they believed we were worshiping icons or animals and punishing ourselves with self-torture. The Sun Dance was seen as self-torture. And yet, look, Jesus fasted. The saints fasted. They purged themselves with whips or whatever. So we could go to jail for the Sun Dance, even past 1934.

It had to be fear. Even the Ghost Dance, Wounded Knee, when they killed all those people, they were merely establishing a new Ghost Dance ceremony. The soldiers thought there was going to be an uprising, and they shot all those people. That was over a religious belief, too. Their lack of control over the Indians filled them with fear.

No One Could Ever Enslave Our Spirits

Whites have always been afraid of the Indians. They tried to enslave us, but they couldn't enslave an Indian.

If Indians had been on those slave ships, every one of them would have jumped off. Every damn one of them. If there had been no way out, they would have run into the guns or jumped off. No one could ever enslave our spirits.

You know what they call the Indians back home? La Savage. The savages. There is a fear of Indians.

People have realized something is missing. Spirits have been broken. It's been a breakdown of the spirit until now. That's why we're going back to the ceremonies.

Forgiving All Enemies

We have the ceremony of seeking a life vision—what'ya going to do the rest of your life. The other one's Throwing the Ball; it's the wisdom-gathering thing. The Sweat Lodge, of course, is prerequisite for almost all these other ones. It's the method of purification or reconciliation. Then there's the Memorial Feast that's held a year after a death. It's for reconciliation. That feast means that you will have forgiven all your enemies, and all your enemies will have forgiven you. You don't go into any of the ceremonies with any grudges. You have to have everybody forgive you and you must forgive everybody. Maybe that's why we were defeated.

You know, with the missionary, you could go up there and get forgiven one week or the next day and go back and do it the next week or that afternoon. You know, with them it's like, if God has forgiven me, why should I bother with you! It's just the opposite with most Indians; it's universal. You can't go to a cross until you've forgiven everybody else, and you do it at memorial. You talk to the people.

People tell us we don't have to do that. Just go to confession and say five Hail Marys, and you don't have to worry about making up with the people. I know people who haven't talked with each other in years, and they still go to their church. Sometimes to the same church.

SACRED CEREMONIES OF THE MIDEWIWIN

In the Midewiwin, the Grand Medicine Society, there are degrees. You go to the third degree, and if you don't have the real gifts, you can't go further. They are not open to anybody but Ojibway. They're very sacred ceremonies.

With the Ojibway, the men on one side and the women on one side, but they still use the tree like the Lakotas because some of the beliefs are universal—like after death the spirit remains on earth for four days. That's pretty universal belief. The tree, also, is living. It lives for four days. We fast and we pray. We tie tobacco ties. We ask that tree spirit, spirit of the plant, to carry our prayers all the way to the spirit in nature with tobacco ties. We all have the tree.

In the Ojibway ceremony we have the round arbor. It's always round. And then you have little stalls in the trees. The trees that go over like this, they form little stalls. The women stay on this side, and the men on that side. In the Ojibway society, the women blow eagle whistles. Sioux women never do it, never blow eagle whistles.

With the Midewiwin, they pick people that have visions or some gift with healing. To be accepted in Midewiwin, you go to the third degree, which means you can use the medicines. But some have healing power in their hands or have visions when they are young. Those go on to the other stages.

At a certain point in a young person's life, they have to go out on a vision quest to find their mission in life.

When they're very young, they will say, "Did you fast today?"

If the children would say, "No," they were shunned.

If they said, "Yes," they would paint the face. Everywhere they went, they would feed them, because it's so common-like; you know, my brother's kids come here, to this day I'd feed them. No big problem. Like his kids could stay here a week, a month, a year, if they wanted to. They are really "our" kids.

OJIBWAY CREATION STORY, THE GREAT MYSTERY

In the Ojibway creation, the Great Mystery, it means God, Creator, but mostly the Great Mystery. There was a woman there. When he created the universe and the earth, he used all the elements in your body ... like the water and the calcium, the rocks. He had this woman. She was lonely. So he gave her a spirit mate. She bore two children with him. It was said they destroyed each other, and then the waters came and destroyed the earth.

Again she went up there to the Great Mystery. She wanted another mate. So he gave her a spirit consort again. Then she came down and lived on the turtle's back. It was during the time that water covered the earth. All the animals tried like the otter to get her some dirt. The lowly little beaver went down and got her some dirt. He was all wiped out, but in his paw was this dirt. She started painting the edges of this turtle. And it formed turtle island, Turtle Island, the United States and Canada from this turtle.

Her children got along this time because of past spirits; both had spirit pasts to them. A conflict arose between the father and the one who got the pipe. This caused the death of his mother. He fought with him for days, but they were so evenly matched that they finally gave in. Still he had the edge over his father because he had the flint, and the birds and animals were on his side.

During that time the animals each gave something. The bear gave healing. He gave his life and he became medicine.

Our pipe is still a pipe of peace and reconciliation.

Prayer with a Universal Pipe

We have the Sun Dances for the ceremonies. How a medicine man conducts the ceremony is according to what that person's vision is, his interpretation. Each medicine man has a variation in the Sun Dance. Some things are universal: the four directions, the tree, and the four days, and prayer with a universal pipe. But there's different things, like the rounds and the songs and the altar. They're all according to that medicine man's vision. That's the way it always was. Go to one medicine man, you like the way he performs his ceremonies, you go to him, you choose that. Doesn't mean the other person's wrong. Just feel that his way helps you achieve your communion with the Creator.

The ceremonies are really, really personal to people who attend them. They're just too personal except like the naming ceremonies. You're supposed to let the whole world know what your name is. The Creator needs to know to call me by that name, ceremonial name. If the Creator does not know your name, you can't go, can't go over.

I am part of the traditional movement. Others, a lot of them, want to structure it. They've written it down, but they haven't gained it through memory like the way we are supposed to. We're supposed to be oral, learn the songs.

How can structuring it and writing it down be so authentic? Some of it we can't tape; it will not record on the tape although the tape recorder is working. They've got the tape recorder going, they have new batteries, I don't care what you do, it won't tape.

We have to learn through the oral and remember through the memory.

In Ceremonies Tobacco Is the Exchange

Tobacco is an exchange, always. If you want a ceremony, you bring tobacco. Sometimes, in addition, a blanket or four yards of material. But nothing is a substitute for tobacco. If you want a story, you bring a cigarette ... tobacco ... an offering. You always give something to get a return. Tobacco in all our ceremonies is the exchange.

After you complete your four-year cycle with the Sun Dance, you have a giveaway. You make things or have things made or buy things to give away in thanksgiving to the people. I'm having star quilts made.

WOMEN HAVE THEIR OWN CEREMONIES

Women have their own ceremonies in Ojibway, and the men have their own ceremonies in their Sun Dance. Then, when they break their fast, the men serve the women.

It's the opposite way around with the Sioux. You'd never catch a Sioux man dead serving a woman.

Used to with the Sioux, the woman would walk two steps behind the man. The only reason I'd walk two steps behind a man is to kick his goddamn ass.

WOMEN ARE EQUAL, SMOKE FEMALE PIPES

Women are equal. There is an equality. The women don't smoke the male pipes. Smoke female pipes. That's to call the spirits. It's also a voice and authority to speak the Midewiwin song that I have.

THE NEAR-DEATH EXPERIENCE IN CHILDBIRTH

When a woman chooses to go into the Sun Dance, she never has to do the vision quest or go to the sweat lodge or anything like that because she already ... each time she gives birth she has that near-death experience.

For her to do the vision quest, it has to be for a very special understanding because it is a very powerful thing for a woman to go on a quest for something. Men have to do those things as a part of the practice and tradition.

They say the medicine people have certain requirements, near-death experience. Some even have out-of-body experiences. Go into the spirit world and they have the constant communication with the spirits. But the woman does this each time she gives birth. It's a near-death experience.

ADVICE OF WOMEN IN SUN DANCE

The Sun Dance chief, he's supposed to be advised by a woman elder. So I serve that part in that Sun Dancing.

The Sun Dance chief has earned the right to have a Sun Dance. So, when you have Sun Dances, you have a leader in there. He's not necessarily a medicine man. He has just earned that right to do that. A medicine man comes in at certain times during the healing portions of the Sun Dance.

SUN DANCE AND WHITE BUFFALO CALF WOMAN

The story of White Buffalo Calf Woman is that she appeared to these two hunters. One had lecherous thoughts and immediately he went toward her. He says, "Well, we'll take advantage of her." The other says, "No, she looks sacred."

"No, I'm going to take her." And as he approached her, he went down and just was a skeleton and turned into dust.

She instructed the other one, "Go back to your people. Have them prepare for me."

There are stories. It could have been four days, four years, or four hundred years, or forty years, but it was four. They do the ceremony in four days because the tree lives four days. So they start the Sun Dance by sending out scouts who represent the two men that found her. They look and they find a certain kind of tree. It has to be poplar. The first day they get the tree, because that man was instructed to prepare an arena, then trees. So they chop the tree and carry it sometimes in the rain and thunder.

Last year they carried that tree two miles down the road in a hundred and ten degrees. We followed; we had to pick up all the leaves. Then they put the tree into the ground; it has the tobacco, the ripe meats, the ceremonial stuff that I have to provide ... acquire. When we put the tree up, the ropes are put to the people that are going to pierce. Then the leaves are wrapped. Then the means of survival, the woman's all-nice sinew is wrapped just like the cross. The tree's put in the ground firm enough so they can pierce from it. Ropes are tied to it. So that's the first day.

Four days before that we take sweats for purification. Those were the instructions of the White Buffalo Calf Woman.

Sprinkling the Plant Berries Slowly

When you get in there, you are mentally and physically prepared. You don't have any food or water from that point on. Some medicine men don't even allow cigarettes. You load your pipes. The woman teaches you to load your pipes. An older woman can, also, hold a pipe in the Sun Dance. So you bring your pipes out and light them up. Some people have no pipes. You have to earn the right to have a pipe. You put the pipes on the rack and then instructions begin.

On the morning we start, we take a young woman and dress her up in white. She comes in from the east, sprinkling the plant berries slowly. I have the responsibility of bringing her in from the east, bringing the pipe. All are waiting for her in the arena. It's an emotional time 'cause you've spent those four days praying and preparing for her just as it was an enactment of the olden days when she actually came. That begins the four days of instructions, teaching the people to heal, to pray, and giving them the medicines. That's the beginning of the Sun Dance.

She dances for the four days. She always has a stand-in in case she begins the monthly flow. Any women that start that have to leave because of the power the woman has at that time. Older women have sage. We wear simple dresses and we tie a shawl around our waist and we dance barefoot.

Second day is probably the hardest where you feel the hunger; second day you passed and you're going into a sense of probably ecstasy, where you have a deep communion. You can feel that presence in there. If you're sick or something, that deep communication overcomes that illness. I seen people jog ten miles a day for two months or fast and things like this come in there and last one day. Then, I've seen those skinny or large women come in there go through the four days like nothing. One year another woman and I were the only two that made it . . . for four days.

You dance every day, four days. Sunup to sundown. You don't take any food. The last day, you're thinking about the watermelon. You do have the sacred food. You have the cherry juice and the buffalo part and you have some of the ground meat with berries. That's how you break your fast. Then you drink the juice of the cherries, choke cherries. After that you think you're really going to eat, but you can't. You lose like ten or fifteen pounds in those two days.

CYCLES OF FOUR

So they do the thing in cycles of four. Each morning you start out at sunrise with the . . . there are two doors of the sweat. You close the lodge tight . . . sunrise to sundown. The only liquid you get is that water blessed with the bitter root. It's a medicine, blessed by the medicine man. Once in each of the twelve months you're preparing. Each new moon you have something for the Sun Dance. The month before, usually the month before the Sun Dance at the solstice in June or else in the fall, the equinox, that's when you have them. They used to know those things, knew the stars.

UP AT THE HEALING TREE

When my grandson was about four years old, he went with a little sprig of sage to the Healing Tree in the center of the arbor ... the tree that we use. Up there at the Healing Tree, they painted him up and got him all cleaned up. He was going in about two weeks to Minneapolis; scoliosis, going to be in a cast for nine months.

A half hour before surgery they canceled him. There'd been some improvement in about three weeks. Been improving ever since, straightening. So my son began dancing. He's now a Sun Dance chief, also.

My son-in-law, he drank quite a bit. I gave him a pipe eight years ago. Hasn't touched a drop of booze since.

Everything's a circle. We're each responsible for our own actions. It will come back.

I have three more sessions, maybe—I say maybe, because it's Midewiwin—three more sessions to get off this insulin. I had a hard time taking it; I really had to check it, because I was going almost hypoglycemic. So I have three more ceremonies to go through. But then I go into the Sun Dances, too, without taking the medications. Of course, you can't. I have two sets of thoughts—thinking one is that faith has to be great, and the other is common sense that if you're not eating, you don't take insulin. You take insulin to take care of your intake. I go into the ceremonies where I fast. I have one more obligation next summer. That's the elders, the Grey Eagles, the Lakota's Sun Dance. I carry the eagle staff in there, which means that when they're piercing I have to stand there, and then I have to follow the ones that drag the skulls around, dragging of the skulls of the Sun Dance.

You reach a point of ecstasy in the Sun Dances.

MEDICINE PEOPLE KNOW HOW TO PRAY

The emotional thing about medicine people is that they know how to pray and they know how to cry. They usually pray until they cry. They remember how they were instructed.

You go on the vision quest. You go with only one blanket. You stay in the winter. You don't eat or drink. Some come and check on you once in a while, but they don't talk to you. You need to reach that one point, to isolate yourself, to reach Original Blessing.

At some point your ego is submerged and you become selfless. Your spirit is out. Suddenly someone from the other world is talking to you and you lose all self.

Your spirit goes out to that spirit. You can use the cedar for purification, but sage is better.

THE BACKWARDS PERSON

The Heyoka person is a backwards person, not like Heyoka sage which is a false sage. The Heyoka is not a false person. They're usually men; there are not many women that would be called that. There was one at Red Lake this year. This is his fourth year of being backward. He danced backward; he did everything backward. He's lost all his possessions, his job, and everything. He made the decision to do that for whatever reason. Danced in powwow in full costume backward. That's a Heyoka. Backwards person.

Some of our Heyoka medicine men are our most powerful medicine men there are. It's given to them in a vision. They go on a vision quest and have to do this because of the message they received. They fast. They fast and pray and get so deep that they have to be shaken to make them continue to live. The most powerful have male and female characteristics. At some time in their life they feel like they can take the female traits on, but they are not homosexual. They just have both and have become completely balanced. They are powerful! Other people have to take care of them.

I can't explain how these things come. They just come.

FASTING TO PUT YOURSELF AT PEACE

When you fast in this modern world, you have to separate yourself from the TV and radio. You have to rid yourself of the outside world. You can exist and fast. Usually you just drink water or tea. You fast for as long as it takes to put yourself at peace.

The fasting leads to the near-death experience. You're saying, "Here I am, God, I ..." Or else you're praying, let's say, what's so hard for a medicine person is this: You have to be willing to give your life to heal. If someone is very, very ill, you're telling the Creator, "Take me, instead, if my sacrifice is not enough. Take me."

That's why you have people that have medicine powers, but it's a very, very profound thing to do it.

You have to love your fellow man so-o-o much that if a total stranger comes in here, you must be willing to trade your life for his.

When you use that medicine for a bad purpose, it's the law, it will come back on the one doing the medicine. So each medicine person realizes the sacred duties and the price that it will cost them. They must be very careful.

COST OF THE PIPE

Some who are given the pipe have lost members of their families. One lost his sister; another lost a family member. They were given the pipe, and they didn't think they had the right to use it. It was a very powerful one. So they met for many days and they decided to take it. But there was a price. They took it for their people, but there was a price, and they knew there would be. The bad tries to attack the good. When people decide to do this, they must almost be a recluse. You have no attachments. If you do have attachments, you must be willing to suffer great pain.

Sometimes the suffering is so great. You can be in the same room with a person who has something wrong with them. For example, if a person has a bad leg, you get up and nearly fall. And then, the thing stays with you. Your inner strength has to be such that you can cast it out.

Most medicine people are really, really understanding of psychology, the minds, and things like that. They know if illnesses are psychosomatic; they know if they're not.

We had a ceremony where this guy had cancer. The medicine man was sick for months after it, and he went to a woman who purged him of this with sage. Sage or cedar is put in a little pan. You light it and then you pass it around, and then you let the smoke go up and you ask, "O, God," or whatever you want to call the Great Mystery, to purge you of the illnesses from the one you helped to be healed.

A medicine person has to be careful of crowds ... sweating and palpitations and hyperventilating ... because of all the bad vibes that are going. That's because there are so many bad vibes and bad feelings and negative things in crowds.

I distract myself by reading. I sew a lot. I go off alone a lot. I go to the park and walk around, stay outside. I don't shop at all.

STICKS INTO MESSAGES

The mind power was so great among my people. My grandmother had little sticks in her hair, and somebody two hundred miles away could move those sticks into a message. That is supposed to be the devil's work; that's what the Catholics said. It was a power to do that, their minds were so great. The Indian people can no longer do that now.

My grandmother was a powerful medicine woman. She warned me of the tornado. I listen to her now, although she is no longer here. There is communication with the spirit world. Our people were even buried with spirit houses on top of the graves. They face east to west. There are openings on the west side so that tobacco

offerings can be placed there. They still bury people out in the woods. They put those little houses up and put food and stuff underneath there.

COMING INTO THE SPIRITUALITY

The Midewiwin are very powerful. There's a lot of ways you can come into the spirituality. I was born into it through my grandmother. I am not a medicine woman. I have certain gifts, but they are not the real power that you can have, which some people can develop. If I wanted to do that, I could go to the Mide or probably fast to see if I was supposed to be doing it.

Some medicine people become arrogant and self-serving. I don't know how they can do that and retain the God-given gifts that we have. They still have the same power. When you're doing the ceremonies, you can come and see this medicine person has no charisma, and you say, "Is that really a medicine person?" You expect blue lights or an aura or something. It doesn't happen that way. It just … all of a sudden when they begin the ceremonies, they somehow or other … become a conduit to the Creator. Suddenly it happens when they pray. At that moment when they're doing the ceremonies, something else comes in. They themselves don't have the power, yet somehow or other God uses them.

Medicine people are channels to God. He picks certain people He knows. They can be people you don't like, but their total concentration is with God. Nothing else exists.

To reach the good you have to do a lot of praying. You have to take the medicine and go on a vision quest until you get your medicine, whatever it is. Usually, it comes through some kind of animal. Of course, the bear is always the healer. Those from the Bear Clan cannot eat bear meat 'cause you don't eat the animal that's your clan animal. So the bear clan, with the Ojibway, is the healers.

STORY OF THE BAD MEDICINE WOMAN

Some of the people from Oklahoma, the men that are called Eagle Catchers, what they do is they know all the herbs and all the medicines. They have to travel till they're sixty and then they get a pipe. I met one of these. And, ah, he then gave me, you know, the power of the Cougar.

He said he found only seven people, and he said, "What's your history? I'll tell you your history." He says, "Somebody in your family was a discipliner. What's a discipliner?" And he says, "Tell me about it."

And I told him about my grandmother. A woman had been using the medicine in the bad way, this one woman was doing that. So, finally, they came to see my grandmother. She got one of her relatives and my father and they went to confront this woman. My grandmother prepared herself. So she told them to take this woman and tie her. So they took her and they tied her to this pole, and they had to completely tie her up and destroy her medicine.

She was foaming at the mouth. She was just like a wild animal. She was breaking the cords; they were cutting into her, that they could hardly tie her because her strength was so great. They burned this medicine. The medicine was screaming and she was screaming. And they burned the medicine. Then, ah, then my grandmother told her that she was never to touch that medicine again.

They had to go and sound the alarm that she was not to get medicines from the herb gatherers. Medicine people usually get people to gather medicines.

So she was a discipliner of medicine people, my grandmother, and that's my gift, too.

So far, he's found only seven of us in the United States and Canada.

THE POWER OF THE DISCIPLINER

A discipliner can see who someone really is. You can see them. You can see the good medicine people and the bad ones.

This medicine man was molesting young boys in a sweat. In the sweat! For some reason or other I just got thrown in with him. My gift just brings me to these places, for some reason or other, gets me there. In this case, well, I have to warn them. I have to tell them, "You mustn't do this anymore or you will suffer the consequences."

I do it. And I found out, much to my amazement, that it works. I am really amazed that I can see it. I'm more amazed that they can't hurt me. See, because my grandmother saw, she also had the gift, she couldn't be hurt by people. It is a power unto itself. So there are probably seven of us that exist.

I was in a tornado in, Jesus, '84. Destroyed everything I had … except a china platter, over a hundred years old. My dad gave it to me. Dad gave it to me about twenty years ago. My mother's china teapot … and yet that tornado dented my refrigerator. So, when I talk to some medicine people, they say I can't own anything, a house or anything, don't get tied down to this land. I don't belong here in this setting. Only the things I could carry survived, not the house ... a platter, a teapot.

The refrigerator got bent, couldn't open the door, and that platter was on top, there, and there was a little shelf on top, and that was where the teapot was.

I have listened to the medicine people since then. Can't buy a home.

A powerful medicine man said, "Everybody has to go back to their roots. The Great Spirit gave all Ojibway great gifts of beauty. You will never have land, but he gave you a mind. You will always lead. There'll be one of you with every tribe."

Look for us and you will find us there.

THE BURDEN OF THE HEALER

This horse, a Morgan mare, had a big lump on her jaw. And what they did was they tied it off. It would just drop off and die like you'd tie a puppy's tail. So they did that. I came out and said, "What the hell are they doing?" I thought he was trying to cut it. "Bring that knife," I said. Just like that, I wasn't even myself. Just like an out-of-body experience. "Bring that knife."

I cut that thing off, and I was told, "It's going to bleed."

I said, "Shut up! Right now! Shut up," I said. There wasn't a drop of blood. That place came off. The hair even grew back. It was about the size of a quarter. I cut that off. No blood.

I got in the house and, "What did I do? Why did I do that?" I couldn't imagine why I did that. Just took over. A number of times that I've done something like that.

A friend is hypoglycemic. She's had some kind of surgery, and she had some sores about this big and they were just filled with pus. They were draining, draining, draining for about a year. She'd go to the doctor and they'd drain them, dress them. She wouldn't tell me. But one day she was telling the youth and elders about her suicide attempt. So she had these sores and I was close to her and I knew they were painful. One day, she announced, "They're gone! All gone!"

Her skin was just soft and, "They're gone."

So I didn't think anything of it till I went to take a bath. I had those damn things right here on my stomach. Still got the scars. They didn't hurt; they didn't itch. I knew they were my friend's sores.

I put a bandage over them so they wouldn't rub on my clothes. They were yellow. There was pus in them. I could see them, but I didn't feel them. They didn't hurt. They weren't sore. They weren't itchy. I couldn't understand it.

I found out that my friend had lost hers and I had just taken them. They healed that way. I put the dressing and I put the salve, and I bandaged them. They healed over but left real dark scars, is all I have now.

I didn't know I was doing that. I felt bad because she had them. I was close to her.

You never know when you get sick if you took it from somebody. Now my heart condition had to be taken from somebody or I wouldn't be getting over it and finding less and less symptoms. So last summer I went to different doctors and "Why are you taking this?"

I says, "I don't know. The other doctor gave them to me."

"You've been on Nitro pads for four years?"

"Yes."

"I can't see that you need them," he says. "Your ankles have never swollen?"

I says, "Nope. My ankles never swell."

The EKG indicates I have a heart problem. They've taken all these tests. And, yet, I don't have all of the symptoms. My ankles never swell. I don't have any angina. I don't have any heart pains. But the EKG and sophisticated equipment says I have it.

The doctor asks why I'm taking this, and suddenly I realize I don't have heart problems; this is somebody else's and it'll go away. I'm on one medication yet as a precaution.

I've got to separate this world from the other world. I've got to walk in this world and walk in that one, too, and see all the mysteries between the two.

The Bible says there's no greater love than to give your life for your fellow man. That's what medicine people do.

CARE OF THE CRYSTALS

There are so many bad medicine people right now. There were problems with a non-Indian psychic at an elders' meeting. He had a crystal that he broke into pieces and gave a piece to each person. He told them to concentrate. By doing that, if everyone follows his instructions, all that power comes to him. This psychic probably got to a certain point where he got bored by the power and wanted to experiment. I think he was trying to tap into the elders' circle, and he had convinced some of these Indian people of his power. But he didn't touch some because they were so centered. He couldn't touch some of us. We're centered. You could tell the ones that he didn't try to influence. But the ones that he did, you could tell they had personal problems that were intruding in their lives; they weren't that centered.

So one night, I don't know why, but I went off alone. During my walk this young person came with all this tobacco and asked me to visit his house. So, I went. They asked me about the sweats, superficial things. But the real reason was that he had one of the crystals. I took it in my fingers and I looked at it. It broke apart.

They wanted to get out of that man's influence. So I gave them the sweet grass and sage from my pipe. I told them they were to keep it and think about it and light it. Light it, light the sage, smoke and purify themselves. That effectively broke that up.

That man planted a tree right in the middle of the night. Says for everyone to put their most precious things in there. One friend put tobacco in a bag. Another had money tied in a bag. Another friend put in her mother's ring. It was just encrusted with diamonds. And her own wedding ring. That was her most precious possession. So she tied that up.

I got hold of them and said, "Hey, hey, put those rings back on." And I said, "Give me that." And I took the tobacco. "What are you guys doing?"

One woman says, "But we'll be hurt."

I says, "Look, give me the stuff." I unwrapped the money, gave it back. Burned the tobacco in the fire.

The clan mothers later decided to dig up the tree. There were even condoms in there. See, when you plant a tree, you put things in there. Tobacco and stuff. So they planted this tree and they sight the directions. Something overtook the whole crowd and they put that tree in.

That psychic was trying to zone in on part of those elders. I didn't talk to anybody about it. I just took the crystal. I have it at the house.

There's an aura. I had a reason to be there.

Indian people from Oklahoma use the crystals to pray with. They want to have the same spirit and mind or power when they're praying. They all have this one crystal; they all pray for that one thing. And it usually happens through the power of the crystals.

Crystals go from generation to generation. And they're really powerful. Now, non-Indians are coming in and picking up this thing and making an entirely new thing out of it looking for God. They pick and choose only the parts they want. They don't have full knowledge of how to use the crystals or run the ceremonies. It's very dangerous for them to pick and choose what they don't know about.

STIRRING UP SPIRITS

One time this Indian group in Chicago called to South Dakota for the medicine man to come. They'd started something and didn't know how to run it. They'd stirred things up. I went with him, because Sun Dancers always protect medicine men. He sat down and I sat in the back. Then he spread his altar. These little sticks that he uses are about the size of a pencil, and he sets the flags, the colors, and the tobacco. When you say flags, they are a cloth with tobacco tied in them. You put the flags on these little sticks and put them on the altar. There's always fours.

So I was sitting in the back. I heard people whispering to each other. I couldn't decipher what they were saying. Suddenly these sticks flew. Something hit and knocked over these sticks. The spirits went on. I knew that nobody that was human picked up those sticks and threw them.

When we started, he said, "Sing a four directions song; can you sing the four directions song?" He couldn't remember it. So he was hesitating and he was stopping.

The people were so packed they couldn't walk up there.

First of all, he said, "The spirits said this is a dirty place. They are not coming back because they don't want to eat here. Too many things are happening here. I couldn't even remember the song. I have sung it about three times a week for ten years, and I can't even remember the words."

He said the ceremony didn't work. Then he said the food was dirty. There were older people from Pine Ridge who had not been in ceremony for a long time. So he said he would instruct them. He told them how to prepare the food, and he would hold another ceremony the next night. We would have to do it at somebody's house who didn't drink.

When you fix a ceremonial meal, you fix a pot and you don't put any seasoning in it. If you take a taste, the whole pot must become a leftover 'cause the spirits get the first, then you eat the whole pot which is the leftover from the spirit food. Anyway, for some reason or other you use the natural animals; you use deer meat. You don't use chicken; you don't use pork. This group had used pork.

It was an old house with an upstairs. So we did it there and everything was fine. The only thing was the medicine man couldn't find me. I thought I went to sleep. He looked all over and he said he couldn't find me. I thought I went to sleep, and he said, "No, no," he says, "you were gone."

I don't know where I was. I thought I was asleep, finally fell asleep; I was tired. I must have actually left. I mean, there were people standing like, in the room like this; there might have been about thirty-five, forty people. So I couldn't walk out. I don't know what happened.

When you go into things, you got to be prepared for the unexplainable.

LIVING WITH UNSEEN PROTECTORS

Sometimes when I walk around in here, my own house, I'm surrounded. I'll feel that, that there's something in here, always is, and there always will be no matter where I go. It doesn't bother me. I know that they're friendly.

You walk clockwise in your house a lot of times if you want or need peace of mind. You use that sage or the black cedar. Find black cedar to purge the spirits. Put it in a frying pan in the room; burn that. Clockwise in every room. Clockwise, the way the clock works. Use just a little bit.

I did this to this house, already. There's things in here. Some come place to place with me. Protectors. They're not always friendly. In an older house they're there. In my house at Bellecourte there are Indian graveyards around it. Some people can't stay there, in that house. But I've stayed there alone; doesn't bother me.

FOLLOWING THE TRACKS IN THE SNOW

One winter there was a big black dog came here. Kept coming around, staying around, going around leaving tracks in the snow. We followed the tracks and they just ended. Didn't know where they came from; there was nowhere where they went. But we saw the dog.

You know, you've heard of St. Elmo's fire, where fires start spontaneously. That happens back home at Turtle Mountain, and I remember hearing people talk about the Druids. Somehow or other the missionaries brought Stonehenge, elements of the beliefs, and used that. There were priests who used all of this stuff that people believed in.

All the Indian people believed some people could change into animals. So the priests used the stories of the werewolf on the people. They said that was direct from Satan. That was a way to undermine the traditional beliefs.

CEREMONY OF THE WIPING OF THE TEARS

We as Indian people dealt with grief with the Wiping of the Tears, that ceremony after someone dies. In that, you have the water and the comb.

Long time ago they used to completely dress you. People wearing mourning clothes used to wear ragged clothes, never have the new clothes while mourning. So they'd come and they'd dress you in new clothes, in the old ceremony, wash your face—that was the wiping of the tears—comb your hair. Somebody'd comb your hair. Just combed your hair and wiped your tears and gave you this water signifying the taking away the grief, the grave, and the death. All the mourning.

Nowadays, in the ceremony, we stand and feed you. That grief and grave and spirit, all the spirituality, goes into that food when they feed people. Give them water, comb their hair, and symbolically wipe their tears with a cloth.

The one carrying the ceremony always takes a little piece of the cloth that we have left over and cuts it and gives it to them. That symbolizes their new clothes. Can't dress them today; can't afford that.

There's another ceremony called Keeping the Soul. For a year you keep the person's things that he liked, like rings, things he wore all the time. At the end of the year, you give these things to people in remembrance. That's at the giveaways. You give one the watch, one the jacket, one the shoes. You think of that person, pray for them while you're wearing or using these things. Giveaway. Everything someone gets; everything in the house is given away.

PIPE CEREMONY AT THE GRAVEYARD

About five or six years ago a friend came and said, "I'm not going to church anymore."

I asked what happened.

She went down to where her husband was buried. She was going to have a pipe ceremony. The pipe ceremony can be held for the spirit in the grave. She set a table and sat on the ground.

So here comes this priest and he is just spewing holy water everywhere, and he was coming towards her and asking, "What are you doing here?"

And she said, "I'm having a pipe ceremony."

He said, "The people have decided you can no longer do this. You will have to go outside of the fence and do it."

So they argued, and my friend told the priest to "Get the hell out of here." And she finished her pipe ceremony.

I say whether it's a pipe or a Eucharist and if the people holding it are fornicators, then God forgives. When we hold that pipe we're sacred, just as sacred as when we're holding that Eucharist. We should not make judgments about those holding them; only God can make judgments.

I am a traditional person, but I was raised a Catholic, and there is nothing in the traditional that is in conflict.

BOXES OF BONES

There's more of us in boxes than are walking around.

In the elders' group, we've been dealing with that. We set aside a forty-acre burial ground. We got back thirty-four skeletons. Only four had died and been interred. The rest had been rendered. Many army forts had rendering pots where they boiled the skin off the skeletons before shipping them. Studies were being done on Indian skulls to determine if they were human or subhuman. What they were doing ... the science of craniology or phrenology, brain size, and they were doing this till, about, in the early 1900s. Thomas Jefferson was one of the first ones to get those skulls.

In 1900, these are people we knew, that we talked to, our grandparents. They were still being rendered at that time.

We figured there were 18,000 at the Smithsonian in boxes. They're very scientific there. They number the skeletons and what area they came from and if they were Sioux and which doctor ordered them. They ordered several hundred of them for overseas. And they dug them up by the hundreds.

They rendered them like you render an animal: take the meat off the bones, boil it out, clean it out.

Some skulls were cleaned and boiled for the Army Medical Museum. Brains were soaked in solutions and shipped, too. They thought we were inferior and would vanish, of course.

They shipped hundreds of Indian remains to the 1893 World Exposition in Chicago, and the artifacts. The artifacts came numbered to correspond to the bodies or the graves they took them from. The pots they were buried with.

At the Sun Dance, after the reburial, we could see them standing up in the hills and kneeling by the trees ... visible to us but in the spirit world.

The spirits don't rest till their remains go back into the earth. They have to be back into the earth with the pipe bags.

The missionaries came and said our ways were witchcraft. They took the pipes, but they didn't burn them. Go to museums and you will see them to this day.

These things have to come back. They have to go back into the earth. That's where they belong.

One thing I'm proud of, our young radical Indians have never once desecrated a white grave. They have too much respect to play with death, and the souls, and the spirits. They could be doing it in retaliation. They don't do that. It's just in their memories to be respectful.

GIFT OF THE GRANDMOTHER

I relate to my grandmother more than anyone else. She ended up with the medicine bundle and was the last one to Sun Dance in my family. Her name meant like, you throw a rock into the water and the ripples are so far-reaching; that's what was her name. She was a medicine woman.

My mother was so fearful, was so indoctrinated by the Catholic Church, was so fearful of my grandmother.

My mother was a tall woman, she was my size, and my grandmother was a tiny woman. She was just fearful of her because of the medicine and what she considered was witchcraft. Not really witchcraft. When you take the medicines, you take the good and the bad. There's no bad medicine; there's only bad people that use it in a bad way.

I was three pounds when I was born. In those days you don't live when you're three pounds. You're either in an incubator or you die. My grandmother, the medicine woman, took me home and put me on the warming oven in a shoe box. And I lived. She took me with the pipe to pray. So I attribute my life to her, really.

CHILDREN ARE SACRED

It was a privilege to have children. It was not a right. The elders, the women, they used to determine even who could have children. Had abortion medicines. And if somebody was abusing a child, they took that child, and the woman couldn't have children anymore. They determined that.

Children are sacred. They are living treasures, gifts from the Great Spirit.

You always treated them as if they didn't belong to you; they belonged to the Creator.

THIS IS THE TIME OF WOMEN

This is the time of women, and there's a new movement across the country. Women are getting up on their hind legs. Women have to rise in the nation and internationally. We have to be more involved in politics and decision making. See what's happening now; women are more involved as a result of Anita Hill. She won in the long run; in the long run she won. It's going to have a far-reaching effect.

Women are getting up and talking.

Women are rising again in our Indian nations.

ELDERS BELONG TO EVERYONE

Elders belong to everyone. We are to instruct our families because they are being destroyed. We need to strengthen our families, plus our communities and our nations. We must strengthen other nations through the prophecies of our society. We must encourage everyone to be there for everyone.

ONEIDA

Maisie Shenandoah

I AM A WOLF CLAN MOTHER for the Oneida Nation. My Indian name is Hul-eegu-wahnay, which means "She Teaches." I am responsible in the ongoing political, spiritual, and traditional preservation of our rich heritage. I have been teaching the traditional ways of the Haudenosaunee, or the Iroquois, for over thirty years.

My life has been so full, it seems it could take months to tell just the highlights. Ever since I was a small girl I have been strongly influenced by my mother, Mary Cornelius-Winder. She was strong, full of life, laughter, and spiritually connected to the Creator. Being a woman who practiced natural medicines, she was known as a midwife and delivered hundreds of babies, including her own.

I was the firstborn to an identical twin named Elizabeth. I was fortunate to have the name of my mother both in English and in Indian. My mother taught me to respect all natural life around me. She taught me to be honest, grateful, to help whenever needed, and above all, to respect the elders. To this day, I pass on these traditions to my children and grandchildren.

When I was young we didn't know any of the modern things that children know today. There was no electricity, running water, telephone, or automobiles. Many nights I remember sitting around a fire telling stories, legends, singing and dancing to our Iroquois chants. Neighbors from all over would join us. Some of my most favorite memories include times when all of us in the family would take potatoes, a frying pan, our lantern, and fishing poles out to the creek with my father. We would cook the fish as they were caught. We were lucky to have such a

caring mother and father who always found a way to take care of so many children.

My mother, who is widely known as the "monarch" of the Oneida Land Claims of New York, had a vision that the Oneida people would one day reunite as one. That has, now, become my vision.

I am proud my children will carry on my dream. They are a strong part of the Oneida community. They treat me with dignity, respect, and if necessary, would give their lives to defend me.

Throughout the years I have experienced many difficult times, but the Creator has always given me the strength to continue on. I have witnessed moments that have caused great stress for our Oneida people. I have spent countless hours in defense of our sovereignty, land, and traditional ways. One day we will again stand before the world as a people who have overcome the odds and survived as a nation.

I remember the first time I met Maisie Shenandoah. As I turned onto the narrow two-lane heading south out of Oneida, New York, on my way to what was left of the original Oneida Territory, the memory of that first encounter almost eight years earlier flashed as clearly in my mind as if it had been just yesterday.

I had been attending a Grand Council meeting of the Iroquois Six Nations Confederacy at Onondaga Territory just south of Syracuse. With the chiefs and most of the clan mothers of the nations in deliberations, I walked across the dirt courtyard from the Longhouse and into the cook house for a cup of coffee. The tables in the eating area were almost deserted, a few diehard coffee drinkers talking politics of the day and sipping their favorite brew, but in the next room there was wild activity. As was always the case, women were laughing and bustling about as they prepared the food for the day, corn soup being the main dish. Maisie was right in the middle of the group, up to her elbows in biscuit dough and the ever-present smile on her face.

As I topped the last, always surprising, quick hill before making a left into the Territory, I remembered the sweat rolling down her face as she opened the door of the huge oven, heat boiling out, to remove a tray of big, golden brown biscuits with one hand and with the other slide in another tray for baking. Her eyes had shone with pride at being so practiced knowing when to make the switch. Her timing had been exact and her movements had been precision-smooth. She couldn't hold back a thundering laugh. With her everything seemed to be a joy and she was always busy doing something.

Now as I walked up to the front door of her enlarged mobile home, I noticed neighborhood kids gathering. Maisie had something going on. Within minutes I was back out front watching as Maisie, with sweat from the July heat rolling down her face, had the children encircling her. In her lap was her Iroquois No-Face Doll. It was story time with her treasures, the children.

IROQUOIS LEGENDS

THIS IS THE LEGEND OF THE NO-FACE DOLL

A long time ago, the Creator, He gave us what we call the Three Sisters, and it's the beans, corn, and squash. They were our sustainers of life.

The Corn Spirit was so thrilled at being one of the sustainers of life, she asked the Creator if there was anything more she could do for her people. So he

told her about a doll that could be formed from her husk. A beautiful doll was made, and she was given a very beautiful face. Now the Iroquois believes that everything has a spirit, and this doll traveled from village to village. When the doll traveled from village to village, everybody told her how beautiful she was. It wasn't long before she became conceited. This means that she thought she was better than everyone there.

One day she heard a voice call her, and it was the Great Creator. And on the way to the Creator's lodge, she passed a pool of water and looked down at herself in the water at her reflection, and she admired herself. She thought, "I really am beautiful."

So when she met the Creator,

the Creator told her, he said, "You have to stop being conceited; you have to stop thinking you're better than everyone else, or I will give you a terrible punishment."

What it was he would not say. And the doll became very frightened.

And so the doll returned to the village again, and once more she traveled from village to village. Everybody started reminding her again how beautiful she was, so it wasn't long before she forgot the Creator's warning. Again the Creator called to her. And so on the way to meet the Creator she passed the pool of water again, and she looked down and admired herself. She finally met the Creator and the

Creator said, "You did not listen to my first warning; now I have to take your face. You can never have a face again."

The doll pleaded with the Creator, but he would not listen. So the doll, on the way back to the town, knew where a pool of water was, and she looked down at the reflection and she didn't see it. And she was very sad.

This is an Iroquois legend on the No-Face Doll, and it's a lesson story that we learned that we should never think we are better than anyone else or a punishment this great could be given to us by the Creator. This is just one of many Iroquois legends.

THE OWL AND WEASEL STORY

Did you ever hear of little people? Well, a long time ago our Creator placed little people here on this earth to watch over and protect us. They dwelled in caves, and in hollow logs, and under rocks. And it's a known fact that only young children and elders can see and talk with them.

Well, in the beginning the owl and weasel would fight all of the time. And one day the owl was so angry that he flew down and snatched up a baby weasel and killed him.

So the weasel went and killed the baby owl. This went on and on, and our Creator became very upset and pulled the little people to guide the weasel and the owl.

One day the owl was chasing the weasel and the weasel went running into a hollow log and the owl flew in right after him. To their surprise they found themselves with all these little people. The little people told them that our Creator said they had to be punished, and they needed to stop fighting and that they would lose their color for fighting. The little people had a corn-husk curtain that they pulled across their doorways and it became very dark inside. The weasel was so scared he put the tip of his tail in his mouth. Because the weasel put the tip of his tail in his mouth, it's the only part of the weasel that is still black.

To this day in the winter they both turn snowy white. This is to remind them never to fight again. The owl and the weasel will never forget what happened in that log deep in the forest.

LEGEND WHY THE EVERGREEN TREE ALWAYS STAYED GREEN

When our Creator made this world, the first thing He made were the trees. He had so many things to do, He asked the trees if they would watch over the land for Him. The trees promised Him that they would. The Creator told the trees that He had to go away but He would be back. So the trees waited and waited for the Creator's return. They began to become very sleepy, and they got sleepier and sleepier. They finally all went to sleep except for the evergreen tree who was still watching over Mother Earth.

The Creator finally returned to find the trees sleeping, and He became very upset with them. He told them because they had broken their promise they would lose all of their leaves in the winter.

To this day whenever we see the evergreen tree we are also reminded never to break a promise.

LEGEND OF TURTLE ISLAND

This is an Iroquois story of Turtle Island. This happened long before the earth was made. There was a place where Good Beings dwelled. This was somewhere very high in the sky and above the clouds. There lived a Woman Being so extremely curious about a strange tree. This tree was different from all of the other trees that she ever had seen. And she would spend her time wondering what was under the tree. She had a strange feeling there was something there.

One day a big, strong wind blew the tree over. She quickly ran over to the hole where the tree once stood. She was in such a rush to see what was there, she fell right into the hole. She fell into a strange darkness. She kept falling and falling; it seemed like it took a long time. Finally, below, she saw a great body of water, what we call the ocean, and she noticed that there was no land and she became very frightened. The animal sea creatures saw her falling, and they wondered how they could help her, and they yelled up to her, "How can we help you?"

She said that she needed something to fall on, some land or some dirt. First, the beaver tried to get some dirt for the woman to fall on, but the water was way too deep. He quickly came back up for air.

The duck also tried; he also failed. The land was too deep below the water. With all his might the otter dove straight down to the bottom of the ocean. The wise old sea turtle asked him, "What are you going to do with all that dirt?"

The otter did not answer. The great sea turtle said, "You may put that dirt on my back so the Sky Woman will have a place to land."

This is why we call the earth Turtle Island.

SENECA

Janice Sundown Hallett and Her Children

Tara, 26 ▾ Renee, 24 ▾ Jill, 21 ▾ Kim, 19 ▾
Ashley, 19 ▾ Thomas, Jr., 13 ▾ Ruby, 7

LIKE A STARTLED FLOCK of geese flapping madly to escape in fright, discord struck Tonawanda in early February 1992. Dissidents attempting to overthrow the centuries-old traditional Longhouse government of chiefs, clan mothers, and faithkeepers stormed the nation's offices, proclaimed themselves the Interim General Council, and declared their self-appointed council the legitimate government of the tiny Seneca reservation twenty-five miles east of Buffalo, New York.

The coup failed. People rallied behind the chiefs and saved the government, a consensus-building participatory democracy based on the Great Law handed down by the Iroquois Peacemaker, the legendary Iroquois messianic figure.

When the dust had settled and the gunfire had ceased, it was obvious that the rebels had lost more than a mere skirmish. Because of their behavior in going against the Original Instructions outlining the way to live in peace and harmony,

certain provisions of the law had to be applied. Every participant in the coup was removed from the tribal rolls by the chiefs and, thereby, stripped of citizenship as a Tonawanda Seneca.

Banished! Permanently! For stepping outside "the circle," they do not, according to Seneca spokesmen, exist anymore.

Somewhat subdued but with her tremendous wit and riotous humor still intact—no coup or anything else could silence her laughter—Janice Sundown Hallett was thrust into the middle of the conflict. In her newly appointed role as faithkeeper, she had to be a beacon for the way of life of the Haudenosaunee, or People of the Longhouse. Ceremonies had to be put through, food had to be prepared, and the Longhouse had to be maintained, and as one of the faithkeepers, Janice worked diligently carrying out her duties during the crisis. The long hours neither slowed her usual quick pace nor dulled her ready laughter—always on the edge of erupting. It could easily be said that she is one of the notorious Tonawanda "music makers" and dearly loved for helping to lift everyone's spirits in spite of trying times.

Somberly, momentarily putting aside humor, Janice states, "The chiefs say there can be no going back. Banishment is permanent. When people try to destroy the government, they have made their decision. Did it to themselves. No one did it to them. They turned their back on the people. They stepped outside the circle."

Always looking for the lighter and brighter elements of any situation, although the serious and thoughtful side is ever-present, Janice does not dwell on the negative. She says, "Our people have had adversities since the first colonists arrived. We have had to endure many fights to maintain our way of life. And I know we will have many more in the future. That just seems to be a fact of our lives. They do seem to get longer and harder as we go along, but our ancestors had it hard, too.

"So why not laugh? It makes life a little easier and more fun, too." And she laughs real hard with a twinkle in her sparkling brown eyes.

Like the traditions handed down through the generations, Janice has passed along those traditions to her children—six girls and one boy. It is obvious they have absorbed much Janice has passed along, because they freely share with those they come in contact with. They are absolutely serious about maintaining their traditional way of life. And to be sure, they have taken after their mother in another way. They laugh, too, and with their laughter the music at Tonawanda continues with another generation.

Janice ▼ A healer told me I'm the type of a person that people will either love me or hate me. There's nothing in between. I will either be their friend or they will hate me. There's nothing in between there. And my life has been that way. It's not with me, it's them. I don't have that attitude.

He said that I was very easygoing, that I was easy to talk to, that anyone could talk with me, but it was with the other people that either liked me or hated me. There was no in between.

I said, "Well, that's their problem, not mine."

MY CHILDREN CAN TALK TO ME

My children have always been able to talk with me about anything, whether it be sex or money or boyfriends or whatever, they can talk with me.

In our tradition, we are not to judge.

We talk about things and I leave the decisions up to them. I figure after a certain age they know right from wrong. So I don't judge them. In our way, even the individual is sovereign.

MARRIAGE IN THE LONGHOUSE IS FOREVER

If you're married in the Longhouse, then there is no divorce. You'll always be married to that person.

I have seen a lot of people that were married in the Longhouse and have gone astray, have gone with someone else. That never lasts. It might go on for twelve years, but it eventually breaks down. They never end up with that person for the rest of their life. The reason why is because they were married in the Longhouse and that's what the Creator tells us. When you get married there, that's for life.

I tell my children, "If you get married in the Longhouse, that's for life. Not for fifteen years and then you go off with somebody else. That's for your whole life."

ON BEING A HOUSEPLANT

I come around here once and I'm not going to waste it. I'm not going to sit home and be a houseplant.

I guess I have that idea because my mom had rheumatoid arthritis when she got older. She was right down in bed like for the last three, four years that she was with us. I don't know what the Creator has in store for me; who knows. Maybe I'll end up like that, but while I've got my faculties and my health, I'm going to go and enjoy myself. That's the way I look at it. At least I can say I was here and was there and didn't just sit home and do nothing. That's the way I look at it. I only go around once in this life.

SEX IS THE TRICK

Sex always seems to do the trick when you first get married. If you get into an argument and you have sex, that makes everything all right. You forget everything, everything that you had been arguing about. If you're satisfied, you forget. If we had an argument and then we made passionate love afterward, I didn't remember or bring it up again. It didn't matter after that.

Like now, once in a while there's passionate lovemaking. Once in a while, not often. Once in a while will do a long time now. No, no it's not passionate anymore. Now, it's, what word am I looking for? Gosh, what am I looking for? It's, ah, it's not all, all the excitement and stuff like that. Gosh, how can I say it? I'm looking for a word for it. Oh, gosh!

Like, like you know it's there, and you can have it anytime. I guess it's less interesting. Well, I don't ... yeah, yeah because you know, you know ... I'm not saying it makes it less interesting, but it's a more comfortable feeling, or at least, I am. I'm more comfortable with it now.

It's that comfort that is there that you know you can get it anytime. To me, I don't think about sex like I guess I used to when I was younger. Now, I don't think about it, because I'm too goddamned tired when I go to bed. When I go to bed, I want to sleep.

SEX IS A POWERFUL FORCE

The sex drive is a powerful force, but as far as sex is concerned, I never really placed a big importance on it. Take it or leave it. I don't think it is that important to me now. Nah.

It might be better now, but I think when we first got married it was more exciting. I guess maybe after a while it's just there, and you know it's there. You know you could probably have it anytime. There's not that urgency for me. My husband might have it, but I don't. He's not changed; no, I don't think so. No. No. Maybe a little less, but ... This is deep stuff.

CHILDREN AS A GIFT FROM THE CREATOR

The Longhouse is the children. The children are the Longhouse along with the chiefs and the faithkeepers.

With children we always have to think about seven generations to come but yet unborn.

It's hard to explain to a non-Indian what it is to be Indian—I wouldn't necessarily say Indian, because there are a lot of Indians that act like non-Indians and hardly know their own traditions.

If you're brought up traditionally, you are taught that having children is what a woman is put down here for, put on this earth. As we call it, visiting here. We are, in our way of life, we are to bear. We're supposed to bear twelve children in order for us to get to the Sky World. If we bear twelve children, then we go from here right straight up. We go right to the Sky World. There's nothing in between that would ever stop us. As you can see, there's a lot of people that don't get that far. Including me!

GOING STRAIGHT TO THE SKY WORLD

That's what made us feel good when my mom passed away, 'cause one of the chiefs came over to the house before they brought her back. He says to us, he said, "If it makes your heart a little easier, you can believe that your mom is gone right to the Sky World." He says, "Because she had more than twelve children and this is what they tell us, that that's where women go if they have twelve children."

That is in our instructions. As far as women go, they bear children; they are the ones that give children directions throughout their life, and they're to be good Longhouse people. Good traditional people. Women are supposed to try to teach children the language.

It's kinda hard right now, in this day and age. Women teach the ways of the

Longhouse, and the Longhouse ways are very strict. There's no gambling. There's no drinking.

THERE'S NO ILLEGITIMATE CHILDREN

There's no shame if someone gets pregnant without being married. No shame. That's the difference between us and those people out there, the way we were brought up. 'Cause from when we were little, that's what we're taught. So we can't say we don't want this one or that one. If you believe in our way, then that's the way you will feel.

You will welcome all children. There is no illegitimacy.

There can't be because we're a matriarchal society and matriarchal is the women.

So, who cares what the man is! We have clans and we go by the mother. There's no bastards in this world. Whatever we are, that's what our children are. If there were six children and six different fathers, that wouldn't matter. In this day and age the father would have responsibilities for the welfare of the child or children, however.

PREGNANT OR NOT, NO BIG DEAL

It doesn't matter if a couple lives together and does not get married. We don't place an importance on pregnancy. If we get pregnant, we are. If we don't, we aren't.

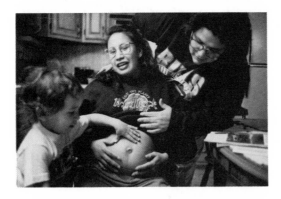

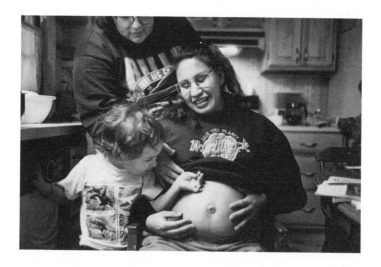

To non-Indians, it's such a big deal. To us, we take it with a grain of salt.

It's like age. Like when people turn forty, they are all up in a dither, because they're forty. To me, forty came and went. I didn't think anything of it. And fifty is fast approaching, and I don't think anything of it.

If our children get pregnant, we're not all in a dither. Should they have an abortion or not? There's only one answer in our way of thinking, and that's to have the baby.

Like with Thomas, when I got pregnant with him. I was thirty-six years old when I was pregnant, and I went to the doctor. He asked me if I would have an ultrasound done. He said because he wanted to see if the baby was all right. That never even entered my mind that he wouldn't be all right.

I said, "No. I don't care how old I am. I would not have it done because whatever the Creator has given me, that's what I take." That's what I told him. He says, "OK."

So I have a little beautiful thirteen-year-old now. I guess that's the difference between us and them is because those are trivial things. When a girl gets pregnant, she gets pregnant. She has that baby whether the father's there or not. That's our upbringing. That's what we're put here for.

LIFE'S TOUGHER FOR WOMEN

It's tougher for women than men. She not only has responsibility for the children, but she has responsibility of taking care of the house. If she's alone, she has responsibility of, if she has a wood stove, of maintaining that wood stove. Making sure there's wood there.

The guy, if he has any sense of decency, he'll help her. But if he don't, he's gone off.

KIDS CAN'T BE EXPECTED TO BE PERFECT

We can teach the children just so much, and the rest is up to them. You can't expect kids to be perfect all their lives. I think they stray once in a while. I guess they wouldn't be kids if they didn't. I carried on some myself.

The girls did turn out real good. I can just tell by the other children their age and what they're doing now. The girls don't do that. I guess it's because they see the values that the Longhouse has, what teachings there are, and they're really strict, really strict teachings. They are good Longhouse people.

I guess it's the way we brought them up, and what we taught them when they were small. That's important, to teach the children when they're small.

Kim is having a baby. She'll have to go it by herself; the boy isn't going to be

around to help her. He's not going to grow with that baby. He's so young, he can't be expected to be responsible when he's a child himself.

Kim's been out of school for like two years, and she realizes that some day she will walk down that road with that child by herself. It probably scares her, but she don't ever talk about it. She knows that I will always be there for her.

I don't know how guys can not care about a child that is theirs. I don't understand.

FULFILLING THE CREATOR'S WISHES

When you bring a baby into this world, you're only fulfilling the Creator's wishes. That's what you do. Last year the kids asked me what I wanted for my birthday; I said to them, "More grandchildren."

ADOPTING A DAUGHTER

Ashley came to live with us in 1987. That wasn't quite a year after her mom died. It was hard after she lost both her parents. Her mom died in March, and she stayed with her mother's sister for a few months. Ashley had to stay home with the smaller kids, because her aunt wouldn't be home. So, she was starting to miss a lot of school. She called me one day and she says, "Can I come and stay with you?"

I said, "Yeah, that'll be all right."

So, that weekend she came and she's been here ever since. She's got her own room now, and I think she's a lot happier. She doesn't ever talk about her mom and dad. She doesn't.

Her mother died in a car accident. Her father committed suicide a year to the day after her mom passed away. Ashley found him. He put a hose in the car from the tail pipe.

Her mom and her dad had divorced before the accident, maybe four years. He had remarried, a non-Indian, and that didn't last. She never talks about it.

PROMISES MADE AT SIXTEEN

When I was sixteen, I made a promise to myself that I would never be an alcoholic or drink like I had seen others do. I've kept that promise to myself.

I probably didn't drink until I was twenty, twenty-one. I never drank to the point where I got drunk. I never ever wanted to get to the point where, when I drank, I got drunk and didn't know what I was doing. Now I don't drink at all. No, not now. It's probably been twenty years. When I did drink, I only had one or two maybe once or twice a year.

POWER OF THE CLAN MOTHER

The clan mother selects the chief for that clan. The chiefs do most of the decision making, with the consent of the clan. If they get stuck or something like that, then they take it back to their clan and have their clan discuss it. The ultimate

decision with a clan comes from the clan mother. Whatever the clan mother decides, goes.

The role that women play in the Longhouse is they carry through with the traditions and ceremonies. The faithkeepers are like the overseers to make sure it does get done. We make sure it is passed on to the little ones.

THE CREATOR HAS HIS THINGS FOR US TO DO

I was selected as a faithkeeper even before I was born. The Creator has His things for us to do while we're here visiting, and it's set up before we are ever born.

We have to work at the Longhouse putting on the ceremonies, helping with them, making sure they go through.

LOSS OF A CLAN

How we're picked, they watch. The other faithkeepers of the Longhouse watch you for years and years. Watch how you perform, how you help, when you

help out, how often. When they picked me, they didn't ask me. They just came and sat me on the bench, but I knew what was coming.

There are faithkeepers for every clan. My clan is Snipe. It is one of the water clans. There are eight clans, but the eighth one, which is Deer, they only have two girls left in it, and those two don't have any children and they're beyond childbearing age. It'll be lost with them when they're gone, 'cause they don't have anyone to carry it on. That's the disadvantage of having church. They both go to church, and they never followed the Longhouse ways, so they never had any children to carry on the Longhouse religion.

THE FAITHKEEPER'S NAME

Usually the faithkeeper names come from your clan. Every clan has names. Like my name came from my mother. She was a faithkeeper. When they go on to the Sky World, their name is put back into the clan to be passed on to someone else.

The name is an Indian name, a faithkeeper Indian name only for faithkeepers. Nobody can use it but a faithkeeper.

I did have another Indian name; I don't anymore. The other name is gone. Once you become a faithkeeper, that's your name. My name right now is Wen-nee-chee-yos-tah.

CEREMONY OF THE ALL NIGHT DANCE

Our All Night Dance is coming up. We don't usually let our kids go until they're like Tom, he's thirteen now; he's changing. He's going into manhood. I will let him go. Like, Ruby's too little yet. She hasn't gone through that transition yet. So, she can't go to it. She doesn't know anything about it. I haven't even talked to her about it. She knows it goes on and she knows she can't go. I would never let the girls go down unless they've had their period first, 'cause that's when they start to become a woman.

The All Night Dance is a feast for the people who have gone on before us. The Dead. We have food, and songs are sung. The first song is about not going to sleep during the dance, because we have all the people there that have gone on before us. Spirits.

LETTING THE SPIRITS DANCE

Then there will be a talk in Indian telling you to leave room between the dancers, so you can let the spirits dance with you. You don't go to sleep, because they could come into your body.

You don't have younger kids come to stuff like that because of "them" being there. A child can see things that adults can't see, and they would know that they're there.

When Tara was maybe two years old, I took her with me for All Night Dance. One of the older women, she's gone now, came over and put black stuff on Tara's face and that keeps "them," the spirits, away from her so they don't bother her and she'll be able to sleep all right.

SONGS BRING BACK THE SPIRITS

They would sing those songs because of all those people being there that have gone on. The songs brings them back.

Tobacco is burned first; then the speaker calls them back. He tells them that they are to be there just to listen to the songs, and that they can dance certain dances. There are certain times that they will dance with us. He tells them not to bother anyone and for us not to be afraid.

SPIRITS LISTENING IN FROM OUTSIDE

The ones who have gone on may not have always come into the Longhouse and participated; they might have stood outside. So when we go through those certain songs, the speaker opens the doors for them so they can listen from the outside. They may come back but still be standing outside.

We've belonged to it probably about twenty-five years. Grandma Nell died in 1960, so it was after that we got initiated into it. I'm in charge on our side. We have water clans and land clans. A person from each side is in charge.

PROTECTIONS FOR CHURCH PEOPLE, TOO

Even though the church people don't participate because it's a feast for the dead, they're very leery when we don't have ceremonies. They realize that they're protected by this, too. A few years back we let our All Night Dance go for that one year. Within that year we lost sixteen people, and the church people were saying, "The Longhouse people have to have that dance; we lost too many people."

If we don't have it, the pull from "them" is so strong. It's for "them." We've had it every year since then.

CEREMONIES ARE FOR THE WORLD

The Longhouse isn't a selfish place. The ceremonies are for everyone. When we thank the Creator, we never, ever, ever say, Can we have this? Can you give us this? Everything has already been given to us and that's why we're thankful.

EVERYTHING IS A CIRCLE

The ceremonies is only one aspect of our lives. Everything is a circle. It continues. It goes on.

As the clock ticked toward midnight, a fine light snow began peppering the ground outside. The wood stove stoked up to ward off the biting February cold while Janice dozed. Daughters Tara, Renee, Jill, and Kim paid no attention. They were still fired up from just having left the bowling alley where they had bowled together on the family team in a league of mostly non-Indians. Not a one was ready for sleep. It was time to talk and laugh among themselves—a ritual played out almost nightly in the Hallett household.

HOME IS LIKE A LITTLE NEST

Renee ▼ It's just like a nest here at home. To us, family is everyone who comes through that door and everyone we meet as soon as we walk out of it. It's just like family to us no matter where we're at. That's because of my mom, my grandparents, and my father. They taught us to take care of each other. It's the traditional way.

Jill ▼ We would die for each other. We'd fight.

Being rich in money is nothing. It's here today and gone tomorrow. As long as you have your family, you're rich in love and that's more than money can buy you.

That's how we were brought up.

PARENTS MAKE YOU WHO YOU ARE

Jill ▼ Your parents are the greatest teachers, because they're the ones that make you who you are.

You don't really appreciate things you have until you don't have them or they're not around.

I was a little brat when I was younger. I would sass back to my parents. I wouldn't respect them or nothing. We were all like that. I finally straightened up.

Ashley came to live with us. Her mom passed away and then her father committed suicide one year to the day after her mom was killed. I thought about it and straightened up, because if my parents went, I want them to go knowing that I wasn't mad at them and that they weren't mad at me.

I thought, that could happen to mine. God forbid! If anything happened to my mom or my dad now, I don't know what I would do. I talk to both of them every day. I love them so much that I don't know what I would do if anything happened to them. Even when they're on vacation, it's like, "Call us! Call when you get there. Call when you leave."

My father used to make me laugh because I would go out and he'd always say, "I don't know what ditch you're in or if you're in a car with someone that's drinking and driving," if you're this or that. I used to always say, "Come on, Dad, I'm old enough to know better, you know!"

He kept saying to us, "You'll understand when you're a parent. You'll understand when you're a parent."

Sometimes I went out with someone who'd been drinking and I'd say, "You've had too much to drink, let me drive." Then, I didn't have a license, but I'd put my butt on the line just to save someone else's life. I would drive.

Now when I go out, I won't drink. There was a time when I did, but I decided it wasn't for me. I've drunk, I've tried marijuana, but I've never taken any pills. I've never snorted anything. My mom knows all this.

I'm high on life. I don't need something chemical. I don't need that kind of stuff to make me feel good about myself or to have fun. I don't need those things.

FIGHTING TO MAINTAIN A WAY OF LIFE

Renee ▼ It's like this new battle we're up against with the so-called Interim General Council that has attempted to overthrow the traditional government. The battles are getting longer and harder. Before it would be a few months; now it's getting longer and longer. It's hard to imagine what we will have to fight against when I am my mother's age.

What we are fighting against now is the white man coming in and just taking us right out. Those people don't realize what they are doing. We should worry about what ceremonies go on in the Longhouse and make sure the children come to the Longhouse and are at those ceremonies to learn so we can carry it on after our speakers and singers and everyone dies.

If you took everyone on the side of the Interim General Council and sat them down and said, "Why are you doing this?" I bet you one thing. In spite of everything, the one answer will be money. And our life is not about money.

Our instructions say there's going to be a whole bunch of people who don't believe in the Longhouse, but there's going to be this little group who believes in some of it. Only a handful will believe in all of it.

They said to me, "What group would you put yourself in?"

I said, "I would be the one who believes in all of it, because I do." I said, "The Creator works in weird ways." I said, "When there's something going wrong, He'll let you know and He'll make those people pay who are doing wrong."

In the Interim General Council—that's the name the group who's trying to take over gave themselves—there are a lot of people who go to church and who have more or less brown skin but are not . . . they're Indians but they're not. They've been assimilated through the church. They don't understand that everything we talk about, everything we say leads back to one thing—the Longhouse. It's not really a religion; it's our way of life. It all comes back to that, and they don't understand that. They just can't grasp it. People are blind when they can't get what they want.

We're sticking to the Longhouse, and a lot more people are coming back to the Longhouse now.

When you're doing something wrong, that man upstairs will let you know. Look at these people who are trying to kick our chiefs out. Two women have lost babies, there's broken legs, heart attacks, one man has gone crazy, others beating each other up, one man poured kerosene on himself on Christmas Eve and set himself on fire.

Jill ▼

> *Our laws are so strong that they aren't even written. It has lasted all these years, handed down from generation to generation to generation.*

Some want to change them, but they still want to be known as sovereign people. The minute they give up all them rights, the minute they let the state or whoever in, that's when they give up their sovereignty.

Once you step outside the Longhouse, you've stepped outside the circle and you have lost everything.

The Four Helpers, the four spirit beings, protect our mind. They're the keepers of the mind. Go against the Good Mind and they'll let you go.

This man went crazy, and one of our chiefs got up in the Longhouse and said that when you go against the Law, this will happen. And it did.

Tara ▼ Our teachings say that when you are born, your duties are set out for you. They're chosen for you ahead of time.

SCIENCE, THE FOREST; MATH, THE STARS

Renee ▼ Our science is going out into the forest and being able to look at a tree and say, "This is for headaches. If you have headaches, you take that." Not many people know that anymore. And that's sad. I'd like to learn it, but there's really no one to teach it. That's our science.

Our math is looking at the stars and telling the moon—what moon is to do what by. We have our own math, we have our own science, but the children don't know it anymore.

We have our own language. It's not necessarily English, but it's our own language. English should be a second language to us; it shouldn't be our first one, which it is to most children nowadays. That's sad.

A lot of our older people were sent to boarding schools. They were told, "You don't talk that language. You don't speak it. If you speak it, we're going to beat you."

Like my grandma. When my grandma was sick, I used to go over there and sit with her at night so one of the daughters could go out and go do what they wanted. I would sit there and I would say, "Grandma, what was it like?"

She goes, "When we were in school, we couldn't speak the language, ever. If we did, we got beat. Us children used to hide in the corner and talk to each other in our language."

So, when they grew up, they never spoke it to their children because they thought it was wrong. Now their children don't know and now we don't know.

WHAT IT'S LIKE TO BE AN INDIAN

Renee ▼ People ask me what it's like to be an Indian, and I say my life is what Indian is, everything that I do. Everything I do is based on my life as an Indian. It's our religion. We have our Original Instructions.

GOING AGAINST THE CREATOR

Renee ▼ Not one day goes by that I don't think if I'm doing something right or wrong against the Longhouse, against the Creator, or against my family, or against myself.

MOM, TELL ME ABOUT THE BIRDS AND BEES

Tara ▼ I didn't know about that, sex, until I was twenty-two. I always asked my mom, "Ma, tell me about the birds and the bees." And she goes, "You could probably tell me more about it." She'd never tell me, and I would ask and ask and ask.

Jill ▼ It's important that there is an openness in the family to be able to talk about anything. I feel that I can talk to my mom about anything. Anything! There was one time that I didn't feel like I could talk to my mom. It was the first

time I had sex, and I knew she didn't like the person I was with. I didn't feel guilty about what I did; I felt guilty because I didn't think I could talk to her.

I wanted to scream out to the world. I always thought that I would wait until I was married and I didn't. Then, I couldn't tell my mom and then I finally told her.

I waited until I was eighteen years old because I wanted it to mean something. I didn't want to be at the age where when I lost my virginity I would become a slut and probably sleep with anybody I could find.

We were both sober. It was something I wanted, something he wanted. I didn't feel bad about it afterward.

I loved him. I shared. I always wanted to be able to say that the only man I ever had was my husband. I've always wanted to say that, but I started thinking about it. One day I started thinking about marriage and being married through our way and our religion. It's something that's forever. You're never supposed to have another man. He's never supposed to have another woman. There's no divorce. And I thought about it, and I thought, Well, what happens if, say, in ten years I start to wonder? Am I going to go off and cheat on him 'cause that's one of the things it says in our ways that you're not supposed to do? Just like in the white man's weddings.

THE GOOD IN US JUST ALWAYS COMES OUT

Renee ▼ The way we talk, it's very open. We can mess around. It's not dirty; it's just fun. We have a real good time doing it. We try not to offend a person. If we do, then, there's nothing we can do about it. We'll just try to laugh it off and go onto something else.

Indians are a lot closer than white people. We're a lot closer-knit kind of people. I can go to another Indian and talk about anything I want to with them.

With a white person, you're hesitant 'cause you don't know if you'll offend in one way or another. That's just the way we've always been. Our parents taught us like that.

I don't know where our humor came from, but it can be the worst situation in the whole world and you can sit there and you can laugh. I guess it's just because the good inside of us always comes out no matter when or where it is.

People's always asking me how I can always be laughing. I say, "You should see my family."

Like at a funeral, it's supposed to be so sad. I mean, we grieve for a little while. Well, then, we'll sit there and we'll think of something that person did or someone did to that person or like a joke they told. We'll sit there and we'll think about it and we'll just laugh and laugh. We'll finally say, "Well, they might be gone but they'll always be here. It makes me want to cry, but it makes me laugh at the same time."

Jill ▼ We can break up the most serious situation with laughter. We'll be anywhere, at my mom's store, constantly people will come in. They'll sit in the back room and talk to my mom, whoever it is. Next thing you know, they're all laughing. About what! Nobody knows, but constantly there's laughter.

GRANDMA'S CHAIR WITH A HOLE IN IT

Jill ▼ When Grandma passed away, the funeral director came to my grandma's house and got all the sisters together to discuss what they wanted. My grandma, before she passed away, she couldn't ... she had an outside bathroom ... she couldn't go out to it so they took a chair and cut a round circle out and put a slop pail under it so she could just go in the house.

And the funeral director was coming and he just ... some people understand the way we live and some people don't, that not everybody has running water or not everybody has electric ... so he was coming and they tell me, "Go sit on that; go sit on that so he don't see it."

So, here I am, stuck on my grandma's slop pail. And we were laughing ... everybody; it was so funny. ...

SPIRITS AND WORKERS OF GOOD AND BAD MEDICINE

Renee ▼ The spirit is always alive. Oh, we know. It's there. They always say the children see, the children can tell you. Some of the adults see once in a while.

When I was about fifteen, I had a dream about one of my aunts, and I described her to a T. I never met her. She died before I was born. The elders told me that she needed to be fed. There would have to be a feast for her.

Spirits come to different people in different ways. My aunt just came to me in a dream.

Some white people say, "Oh, no, ghosts don't exist."

"Oh, yeah, they do!" I say. You can't explain to them what it is, because they won't believe you for one, and for two, they just don't have that inner sense to feel it or to know it. We know it exists. We believe in that way.

People can use the spirits. They may want something you have, so they use them.

Jill ▼ It's happened to me. Somebody tried to make me go crazy. Messed with my mind, because they wanted me to go with their son when I was with someone else. It happens. You can feel it. You know something's going on. You don't act yourself.

When it happens, you go to somebody who can help you, like a seer.

Scott and I, one night, we almost killed ourselves together, the both of us sitting there bawling our eyes out. It was Scott who asked to do it. First he told me he wanted to kill himself. Then, he said, "Do it with me."

I said, "O.K., if that's what you want, then I'll do it."

We sat there in tears for a long time in the middle of the night crying, hugging each other, and we were ready to do it. But, he snapped out of it. He closed his eyes and like a flash he saw a silhouette of an old woman. He said, "Someone's doing this to us."

I don't remember what happened after that. That whole thing was one big blur. As we were driving away from that place, the farther we got the better we felt. If we touched each other, we'd jump. You could just feel it. It was like being in a smoke-filled room and when you get out, you're like, *Whew!* The farther we got from it, the more we felt like ourselves.

BEING A TRADITIONAL INDIAN

Renee ▼

It's hard being an Indian. You have to live up to such high standards as an Indian; plus you've got to live up to white man's standards.

I don't really care about white man's standards. I care about being the best person I can for my elders.

I want to be known as a good-hearted Longhouse person who takes care of her family.

Nowadays a traditional Indian is like a needle in the haystack. Everybody's getting so assimilated with white people that you got to really push and shove to stay to our way. I want my children to be that way and my grandchildren and my grandchildren's grandchildren to be that way.

It's hard, but it seems the more we try, the easier it gets. The harder we push, the easier it's going to be.

YES, WE EXIST

I met a lady from Louisiana in the shop, and she goes, "You're really Indian!"

And I said, "Where do you live?"

She goes, "Louisiana."

I said, "You got to be kidding me! You've never met an Indian before in your own life?"

In college a girl came to my room and said, "Can I ask you something?"

I said, "Sure."

She goes, "Do you Indians sleep in tepees?"

I'm, like, a nineteen-year-old girl who lives in western New York and has the whole Iroquois Confederacy here. She even asked me if I had a different way I brushed my teeth. No lie! That shows how much the white people don't teach their children what there is.

We're here. We're proud.

I want to let it be known.

GAI'WIIO' ▾ THE CODE OF THE IROQUOIS PROPHET

Tara ▾ The Gai'wiio' is our way of life. It tells what's right and wrong. It tells what you can and can't do. It tells the woman where her place is. It tells the man where his place is. It's just everything. It's laid right out for you. It's the life the Creator's telling you that you should live to be a good person.

Being an Indian is hard to define.

You have to understand that you yourself is just as important as the snow on the ground, as the leaves on the trees, as the berries on the bushes.

You have to understand that you're just as important as they are, and they're not any less important. The same as the worms and bugs and everything else.

Everything really is equal. The Creator doesn't look at me any better than He looks at the trees. We're all the same.

No one should think they're better than anyone else. You're just the same as everybody else.

Some take parts of the instructions and leave off others. I don't like that. He didn't give it to us to pick and choose what suits us. He gave us the way it is, and that's the way we're supposed to use it and not to pick and choose what suits us.

When I repented, I did it in the Longhouse. To repent, they have a whole mess of strings of wampum. There are different beads and they go down through them. Each bead is a lesson. Each lesson He gives us. When they do Gai'wiio̓, that's what they do. It's for five days. Every strand of wampum is a different lesson.

There are people who are born to preach Gai'wiio̓. They may go for a certain time and then realize that is their purpose—that the Creator put them here to preach Gai'wiio'. What they do is, the person who's doing the preaching comes around and you hold the wampum, and it's your doorway between you and the Creator by holding that wampum. It's all done while you're holding the wampum with the other person.

When I was pregnant, every night before I went to bed, I would repent. Then, I would try to be the first person out to greet the morning. I always tried to be the first person to be awake in the morning and be out the door. If I couldn't be out the door, I would at least be at the window and look out at the morning. Then, that night I would repent and just give thanks for my day.

Even now I'll still do it. A lot of the older people, that's the way they were when they were younger, and it just became habit for them. It was the way of life; it was the way you were supposed to be.

The people who are jealous are that way because they know some who follow the Law and they don't or they can't, that they don't have what it takes to follow it. We try to follow it as close as we can.

Jill ▼ We're all on the same level. We are not better than, say, an anthill outside. We're not better than they are and they're no better than us.

We have to give thanks, like when you're pregnant; we are taught that it helps when the baby makes his entry into the world. The baby doesn't get his spirit until the sixth month. So between the time of conception and up until it gets its spirit, it doesn't know if it's going to stay here or if the Creator wants it to come back home to where He is.

If we don't give thanks, the gifts from the Creator may be taken away. If we don't have our Sap Dance, the next year the trees won't make the sap to make the maple syrup.

If we don't have our thanksgiving for the strawberries, the next year He can, just like that, stop everything. That's why there are hurricanes and tornadoes and volcanoes and all those things, because there's something so much greater than all of us that in a split second He could wipe every single one of us out.

The elders say when it snowstorms or rains really fierce that He's reminding us there's a force greater, greater than us. He's reminding us of that. You could get a big head and think you're all high and mighty, but He reminds us that we're no greater than anyone or anything else.

We don't follow nothing but what the Creator has given us. That's our Law.

WELFARE FOR THE SEVENTH GENERATION TO COME

Jill ▼ We are taught that we are to look out for the welfare of the seventh generation. I am the seventh generation of my elders from the past. What I'm doing today is I'm looking at the seventh generation, the faces that are yet unborn.

Somebody back there was looking out for me. Now I'm not even thinking of myself as a seventh generation; I'm thinking of seven generations down the road.

When I thought of that, I felt so good inside.

KNOWLEDGE FROM THE ELDERS AND THE CHILDREN

Tara ▼ Respect. Respect is a very big thing. Everybody's important, but you have to value your children and you have to value your elders. They're irreplaceable. The knowledge you can get from both of them is a knowledge you can't get from anywhere else.

Kids are the best. They see the world differently. Their minds aren't polluted. We are taught that when a woman's pregnant, she's not to hold onto a child for three years. A child's tie to the Creator is still very strong for that period of time. A child in the womb is still in the Creator's world. He's not here yet. So if a pregnant woman holds onto a born baby, that child still has that pull to the Creator. It makes it hard for the Creator, because that's where it belongs. That pull can be so strong that that can help the Creator to take that born baby back.

That's why young children are so priceless, because they still have that close tie between this world and the Creator. That's why they're so important.

If a baby stays in this world or returns to the Creator is not up to us. You have to take care of them best you can take care of them, but if He chooses ...

People ask me if I'm not scared to have a child at home. I say no, 'cause if the Creator means for me to have the child, I will have it. There's nothing anybody, I, or any doctor or anybody, can do. If He wants that baby to be with Him, He'll take that baby. You can't change it. If He wants that baby, there's nobody else who's going to overrule what He wants. That's just the way it is.

People might think it's hard and it's cruel, but that's just the way it is. You have to accept it or you don't accept it. If you accept it, you have to realize that what He has for you is what He has for you no matter how hard you try to fight it or go against it. It's going to happen.

I had a midwife and she gave me a lot of Indian medicines, and I did all that I was supposed to do. I really became aware.

My sisters look at my son, His-tee, as being their nephew, but they also look at him as being their very own. We went through the whole pregnancy and childbirth together. All five of us girls were together through the whole experience of the pregnancy and the birth and everything afterward. There's always going to be that very, very close tight bond between him and my sisters. They're like his second mothers. All of them.

Maybe three weeks after he was born my mom came home and she said, "I got his name today." From that day forth he's always been called that—His-tee.

I kept him in a cradleboard for a really long time. This woman said, "Isn't that cruel. You can't touch him. You can't hold him. You can't do any of that stuff."

I said, "Hey, I breast-feed him. He's almost four years old. He still nurses. When he was in that cradleboard, I can touch him. I can hold him. I can nurse him. I can do all that, but he always has that security of feeling somebody was holding him by being wrapped in that board."

That wasn't cruel. He always had that security of knowing that he was being held.

When he's nursing, I feel contented. It's like I know he still needs me. The first time he stayed away from me all night, I couldn't sleep. It was like now he doesn't need his mother anymore. This was his first stage of breaking away from his mother. I really feared that.

I asked my mother how it felt to have me. She said, "I don't know. I was dead from the waist down, Tara. I didn't want to feel nothing."

I was disappointed. I cried. I cried, because it's the greatest gift a woman can be given. To have your body numbed and dulled and have no feeling whatsoever, I couldn't see it.

Nursing! She only nursed me for six months. And, I was the longest. I was told I was lucky.

The expectations of women changed so much between the time she was having children and I was having children. Then, it was give her a shot, put her legs in a stirrup, and that's that. Now it's getting back to where it's all natural. The pain you feel, once you see that baby, it all goes away. It was all worth it. How can you appreciate a child if you didn't even feel the pain when it was coming?

CHILDBIRTH AT HOME

Tara ▼ My labor was only two hours from start to finish. It was funny, because nobody else knew what to do. I was like standing up, sitting down, walking around, tried to do all these things. I did a lot of reading. I did a lot of talking with my midwife to tell me things I should do and shouldn't do.

When I went through transition, I shook uncontrollably. My sister Jill thought I was having seizures, and Ma was over there yelling at me. Ma was yelling, "Tara, relax. Relax. Just relax."

Every woman's body reacts differently to the whole process. Some women will be the biggest bitches in the world, and then, there's other women who always have to have somebody touching them. That's the way I was. I hated to be left alone. I always had to have somebody touching me.

When my body started pushing, Ma says, "You can't push. It's too early. You got lots of time left. You can't push."

I said, "Mom, my body's doing it on its own. I can't stop it."

Then, I went back to my breathing, trying to work with the contractions to make them a little easier. Right after that I went from the couch to the toilet. I could remember the midwife telling me that when you get toward the end, sit on the stool in the bathroom because it helps to open you a little better.

From the very beginning I had a fear of tearing. The midwife told me that with all the pressure, if I did tear I would not even feel it.

I was sitting on the toilet and I was sitting on the toilet and that's when Mom said, "You get where you're going to have this kid."

When it got time, it was like only minutes before he came. When he started out, someone said it was the cord. I said, "It's not the cord, it's the head! It's not his cord. Don't worry about it." Then, Mom didn't even catch him. He shot across the floor and landed right next to Mom's foot.

It was like maybe two, three, maybe four pushes after that he was skidding across the floor.

Mom said to me how when I was in labor with His-tee, I said, "Holy mackerel, this hurts," and she goes, "You should have thought about that nine months ago!"

I knew it was going to hurt, but see, whenever I had my period or anything, I never had really wicked cramps or anything, so I never knew what it was like. That was my experience of cramps for the first time. I only bitched a couple times.

His-tee's father only donated the sperm. That was his only function. I don't care for him because after he found out I was pregnant with His-tee, he wanted me to have an abortion. So I don't care for him.

I believe this is your life and you live it the way you want to live it. Nobody else has got to deal with the repercussions but you.

BIRTH CONTROL AND THE GAI'WIIO'

Tara ▼ A woman's duty is to have children; that's why you can't use birth control. See, you could use condoms and it's not you using birth control; it's the man. You have no control over what that other person does.

Jill ▼ If the world was the way it was two hundred years ago, then don't use birth control, because we are firm believers in not using condoms, birth control pills. Nowadays, it's kind of unavoidable not to use something unless you want to end up in two months having herpes, having some kind of venereal disease or AIDS.

Most girls have to tell men, "Put this on."

They say that when you sleep with someone, you're sleeping with everyone that that person slept with. It's such a horrible cycle that three persons down that person could have AIDS or that person could have herpes.

Kim ▼ I say that the Creator does things for a reason. If you end up with AIDS or herpes or something else that's going to end up killing you, it's for a reason. You're going to get that whether you're careful who you sleep with or not. If it's meant to be, it'll happen.

Jill ▼ The best thing is to keep your legs closed in the first place. Like Kim told me today that her feet were so swollen, and I told her, "Well, you should have thought about that before that other thing got swollen."

Mom wishes we were horny, 'cause she wants more grandkids. She drills it into our heads: "You're horny."

That's why probably she sleeps all day long, and she runs around the house all night whispering in our ears, "You're horny, you're horny," in our sleep.

RELATIONSHIPS WITH MEN

Jill ▼ I'm not married. Scott and I are best friends. He won't go home. He won't. He won't go home. I tell him, "Go home. Go home and stay with your mom."

He likes my mom's house. He's an only child. When we first got together, he

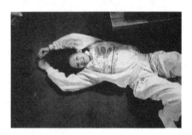

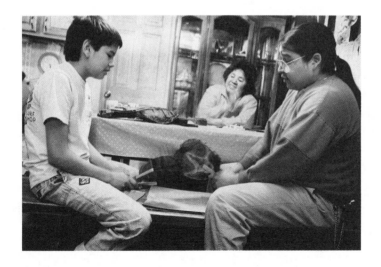

drank a lot. I didn't. We were like best of friends. We would stay up all night watching movies at the house. We would go to the airport and just watch the planes land and take off.

Scott and I just ended up together. We've gone through a lot together for me to be able to just look at him and turn around and say, "I don't want to be with you anymore." I can't do that.

Right now, I've told him I need my time because I do want to marry him, but when I do marry him, it's going to be me and him and me and him alone. I don't want to cheat on him, and I don't want him to cheat on me, so I told him I just need my space. But he won't go home.

Scott likes my mom's house. He says it's the kind of place when you walk in you don't want to walk back out.

I don't want to marry him now. I don't want to hurt his feelings, so I don't date anyone else.

You don't sleep around. I don't like using condoms; it's against our religion to use birth control. So, you tell him, "Pull it out."

Or you can tell him to go home and take a shower. We can cool off like that. Women are different than men. Men get it in their mind and that's it. They want one thing.

DATING WHITE MEN

Jill ▼ I dated a white man. I couldn't talk to him about the things I could talk to an Indian with. They don't understand, like, with our ceremonies. They don't understand. And there's things that we can't tell them.

The white guy I was dating got to the point where he said he loved me. And I said, "Well, wait a minute here," because I couldn't say it to him. Saying something to someone and not meaning it hurts more than saying nothing at all. I could say I love you, but I don't mean it. That's going to hurt more than not saying I love you at all.

I said to him, "Why don't we just stop and be friends?"

He said, "Why don't you just fall in love with me and marry me and we could live happily ever after."

I said, "No, I can't do that." 'Cause I couldn't. I'd be turning my back against my people. I can't.

Renee ▼ Ashley is seeing a white guy. She told him there will always be a barrier between them because she's Indian and he's white. He said he knows a lot and that he can learn.

She told him, "You can learn all you want, but there'll always be something I know that you won't understand and you won't be able to figure out. There'll always be that something, and you'll never be able to find it, and that's what's going to be the difference between me and you. It will always be there and you can't change it."

MEMORIES OF GRANDMA

Tara ▼ My grandma died in 1983. I don't think a day goes by when I don't think about her. I didn't get a chance to be close to her until it was too late. I got to realize just what a wonderful person she was. We used to go to the movies together, shopping. My aunts would want to go out, and I would go spend the night with her. They would say, "Do you want to baby-sit your grandma?"

I'd say, "It's not baby-sitting my grandma. It's giving me a chance to have time to spend with her."

I went to college right after she died. I was so lonely; there was no other Indian people there, nobody who understood what it was to be Indian, so I used to go out on really long walks. I would talk up a storm to her and I always felt so much better. That's one of the things that I'm looking forward to when I do go and get to see her again.

The first time I came home, my dad picked me up at school to bring me home. When we hit the reservation line, I just breathed like a sigh of relief. I was home. I belonged.

PUNISHMENT

With Gai'wiio' and repenting, you know you're going to pay for the things you do here. One of my cousins died, got run over by her boyfriend. That was Ashley's mother. He was like our uncle; it was like we grew up with him. We talked to him. We treated him the same as we always did, and we were never cruel or rude or anything. And my cousin said, "How can you do that? He killed Molly M. Don't you love Molly M?" We said, "Yes, we love Molly M, but if he did anything wrong, it's not for us to punish him or judge him. He'll get that when he goes to the Sky World or goes down to the Punisher's House. That's when he'll get his punishment. Everything we could do to him here would be nothing compared to what he's going to get there."

The Punisher's House is where you go if you're bad. You get your punishment there for whatever it is you've done, like playing cards, gambling, school. White man's education—you get punished for that. You get punished for drinking. You get punished for beating your wife, hitting your children, murder, birth control.

It's like my ma said, "If they're wrong, you have to understand that the Creator will punish them for what they've done. You have to really believe that and just leave it up to Him." So basically that's where it's been.

VISUALIZING AMERICA, GREAT TURTLE ISLAND, BEFORE CONQUEST

Jill ▼ Look at everything that man has done. Tell me, two hundred years ago, AIDS, what was AIDS? When the white man stepped foot here, we didn't have any of this stuff. He brought new diseases, he brought alcohol, he brought gambling, he brought the money.

I will be driving down the road and I will think, "I wonder what this place looked like a hundred years ago." When I go to Niagara Falls, I sit there and I'll think, "Two hundred years ago Indians would come here and just sit in a tree, sit on the bank, and now I have to sit on cement." There's nothing but buildings. Imagine how much more beautiful that looked before they put all that there.

Every morning, with us, we step out this door and we step onto that Mother Earth, we know that no one can take that away from us. We can walk on this because we know it ain't ours to own; it ain't ours. It's ours to take care of.

I don't like to say "white people" because it's like putting all white people together, and every white person is not the same. It's stereotyping. I bet that someone that could be an Indian hater, I bet you ten to one they got Indian blood in them, somewhere way, way down the line, say great-great-great-great-grandfather could have been an Indian.

Renee ▼ Not being able to speak my language hurts. It makes me want to cry. We didn't have anything to do with not being taught. It leaves a vacuum.

When you start to learn and you listen to the speaker in the Longhouse, you can pick out words here and there and you're like, oh my God, I understood him. Picking up one or two words at each ceremony means that you're going to pick up others at the next ceremony.

We know we're giving it a shot now.

We are told that the babies born in the 1980s are the special ones because that's the elders who had died before and are coming back. They look different, their eyes; they have bigger heads. If you look at those children like that, you'll notice it because they act different. They look wise. You'll think they look old, and then you'll say that *is* an old man, but it's just a baby.

BEARING THE BURDEN OF BEING A CHIEF

Renee ▼ Our chiefs have to put up with so much. They don't have to just take care of themselves and their families; they've got to take care of every person on the reserve, every one of them people. They're not even a husband anymore;

they're not a father anymore; they're working for all the people.

Kim ▼ When the white man first came here, the Indians laughed at them because they fenced in an area and called it theirs. They said, "This is mine," but to Indians it wasn't. You stayed here for a while, then you moved on, never owned it.

I talked to somebody about learning Indian medicine. They said, "If you learn the good, you have to learn the bad." That's scary. I don't even want to know what the bad looks like. I don't want to know how to do that.

Those people who were not brought up in the Longhouse, they don't see the chiefs for what they really are. They don't take all their knowledge for what it should be. They look at them just as another person. If they're chiefs, they're there for a reason. They were given something to be there. They don't look at them like that, and they'll shit on them like nothing. They'll call them names and say all kind of things about them. It's because they don't care.

When chiefs come, you sit there and listen to them, respect. You don't even have to know who they are for that matter, but just to know that they're a chief.

HOH

Mary Leitka

DRENCHED AND RED-NOSED from the early morning chill, Mary bursts through her front door. She is still in her high-waters, rubber pants, and old fishing coat. The odor of the river and fish trail her as she makes for the nearly overflowing coffee pot she brewed before leaving at the crack of dawn to go fishing.

Gulping down a few swallows of the hot, black liquid to cut the dampness of the rain forest from her aching joints and the numbness from her cold, water-chafed hands, she laughs, bragging unashamedly of the aroma she has added to her dining room, "This old coat has served me well. I've fished in it over five years. See how it's torn, but even when it's wet out it still keeps me warm. But it has had it, and I guess I'm going to have to let it go one day."

Within an hour she is ready to go back down to the river to check her nets. Following the muddy path through the forest to the river that bears the name of her people, Mary—chair of the tiny Hoh Nation situated in America's premier rain forest on Washington's Olympic Peninsula—walks right through puddles and dark sticky ooze. Water, fog, low dark clouds, and lots of mud are the norm. Only sunshine is rare in this area, which gets around 132 inches of rain a year.

Ferns and fallen, rotting trees cover the ground she quickly traverses on the way to her inherited fishing spot at the bend of the river. Moss highlights and outlines the trees of this enchanting darkness where soft light seems to glow from the forest floor up. Moving deeper into the wood, the greens keep rising with each new step. Here the sun doesn't shine; only diffused angular rays peek through the evergreen canopy shrouding this misty, isolated primeval world of velvet.

Down at the river, the forest abruptly ending with the roar of the mighty glacier-fed Hoh, Mary observes, missing absolutely nothing. Her eyes cut through the monotones of the gray mists, sky and river one. Up the river, Judge, a childhood friend and lifelong friendly rival, is standing, pulling in his nets, as the boat he is riding drifts at a hearty clip down the river. Mary squints, eyeing the salmon he is untangling from his net. She openly admires his catch and silently envies the three, maybe five, forty-pound salmon fighting against the mesh of the net as Judge quickly throws them aboard.

Having watched intently but unmoving for a long time, she suddenly steps briskly to the bank's edge, grabs the rope anchoring her boat and skittles on her butt down the muddy ledge as if on a greased sliding board. It's a fast trip to the bottom. "Got to be careful at the edge," she says. "There is no stopping out into

the deep part. One step into the water, and the drop just at the bank could be ten feet or more, with your next stop being the ocean, if you came up at all. You could get a quick education, but one you may not have a chance to remember."

Rivers in this part of the country are fierce. They are hungry for anything getting in their way. Mighty trees are evidence of that. Their remains literally are stacked one on top of the other at the rivers' mouths as the Pacific's waves and the rivers' currents battle for dominance.

Casting off, Mary expertly maneuvers her aluminum boat along her net. She knows she has fish but takes her time carefully cleaning out debris trapped in the mesh-imprisoned cove. Then, at just the right time—her time—she begins pulling up the thirty to forty pounders, clubs each one to death so she can avoid being unbalanced by their mighty tails possibly flipping her and themselves into the speeding currents. This struggle for life, food for Mary's family or breath for the salmon, is part of her ancient traditions, and this very act is imbedded in the Hoh's thanksgiving ceremonies to the Creator for the food, with the salmon praised for giving its life for the people to survive.

As she works, she espies the river and the other fishermen. This river of her ancestors is not just the river of her people today; it is her river and its life-giving waters flow through her veins, sustaining her physically and spiritually.

Ready to leave, Mary takes a quick look about. Her net moves. Another fish is trapped. Leaving is delayed while she climbs back into the boat. Deftly she pulls the smaller pink salmon aboard. This one, she decides, will be dinner.

Having completed her tasks for the time being—there'll still be another trek back to the river today—she picks up the path away from the river again. Making a sharp turn on the path, the river comes back into her view, and sure enough, she pauses again to survey the river and watch another fisherman slap the water with a paddle to scare or startle fish from the banks and hopefully into waiting nets.

Back at home and out of the bone-chilling dampness of the mist, Mary grabs for the coffee pot and a short rest before beginning the necessary cleaning—one for dinner, several others destined for the smokehouse and drying.

Much of the traditions and knowledge has been lost at Hoh. Mary knows and remembers a lot, however, and has been more shy than reluctant to pick up the singing and drumming, but she has, nevertheless. In some ways she has not revived the old ways but reintroduced them to a generation whose parents, and even grandparents, never shared the wisdom. Today Mary teaches the youth elements of their heritage, an experience they are having for the first time. At the center of her teachings is the river, her nation's birthright and lifeblood.

THE RIVER IS ALL THAT MY ANCESTORS KNEW

This river is all that my ancestors knew, and it is still all that many of my people know. We never had a name for the river before the white man.

The best times I have had have been down by the river. It's so beautiful. In the evenings I go down by the river. I say to myself that I will not stay till dark. Then, what do I do? I stay anyway. I end up heading out on my trail home in the dark. Since this is part of the rain forest, the growth is so thick it's hard to see. It's a trail of darkness. I always get home. I can sense the way.

As a young girl I was so quiet. Everything I was learning, I kept within myself. The peace I would find would come through the ocean. I would sit down there day after day and play the flute.

I had a special place I would go when someone died. I would go there and cry and pray and try to ask the Creator for help to get me through it. Later, when I got older, I switched to the river. Now I have that special place on the river.

My knowledge is the river. I know its moods. I feel comfortable with the river, even when it gets rough and the river is pushing all the trees down. It is alive.

THE SALMON GIVER

There are many stories about the salmon. The Salmon Giver is one of them. We have a society and a special song for him. When we have a dinner, I go to the river to sing the fish song. The skeleton of the first spring salmon is laid into the river so he will go up that river and spawn and come back. He'll bring more fish for us next year. Without that song to honor him, he won't bring more fish.

Some of us compete against each other for the first spring fish, and after that for the biggest of each catch. We'll cook the fish and then we'll eat it, and I'll take the skeleton down to the river.

One time this man asked what I was doing. I said, "I'm an Indian! I'm singing to my fish that I put back into the river. It will go up there and bring back all these fish."

Then, I took my net out of the river and there were four fish in there. He didn't have any. He said, "Hey, I got to learn that song from you."

THEY BROUGHT EVERYTHING POLITICAL

What I hate most that was brought to this world, brought to the Native American world was ... not only did they bring the roads, the lights, and everything else, but they brought everything political with them.

Now that's the things that hurt our children. That's the things that make the other people hate each other. It's all because of this ... the political for the fish, for the elk, political for anything that we eat or do now. Dig clams. I can't even go down there, dig clams on the beach, without people harassing me.

It's all political. That's what I hate most of all.

If I had my choice, I would not want the roads into here now. I really liked it, how it was.

We have some really political issues we have to deal with here. I have told state officials about how much pride my people have. "Listen to them," I say.

We have been cutting back our fishing for years, from seven days to six days to five days to four days to three days to two and one. Now we're only fishing one or two days, because we need to let fish escape up the river so they can spawn. The more that goes out, the more comes back. But nobody's watching up the river, beyond our territorial borders. The state says it does not have enforcement. We can't enforce laws on the fishers up there; they're non-Indians. They're open twenty-four hours a day; they're open all year around. But the tribe has to shut down.

It makes me so angry because we're closing, because we want to enhance the escapement goal, but nobody else is worried about it. Not the state. Not the sports fishers. They'll fish it out. They've listed the whole river as the fishing capital of the world for sports fishermen. When I go down to go fishing, there's three boats right there. They will not move. I'll just go in and I'll make all the noise in the world to try to get them out.

We were told by the state we've got to close our river. I said, "You're being paid all this money to protect the economic social status of these people and they are not benefiting. They're leaving, my people. They're totally being destroyed. And the ones that stay here are the ones not educated. They did not continue their education because they're going to be fishermen. And how can they survive? Why don't you go and ask them?

"Ask my people how they survive when we close this river. Ask how often they have to go to court to keep from getting thrown out of their house because they can't pay their rent. Ask where they have to go to get food and clothing for their children. To clothing banks! Food banks!

"Ask them who they have to ask for help when they need some money so their lights won't be turned off, so they're not being kicked out of the house."

I said, "It's me. I give money out of my heart. I don't ask for it back because I know what they're going through."

We've always lived along this river. It's the river of our ancestors. We always thought there'd be fishing here. You've got the older ones that's too old, period, to go back to school. They have pride! They don't want to ask for food, for money, for food, for anything.

Sometimes they eat tuna casserole all week. Unless somebody else comes over and tells me, I don't know it. They're too proud to say anything. And I tell them, "Don't ever do this to your children. Let me know. I've got a freezer."

Washington, California, Oregon, Alaska, Canada ... if they're worried about this enhancement on this river, they better cut back out on that ocean; they better start managing this river. They say we, the Hoh Tribe, are co-managers. We are not co-managers!

People say we're the bad ones, that we fish day after day with nets from bank to bank. They don't know we fish only one day, two days. They don't know how often we're closed.

We count all the fish we catch here, even the ones for ceremonial use. We scale them, measure them. We know if they're male or female, if they're hatchery or native. But we do not know one thing about upriver. All we know is the state says they're on the honor system and the punch card. If you catch a fish, you punch it on your own honor. Ha!

We've been pushed back all our lives. We've lost almost all our land. Just this one little square is left. We've been pushed back for fishing. Now, the state is giving us pressure on the hunting, on the clams.

I told the state, "When I see that old man down there, he'll be eighty next year, throwing a net out there, trying to catch a fish so he can eat it, something that he's eaten all his life, and you're telling him he can't eat it. Are you going to be the one to tell him to take that net out? Because I'm not. As tribal chair, I am not going to. I'm going to tell the enforcement officer to leave him alone."

Fishing is what he's done all his life. I've lived on fish from since I was born ... fish, elk, seal. I want my fish. My people want their fish. We're going to have it, too. It's our way of life.

DIGGING CLAMS, FOLLOWING MY FOREFATHERS

I was down by the ocean digging clams one day. This man stopped by and said, "You Indians think that you can take everything in this world as yours, just like digging these clams. You're digging all these clams."

When I'm digging clams and seafood, I'm doing what my grandfathers, what my forefathers before did. I'll do this until the day that I die, and I'll teach my children the same way. I came to the ocean and the river to get food for what I ate as a young girl, and I'll continue to do this. That is my right. There is no one in this world that can tell me to stop eating these things that I've always loved.

HATRED IS STILL HERE TODAY

Hatred is still here today, directed against us from the outside. The Ku Klux Klan is still out there. The white supremists. They're teaching one to the other to the other and more and more. Hatred breeds hatred.

I cannot understand this. The white supremists can gather and have an organization. The Ku Klux Klan can have one. The minute we have an Indian organization to regain our rights, we're renegades. We're watched, bugged, traced, and tracked. That's something. Indians want to be recognized. We are sovereign nations. We want to be left alone.

I wish we could go back to the way my ancestors had it, because of the closeness we had then. A lot of it's lost. But it's coming back; it's turning around now.

I moved back home three months before my mother died, but she died the day I graduated from college. I wanted so bad for her to see me in cap and gown. Be proud of me of what I achieved.

After getting all this education, I come back and applied for jobs at Forks. Not one of them thought I had the education, thinking, "Indian with an education? Indians don't have educations. They're too busy drinking their alcohol." That's the attitude toward Indians in Forks.

So I started working with our children. They'd say, "We want to learn to dance. Can we dance with you, Auntie?"

I love everybody in this world. There is no difference between color and nationality. I was brought up to have respect for everyone. Everyone is a human being. There is nothing that separates me from them.

I don't hate the people who hate. I feel sorry for them.

WE KNOW THERE ARE BALANCES

In our society we know that there are balances. We know that there are individuals who have characteristics of the opposite sex. This has been acceptable.

This man came to talk to me and he said, "When I was born, I was born part a woman. I am never going to hide that from this world. I will admit that from the day I was born, I wished that I was a woman. There is no way that I can continue on throughout my life without admitting to the world and to myself that my wish is still there."

Men like this have maternal instincts. They are motherly types. They see life from that viewpoint. It's not shameful.

THE EAGLE COMES IN TIMES OF TROUBLE

When stress from all the pressures gets to me, I go down to the river. I sing. I cry and pray and talk to my mom and my grandfather, just saying, "Give me the strength."

Many times when I'm sitting there, here comes an eagle, and he's flying, and he's across the river. He sits on a tree right across from me. I said, "You're there when I need you. You always seem to know."

That really gives me a peace of mind, the strength. And I feel so much better.

When I go off and do these things by myself, that's where I get my strength, my peace of mind. That's where I have a chance to have someone that I can talk to.

We Always Made Decisions Based on Our Traditions

Before the elected system, we made decisions based on our traditions, the way that was handed down by our ancestors.

Before the government system came in and the roads came in, we would just throw our fish up on the banks and everybody knew who it belonged to. Nobody bothered them. After the roads came in, outsiders came in and stole people's gear and fish. They thought, "This is easy." Steal from here, steal from there. Never used to happen before.

The outsiders hadn't been taught the teachings, like how to respect each other. We knew all this. We grew up with it. Then others came in who hadn't been taught.

Out there it's take it. It's take it. Don't even ask, just take it. As long as it's out there, well, why not, they're not taking care of it. I'll just take it.

The first thing that's lost is the teaching from the elders to your children. If that's not taught, it's gone.

The Witch Doctor and Stick Indians

My children come and ask me to tell them about Daskiya. So we all get on the couch and I start to tell them, and then I say, "Get the blanket. Let's cover our heads." So we do. Soon they say, "Enough. Don't tell us anymore!"

Q'wãəti' was the Maker. He was called the Maker because he made a lot of things. Stories are told how the land was made, how Q'wãəti' made it. Lots of stories are told about landmark areas, boulders, and about how Q'wãəti' had done it.

Daskiya was a woman witch doctor who used her powers to destroy what Q'wãəti' made and harm people who got in her way. We were told, "If you're bad, Daskiya will put pitch on your eyes and take you and use you for a slave."

Talk about being good!

The Stick Indians were just a spirit people. They weren't there to harm, but they were scared of what was happening. There was too much civilization coming closer.

People have seen the Stick Indians. My stepfather saw them. The car had broken down. It was getting dark. He and a friend who was with him started walking down the road to get help, and all of a sudden they saw these little people, and then, they went blind. So they held onto each other and going like this to feel the sides of the road to make sure they were not going into the ditch. After they walked a long way, they started receiving their sight back. They said that they couldn't explain what they saw to anybody.

When you're walking and hear them in the bushes, you just say, "Leave me alone. I'm not bothering you."

I have done it. I know! Talk about awfully quiet; even the frogs stop croaking.

I still remember the stories. I do.

THE DRUM WAS HERE BEFORE WHITE MAN

Crossing yourself in the name of the Father, the Son, and the Holy Ghost. Where did these things come from! Before white man came, it was never there. We had no Father, Son, and Holy Ghost. We had the Creator, we had Mother Earth, we had the moon and the sun and the stars. All these things.

When I joined the Shakers as a young girl, I couldn't use the drum. I couldn't sing any Indian songs.

This drum was here before the white man. We sang our songs with it. We got our spiritual help through drumming and singing.

This cross was never here. These bells were never here. This came with a group of "civilized" people.

I believe like my mother did. There is only one Creator. There is not many gods. There is only one Creator.

Don't say things about my drum. That would cause me to feel hurt.

Don't judge what I do with my culture and my religion.

I Cried When I Looked into the Mirror

When I came to that point in my life where I had decided to stop drinking and straighten out my life, I always cried when I looked into the mirror. I wished I could see that young girl I used to be before my mind was controlled by the alcohol. As a young girl, I remembered how caring, how happy I was. Every time I looked in the mirror I thought I would never see that girl again. Maybe so, I thought, but I knew that I could change. And I did. I just quit. That caring, happy part of that little girl did come back.

So I was surprised when this medicine man came to visit. As we talked, I got up to get coffee and suddenly he said, "Mary, when you got up and turned a certain way, there's a young girl behind you following you."

There was no one else in the house, so I didn't know what he was talking about. Then I remembered the happy and caring young girl I had thought about when I looked into the mirror. He said maybe that young girl had returned.

Just because I stopped doing those things doesn't make me perfect. I'll always regret doing those things in my life. The drinking and things. Until the day I die, I will never claim to be perfect. I never was and I never will be.

I know I can use the mistakes that I made as an example to help guide the rest of my life.

I had so much anger during the time that I drank. I broke my hand fighting. I beat up a woman. I was terrible. I would fight with bikers. When you drink, something brings the anger out. After we'd come home, I'd look in the mirror and

I'd hate myself for being that person. That's when I'd wish I was that young girl who was so quiet, that used to use the beaches as a haven, her place that she could go to ... to release all her feelings to the ocean and the river and to the clouds. That was my place where I could sit there and look at the clouds and see many things. The fog. When the fog would come in, rolling in, so thick you can't even see. Just walk through the fog.

WOMEN KNOW MORE ABOUT LOVE

Women know more about love than men do.

You can't cocoon the other one. That's smothering. Love is talking. Love is sharing. Love is learning things about each other.

In a traditional marriage, a man would want a woman as a wife and she would have no say. The girl's father would trade her for so many blankets. The man would wrap her in another blanket and carry her off. They were married.

My grandfather wanted to marry off his daughter, my aunt, through the Indian ways. He was going to give his daughter to this man and get things in return. She didn't want to and she hid from this man, and she came back singing a song about how she didn't want to be married to that man.

To get traditional divorced, all they would do would cut the blanket in half and they were divorced.

CHILDREN SHOULD BE HUGGED

Children should be hugged and told they are loved. My dad used to hug me and hold me and really loved me. My mother, even as I got older, when I needed a hug she would hug me. They were there for me when I needed them.

You really have to show the children you love them.

We have seven daughters. Each has her own personality. I have shown my love by hugging and holding and a lot of talking and telling each child I love her. Nothing will change that love. Each child has to know people will like them for who they are, not for someone they try to be. Be yourself. You make yourself. You mold yourself.

So Much Is Being Lost

So much in our culture is being lost. So many of our people are dying and taking the knowledge with them. What they took with them, that wisdom, can never be replaced. It's lost unless we listen to the elders we have left.

We were put on this earth for a reason, and it's not our decision to make when we come here and when we leave.

We'll see the loved ones again.

To deal with the mourning, I go down on that river. I sit there and sing and cry and pray and talk to my mother, talk to my grandfather, saying, "Give me the strength."

You Don't Cry for the Dead

Mom told me, "You don't cry for the dead. And you don't ask them to come back, especially when you are drinking. Don't be there sitting alone and crying for the dead to bring them back; that'll only bring evilness back to you."

One time I could smell that, like death smell, in the corner of my house. I took everything out of the corner. I cleaned the rug. I did everything. It did no good. My kids were scared. They were walking out the door, and they were asleep. I would holler that yell that just comes out of the stomach. All my people know what it is; it's in our culture. I hollered more and more. And I couldn't stop.

My mom called an Indian doctor, a Lummi, to come down and help us. We didn't tell him nothing, just that something was wrong. He knew somebody, something was bothering us. He just knew. Then, I told him I was doing the hollering that just comes out on its own, and I didn't know why.

He said, "But it's you!" He came over to me and started singing; then he started working his medicine. He said, "It's you who's doing this. That smell you smell, that's the death. That's the doorway that you opened to your home to people who died, people you must have been really close to. But they need to leave. You need to let them go."

There were three spirits wandering around in the house. There was my brother; he passed away first. Then, my first cousin; she passed away next. She had an enlarged heart and she was a young girl. Then, Mona, my sister, died in a car accident. Two of them died from alcohol.

I cried. I said, "It's true." Yes, it was true. I didn't want them to go.

Mom said, "You can't do that. You can't keep them here."

I had to purify my heart and my mind.

The Indian doctor did ceremonies to take the death out of the house. Then he told me that I, in my heart, had to let go. There must be a releasing of the spirit.

There's an in-between world people end up in, in between the beyond where they're going and this world, because of people holding them. They wander because they can't go on.

Not forgiving someone holds that person here. Like a man who murdered some people; it's hard to forgive a man like that. That holds the spirit here. Got to learn to forgive.

So, my mom talked to me about death: "Be prepared when I die. Don't do this to me. Let go. Tell my children, tell my grandchildren. Don't hang onto me. I've got to go on."

I had to learn to accept that my mother was going to die. She was sick. She knew it. At Christmas she said she was going to give her jewelry to her children. She said, "I want you to understand that I'm happy with the life the Creator has given me to be here with all of you, but I'm going to give you this. That doesn't mean I'm going to die tomorrow. It just means I'm thinking ahead and preparing you to accept and let me go on to the next world."

SONGS COME DIRECTLY FROM THE CREATOR

My mother gave me a song that belonged only to her. There's no one else that can claim it or, even, sing it without permission, because songs come to a person directly from the Creator. They can be passed down or given away.

When I first heard it, I cried, and she really cried with me. She explained in Indian why she was giving me this song, because I loved it so much. She was right.

She said this is the reason behind this song, how my grandfather must have felt during that time he received the song. It was when one of his daughters died and he received the song to help her to go on into the spirit world. It's a sad song. Really sad.

Songs are a way to communicate with the spirit world. There's meanings in every song and every song is important.

There's a berry song I sing when I go down by the river. I have a campsite there where I go when I want to hide. This song, it's kind of a sad song, but it has meaning to it. It says, "I hear the coming of the berries; I hear the brushes of the coming of the berries. The brushes, they talk to me of the coming of the berries. I can hear the brushes; I can hear the growing; I can smell the coming of the berries. I can smell the strawberries and salmon berries. The brushes are announcing the coming of the berries; the brushes are talking and saying the berries are coming. I can hear the coming of the berries."

SONGS ARE YOUR HELP, YOUR MEDICINE

Your Help. It's like your medicine. Your medicine to help somebody. Your power, your medicine. It was called your Help.

It helps you to do some kind of work to help someone else. Each song was part of what you would use to help someone else, to help someone that was sick, in death.

My grandfather received a song to help him go through the stages of accepting the death of his daughter. He went down to the river for three days, and then all of a sudden he saw in the top of the trees this canoe.

In the canoe is his daughter and some men going up on top of it, the top of the trees, in the clouds. The canoe was carrying her into the other world. It's really a sad song. That's the song my mother gave to me. And to this day when I sing it, it brings tears and it's like I hear my mother.

For you to get your Power, your Help, to get your song, you have to go out to receive it. You have to go and work in the mountains, in the rivers, to get this power.

THROWING POWER

Sometimes when people argue with each other, or are mad at each other, they just throw power. Knock each other down. Just knock them down! Mom said she had seen that power, same as using your power stick.

Word got around about Esau Penn, my grandfather. One time Esau had used the stick on this man because he was doubting the power. He told him, "I doubt you can do anything. I don't believe you. You can't."

So Esau said, "Take your shirt off and kneel down here. Stay here. Kneel here and hold the stick." So he did it.

Esau started singing his song and motioning toward the stick, and the stick started jumping around. This man is trying to hold this stick and the stick is jumping, and he's holding it and it's moving. He said, "No! Make it stop. I believe you. I believe you have these powers."

The Help, itself, is the songs. This is your Help that goes with your medicine. You need those songs, though.

Some medicine men are very strong. They can sing their Help songs, their medicine songs, and take red-hot charcoal and put it in their mouths. No harm comes to their bodies.

These powers are always passed on through the family. I have had the offer. I was told that I could have this power; all I would have to do is reach out and get it. I was not ready for it at that time, so I didn't accept it. It was offered at a very vulnerable time in my life. I refused it. I couldn't do that; I was not ready for it.

RECEIVING THE GIFT

This is a dream I had about Papa after he disappeared on January second but before we found his shoe on the beach. The ocean just took him. He must have been drinking, and we were having ten-foot waves.

In the dream I walked down to the Longhouse in the village. Papa's sitting there looking in the Longhouse window.

I stood by him, and I looked in that window and I says, "What are you doing, Papa? We were looking for you."

He said, "There's twelve drums and twelve singers."

I looked in there again and I asked, "What kind of dancers are them? I'd never seen them kind before."

He said, "They're no good. They're bad. They're evil. You don't be with them. Don't join them. They're no good."

I said, "Well, what kind are they?" The way they were painted and things, I'd never seen them.

He repeated, "There's twelve drums and twelve singers."

Just then the two of them dancing looked up at us and pointed at me. Just like that. I said, "No. Not me. No."

I started to leave. My father grabbed my arm and pulled me by him. He said, "Don't ever run. No matter where you go on this earth, they're going to find you, and they're going to take you with them. You got to learn how to be strong, because if you don't, they're going to take you."

And they came and they grabbed my arms and they're taking me. I thought again, "Oh, geez, what am I going to do now?"

I started praying and singing and praying. I'm standing there and I'm going, "What? Papa!"

"You've got to be strong all the time."

I was told that what had happened to me was that I received the gift.

The Indian doctor said, "You had this gift all along, but you're receiving more. There's a lady that's going to help you and guide you as you go along. She's here with you now. In your spirit and mind, she's already with you."

I SAY WHAT'S TRUE IN MY HEART

I always say what's true in my heart. That's the thing. If everyone could understand, they would know how I feel. Other people, if they continue to go on with their culture and the ways of life, they would know these things.

Sometimes people say I'm playing Indian again. Oh, that's sad.

I don't think I have to play or act like an Indian. I am one. That's me. Who I am. And I'm proud.

SPIRITUAL POWER IS NOT TO BE PLAYED WITH

You have to be careful. Spiritual power is not to be played with. To accept the power, you have to cleanse yourself and make sure you don't use it to harm, just to help.

Right now in this country there is something going on. Non-Indians are interested in Indian culture and medicine, but Indians are not unique in having this power. Every people on earth had this power in the beginning. We never lost ours; it is still being carried on. Every nationality and race must find their own, trace their roots, because people may be able to learn from us, but to really grow spiritually they must find their own past. Ancestry is important. If they reached back to their ancestors, they would find out where they came from and a part of who they are. Finding their homeland, that's important. Some think it is only in the color of the skin. Wrong! You may have been born by the color of your skin or whatever, but somewhere in your family tree you'll find out what nationality and race you are. It is going back to your ancestors' nationality—that membership in a group of people with its own culture, religion, and language.

We were all created by one Creator. There are not many gods. There's only one. To us, He's the Creator. To the white people, He was God. To the Orientals, He might have been Buddha. But there is only one. There was no difference. The only difference may be the difference in the color of the skin, the hair, the eyes. There was no difference in who they were. They're all people of this earth. Everything in this earth is all part of the Creator.

JOINING THE BLACK FACE SOCIETY

To join the Black Face you have to have in your mind, in your heart, deep down inside of you, you've got to know that it is what you want, that you are really serious about doing it, you are not going to play with this, you are not going to turn back. You must really mean that you will continue on. You do not go into the smokehouse or the Longhouse to watch. If you go in, you must go in to participate.

To get the joiners to come in, I have heard stories that some Black Face elders would do what they would call grabbing or clubbing to steal people or wait for them to come out from some place and say, "Let's go visit my sister," and then grab them and take them and make them stay in the smokehouse or Longhouse. When they did this, parents did not approve. Only certain places clubbed. They would knock them in the head if they had to. Literally. Didn't have a choice.

When my mom was in it, it was people going through on their own will and decision and be serious about it.

I'm going to follow all the rules and things they say I must do to achieve what I want as far as medicine and Help.

The leaders of the Black Face were heads of clans. Whatever that person said, went. He was the head man that decided things. Anything dealing with each other was taken to the leader, and he was the one who would take care of it.

POWER OF THE BLACK FACE

The strongest people I know of on the Power are the Black Face in Canada. They say you can come over here to learn. You have to be serious.

With the Black Face you have medicine men, strong medicine men. I've seen some work. One came over to my family and helped me out. He talked to me a lot about right and wrong, good and bad Black Face. He knew that I was thinking, One day I'm going to be in there, to be part of it. He had said, "Well, look at this group here; that is the wrong kind of Black Face. You don't want to become part of that."

Some use the Power in a bad way. It's sad. Mom used to say, "Don't play with it. Sometimes you can do harm to your own self by opening something you don't know about."

When you go in the Longhouse there's certain things that you can't do. You can't continue your education during that four-year process. You can't participate in many things during that time you're being "babysitted."

I BATHE IN THE CREEK

I bathe in the creek. Go clear down under the water four times. During the morning before it even gets daybreak. I face toward the daybreak and pray during that time.

There is a power that takes over when you do this every morning. There were times I was so down, just … just pushed down with all the things that was happening, that I had to get over there. I felt so good going in the mornings.

With the Black Face you start out being called a "baby," still a baby yet. There's a four-year period that you go through all these training times. When you're done with the four years, what you're called is a "baby"; you're being born again. This is a rebirth of your whole life.

ALL HAVE THEIR OWN SPIRITUAL HELP

Everybody has their own spiritual help. Some people might not know it, but they have their own spiritual help. Everyone in this world.

I don't claim to be a spiritual worker. I don't call myself a spiritual doctor. I have a long ways to go. I'm learning, but everybody has in their own heart and their body, soul, their own kind of help. They can go out and search and find whatever it is.

FEELING THE POWER

I was instructed not to go into Black Face, not to be near, unless I was ready to be part of it, to participate and give the rest of my life over to it. I was never to go into the Longhouse just to watch and see what was going on.

I feel the power when I would get near it, though. Like the time my mom went over to Canada for the ceremony and she took me. I was just a real young girl.

The Indian doctor came by me. He was dancing. He had like a holler within your soul. That holler just comes out on its own; there's no controlling it. It's really weird. It's not, not a scream holler; it's a soul-holler holler. It's just funny how it just comes out. So when he came by, he would holler and I would answer him with a holler that just came from nowhere, but it came out of me. And my mom says, "You get behind me."

So I went behind her, and he went and danced clear around the other end, and he hollered again and I answered him. And my mom says, "Go back to your room. Don't go near him."

He had this stick, kind of like had handles on it. So he would work with that stick and sing his songs. They were going to go out to the river to search for someone. Somebody had been killed, drowned or something. She said, "Don't get close to him, where they're working."

I said, "Oh, OK."

Next thing, I don't know how, but I'm up there, right beside him, right where they're at. Mom just came over and brought me back, and she said, "You stay way back here!"

"Mom, I don't know how."

She said, "I know you don't know how; that's why I said I don't want you to be close."

I was so easily brought into it. I don't know how. There's power in it. Once this spiritual doctor made this white man holler. He won't doubt Indian doctors again. That doctor made him holler for almost three weeks. He'd holler in the stores, anywhere, and people looked at him like, "Something's wrong with him; something's very wrong."

The Indian doctor wasn't anywhere around, but he told the white man before he left, "You were doubting in your mind that I could have any powers. You were interfering with me. You'll see! I have my Help and you'll see."

That night, sure enough, he started, and my sister was beyond belief like, "Mom! Make it quit!"

She said, "I can't. That doctor's the one that put that on him to make sure he's going to believe what he can do."

Three weeks later, my brother-in-law comes over. "Mom, you call him over and you tell him I believe in him!"

And he stopped.

THE SPIRITUAL SEARCH, TOMANAWIS COMES TO YOU

My mother was in Black Face, but Mom's gone. And I'm lost. No one's here to teach me. None of the elders know anything about it, because they stopped doing the Black Face here at Hoh about the time they brought in all these things like the stores and the roads and everything. They knew the Black Face would never be accepted, and the law under the United States stopped it. Now I'm wondering and I'm asking people and I'm talking to spiritual doctors and asking what'd I do next.

I got a letter asking me to join the Ghost Dance, and I remembered what Mom told me, "You have to work with what was here. Don't lose that. Don't go off somewhere else to say I'm going to learn this other society."

Indian medicine, the Tomanawis itself, comes to you; it'll come to you. It's going to come to me.

You have to be really patient with yourself, with your life, for Tomanawis to come, because otherwise you're going to keep thinking and asking and wondering.

THE PREPARING OF RECEIVING YOUR HELP

Mom said that the, the, ah, the preparing of receiving your Help was by going through the cleansing process of, in the mornings, bathing yourself, then waiting for the sun to come up or daybreak to come and going by yourself for so many days, the fasting, the sweats, everything to go with it. Not to have contact with the outside, just go by yourself. She said that's what her dad used to do all the time. She said that her dad used to eat like raw, raw elk and drink the blood because that was part of his receiving of the, how he would receive his medicine.

Mom told me how I would know when my time would be, time for me to be part of it. In my heart I would know. Now I am ready. I have been preparing myself in the morning, the rituals in the river to cleanse myself.

STARTING THE HOLLERING

I started where I would holler. When I'm driving, when I'm going to sleep, I just holler. I'd scare my husband out of his sleep, and he'd like just jump straight up, "Are you awake?"

Hollering is kind of like the inner part of your, your Help. And it's something that I still do sometimes when I know something's going to happen. My husband's wondering, "Now are you doing this tonight?"

I just kept doing this, and I would have so much dreams that I would dream like three nights in a row that I'm going walking in . . . it's dark, but I'm not going anywhere. Someone's behind me. I can never tell who the voice is, telling me, "You know what you have to do. You know what you have to do. You know!"

I'm trying to turn around, and no one's with me. Next night it's the same thing. Finally, after the third night, I told my husband, "Once more and I'm going to a medicine doctor. I've got to know the reason why behind this."

I was spending so much of my time trying to search for spiritual help. Something to show me the way.

I was living by fear. I realized that all the deaths, alcoholism, politics, discrimination, all the experiences in my life had brought me to the place it was time for me to get to my spiritual teacher. It was time to get to the Black Face elder.

COWICHAN

Ethel Wilson

LONG BEFORE the slow dawning of the rain forest's murky light, Mary and husband John, darting silhouettes in the Hoh mists, quickly loaded their bags into the car. By the first hint of daybreak, having traveled the twisting two-lane blacktop along the Pacific Northwest Coast under a heavy blanket of fog, Mary's long-hoped-for pilgrimage to connect with her Black Face spiritual roots was well under way.

Rushing in the wee hours of the morning for the first ferry from Port Angeles, Washington, to British Columbia's Vancouver Island had paid off. John and Mary had arrived early enough to be at the front of the line. Now squinting through heavy sleepless eyes, Mary watched the loading knowingly. Crossing the Strait of Juan de Fuca would be eliminating the last barrier between her and her acknowledged teacher—Cowichan elder Ethel Wilson.

"Neah Bay." Mary broke the silence at about the same time the flag man started directing row after row of cars, vans, and eighteen-wheel trucks into the belly of the ship. "That's where we met, Ethel and me. I was at a potlatch at Neah Bay. I believe it was a memorial feast. It was after my mom died. Ethel was an elder in the Black Face Society and a friend of my mother. She was at the dinner. We were drawn together immediately. Both her and I just literally started crying. Just took one look at each other, and we both started crying. Running toward each other to hug. I was so ready for something like that to happen. I just knew right then she was supposed to be my spiritual teacher."

Waiting bumper to bumper in the smoky hull, Mary reminisced, "During the changing of the earth is the time of the Black Face ceremonies. Winter solstice.

Even the elders used to know that. So that's when they would be doing the Black Face until ... I know up there in Canada they always say until the frogs ... some of them use the frogs, the croaking, as timing when they start and end the ceremonies. And that's when I saw her."

Pausing, excited, to catch her breath, she added, "Ethel said, 'Well, you know ... I really ... you got to come over or I'm going to come down to your place.'

"And I really cried. I mean ... I just ... I didn't know what it was.

"Then Ethel said, 'Well, you know, you've got to come over. We're having our Black Face this year. During the opening up you can come over and stay with me for a while.'"

Coming over, for Mary, was more than crossing over into Canada; it was a journey back to an ancestral past and a reconnecting with an ancient spiritual base her mother had maintained and, yet, had warned her to avoid until she was ready. Her own questioning of her readiness to begin her personal odyssey had delayed

this trip, and her apprehension showed as she sipped morning coffee in the snack bar. Behind her, rain and the open waters had consumed Port Angeles, leaving her to ponder what she would face in Duncan—home for Ethel, site of the Cowichan Big House, and heart of the area's Black Face Society.

Fear—not so much that she had been told spirits still walked the hallowed grounds of the Cowichan, but rumors about what goes on in the Big House during ceremony—had made her hold back, hesitate. During the last several years some deaths of initiates participating in the rituals and reports of others being bitten over parts of their body while being "worked on" during the rites had made the headlines of area newspapers. Word from Big House supporters had been spread that those who died just did not have the physical stamina to go through the rituals, that they were not able to stand the test because of being too much a part of this material world and weakened from the foods of today, that there had been too much alcohol and sugar or bad medicine in the body. It all had to come out during the rituals.

Letters of warning, some say by religious groups opposed to the traditional practices, had been sent to prospective disciples to be aware that if they did not attend or appear when called for by the elders, they could be incarcerated in the Big House without their consent and for as long as the leaders wanted to detain them. Suspicion had created a cloud of terror over the Big House and the activities unfolding under the high rough wooden beams, behind the creaking, aging doors, and within unpainted plank walls.

Still, by her own admission, the concept of the Big House drew her. Before modern single family homes, the Big House was home to many families—a cultural way of life practiced by many peoples along a narrow coastal strip of land about 150 miles wide and running from Northern California all the way to the Queen Charlotte Islands in Canada. Common customs and beliefs, shared ceremonial religious practices and medicine societies, intermarriage, and swapping mostly women to unite and insure peaceful solutions to conflict had bound the many communities together as distant relatives all sharing a common heritage and future. Now the Big House was the symbol of the people's spiritual home. It was where they rest, where they "make their bed," so to speak, and where the teachings were given, stories were told, tears were wiped away, where they healed, and, finally, were brought to in death. It was the center. Mary had been told that this was where she was to be reborn, where she was to "live" spiritually, and where she would ultimately find peace.

Finally, Mary's years of waiting and wondering, building inner resolve to make the first step, were over. Nervously she took a last deep breath as she slid out of the car and walked toward Ethel's crumbling government-built house in a neighborhood of houses all in the same condition and just alike in design. The little lady, prone to keeping a daily schedule of knitting flawless sweaters and playing bingo with a passion, met her at the door and immediately, with her humble dress and manner, put her at ease. It was as if Mary was home.

After some small talk, Mary asked Ethel what she should do. She yells out, she said, and feels it in her chest. Ethel told her it must come out; you must go in the Big House. It is calling, and if you don't do it, then something will happen to you that happened to those old women whose husbands would not let them go in. They just creep along now, all drawn over (she holds her hand up, palm facing out from her, and crooks her index finger). Not getting it out can kill you. Your song is wanting out.

Mary listened, then started talking again—hearing but not hearing.

"I've been hollering a lot. It seems to be during the time of death. That's why I've been wanting to come and stay with you. If I'm going far from home or if I'm going to go to sleep, I holler. So I didn't know what to do. The times that I've been here on the island, Mom wouldn't let me go in there. She said not until I'm going to be part of it. I was told that I was not going to stand and watch. Every time I would come near, that first time, I watched the dancers with Mom.

"One dancer came by with a mask, and he'd holler at me and I hollered back. Mom pushed me back. But he went down to the other end, and he'd holler again at me and I'd holler back at him. Mom made me go to the house and wait for her. I never did get to see or participate.

"The times that they asked me to baby-sit the initiates in the Big House, I said that I never got instructions. I never got to go inside. I said I couldn't go in there. After they asked me, they told me what to do to baby-sit the babies, that's what they called the new ones in there. When I was going home, I started crying. I started singing some of Mom's songs. I'd sing and I'd cry. I was just so happy to sing and to hear the songs again."

Ethel Wilson ▼ You have to watch it when you get that way. When I first felt it, I thought I was overworked because I was awake from four in the morning until two the next morning helping the dancers. I told that guy I was living with at that time, "Whew, my chest was really sore." So I got myself Anacin, thinking that would help. It didn't. It was right in the middle of my chest. Then that night, *swish,* it just come out like that. They came and got me right away and sat me down. Then they started to sing them songs there. Pretty soon I could feel them taking me up like I was out of my body or floating. Then they got the old man to come sit by me; I was scared. He went, "um-m-m-rrh," like that. Then they say, "Now you can sing your song. You're all made up new."

I'm Black Face. We have our own, we have to fix our own paint. I got sick from that, the hollering, the crying out. I had two childrens already. I was sick for

four days. They come and helped me. Then I was OK for about ten, fifteen years.
Then, when I started working down the Big House, down this way, I was cooking.
Stacking the dishes. And everybody was busy dancing; the drums was going. And
somebody come and stand just behind my back, and I was setting the table by the
door when the drummers come running in. One lady there, she was drumming
behind me, and my sick come back. And I just hollered that night. Then they fixed
me up. That's the reason why I'm in there. And a lucky thing there that it come out
just like that, or otherwise I'd been gone a long time ago if it didn't come out just
like that. I would've been like that lady that got sick.

There used to be an old man called Charlie down here. He used to just sit one down over there like that and he'd drum over here. He used to find out what kind of disease you have. They got a lady over here, her eyes used to swell up, all over here. And the doctors doesn't know what was wrong with her. She goes to doctors and tells the doctors, "My eyes swell up." But when she lost husband she c-r-i-e-d, and she become sick of the hollering, she got sick of that. So that old man told her son and her sisters, "If you don't put this woman in holler, if you don't put her down into the Big House, she's going to die. So you better do something about it and put her in holler. So they worked on it, and then they put her down there and made a dancer out of her. She come out Red Face; she come out with a real beautiful song. She's still alive yet. And the other one that wasn't put in there, she was sick way before that from the hollering, and they both live in same place. The other one that was really sick and she wasn't put into the Big House there, she died. She just died. She just went skinny and then she left. You should have see her when she's walking out of the Big House and you got to help her. And the doctors can't find out what was wrong with her. But our Indians, they know what was wrong with her. But the husband didn't want her in.

When my mamma was losing her babies, she cried and cried and she got sick. Indian doctors said there was nothing they could do to help her. The only thing they could do was put her into the Big House. So they put her in, and like her song, she become Red Face. It seems to happen from a hurt feeling and red face all the time when they cry. It just builds up until you gradually get sore, really sore.

When your father or your mother passes away, then you been crying, too. You start hollering then. It seems like it's taking forever to get over, you know, you were so fond of them, and taking a long time that every once in a while your tears just come down. You've thought of her or him. In the Indian way, then, you're going to have to put up a dance and put up a memorial and spend all this money and give blankets away. Whatever you got, then you give it away. That's supposed to wipe the tears away. After, when you get done with your memorial there and no more tears, you let it go. You wipe your tears away, and that's the last time you going to cry for that person, because you worked on it. You stop crying. Your thoughts are clear. You cried that night, and you cried for that person for the last, last time. Tomorrow will be, ah, different, entirely different day tomorrow when it comes because you have gotten, taken that away. It was overloading you. When you let it go that night, you let it go all together. You that much, much, much lighter the next day. That's what the memorial is all about. When you let it go, you wipe the tears away with that memorial, your hollering will stop.

THE BLACK FACE IS STILL GOING ON

The Black Face is still going on. There's black paint and Red Face and two Black Face, two different things. I can't explain that one there because it's ... the government's tried to stop that one. But it's the only thing that we've got left. The only, only one thing that we got left there. We can't let it go. There's a lot of things that are used. It's used for memorial, and it's used for Indian naming, and it's supposed to be used for young girl who has become thirteen, but that one don't come out anymore. They used to do that.

Black Face. The paint. When the times comes and if you got a reason, there's quite a few reasons why you want your son or your daughter to be a dancer. Some of them puts them to be a dancer because they went wild, they can't control them. Maybe they think that the Big House will help. They put them in the Big House and make them become dancers. When they become dancers, then they receive the song when it's from the sea or from the mountain, whatever it is. The girl will have to decide which color of paint she wants, what kind of song she will receive. So she receives a real beautiful song of a red paint. You have to paint her up.

Each color comes from the sea or animals up in the woods. So they receive the black paint. They work on them for four days. Then they give it, and then they come out with a real beautiful song. Sometimes you don't even have to ask him or her what kind of animals. Sometimes the words are in the songs. Then you will know what kind of animal they have. And you know what kind of outfit they going to wear, as they each will wear either the red one, grass, or what you call the wolf. And there's all kind of beautiful songs.

POWER COMES FROM THE SONGS

Your power comes from the songs. We've lost out on a real beautiful one. I don't know what it's called in English, this bird. But it had really beautiful songs. But nobody seems to receive it anymore. Nobody's received it anymore. And it's really beautiful. They're way up like that and up like that and then they go a-l-l like that. And it's really beautiful, and after, when it's finished, then they go like that and go like that. They've lost it, we've lost it, and I don't know what happened to that one, but nobody's received it anymore. Each of these reserves has their own groups, and when they bring them into the Big House, each one receives their own songs. Nobody else can use that song. Each one's got its own.

Sometime people just lay there and they say, "I got no song. I got no song. I got no song." They're confused. Then they come and get me, and I talk to them. I tell them, all you have to do is cry. Think about what you really feel bad about in the past and cry it out. That song will come to you. Each individual got their own song. It's their cry like when you cried for your mamma, and then you got something in there, it comes out. It will come out.

When it comes out, it gives you strength.

LOSING THE SPIRITUALITY

Losing the spiritual connection with things, that's what I'm always feeling bad about. We've almost completely lost that connection. There's a lot of things happening now, not only with just my grandchildren but with all the other kids here on the reserve and all the different reserves.

When you go to the gatherings, the young ones are told not to walk in front of the old people, and here they just run without even respecting the old people, just run in front of them. They don't even say "Excuse me." Only one out of ten will say "Excuse me" before they go by the old ones. The rest just runs. We were taught in our days to excuse ourselves or not to go in front of the elders but supposed to find other ways to go where we want to go.

THEY DIDN'T HAVE TO SHOOT THEMSELVES

It's because we're losing out on everything we have as Indians that there's been a lot of suicides with young mens over here.

Young boy, this one was hanging, they found him hanging down there. And not too far from over here, just across the street, one shot himself. And the other guy that's next door to my daughter, I don't know what he done with himself, but committed suicide, too. They shoulda went and talked to somebody to let out the troubles they were having so they didn't have to shoot themselves.

PEOPLE USED TO LIVE IN THE BIG HOUSE

Long time ago the people used to live in the Big Houses. One family would get together, maybe eight or nine or ten of them, and they used to build them by the hands. Then there was no power saw and just handmade tools, and they used to build those Big Houses. When they get that done and the ones that took part building it, they get to move in there. That's how they used to live in there, all the Cowichan Big Houses. There was no radio, no TV, and each evening they got to one corner of the Big House and they'd set the one old man down and all the little kids would sit around there and the old man would tell stories for two, three hours, and the kids just listens. That's how they kept it alive, the true story that happened a long time ago with the animals like the eagles or the whales or whatever. And they kept it alive by doing that. Now they'd rather watch TV than listen to anything. Even when you're talking to them they want to watch, the little ones wants to watch cartoons. They got no time to listen to the old stories. So that all died away.

STORY OF THE GIRL WITH HER HAND IN THE WATER

Long time ago they used to use the canoes. They would row wherever they're going. And there was this young girl—she had her hands in the water as the canoe was going. She was kind of wishing a boyfriend. She was playing with the water like that. This is what I hear from my grandfather. This actually happened long time ago.

She still had her hands in the water when the canoe was going. Somebody, something held her hands. And she was happy about it that something was holding onto her hands, and she didn't let on to the ones rowing there, but she had her hands in the water there and something was holding onto it.

They got home and they went into the Big House where they lived there. So this girl, she went to sleep. See, she was still sleeping there and all of a sudden they come and woke her up like this. There was a, there was a guy there. He was the one that held her hands in the canoe. He changed, changed himself to a guy, come and visited her. She was happy about it. Kept it a secret. I don't know how long it went on there with him come and visited her.

All of a sudden the wind r-e-a-l-l-y blow and the sea was rough, r-e-a-l r-o-u-g-h, and all the fish come into the shore and was just laying there. And everybody was going down to the beach, and they had buckets and they were putting the fish in, they were really happy that the food just come into the beach. And this, this fish there that changes himself to, to the guy there, was ready to take that girl. He was the one that gave all the seafood to the whole village first before he took that girl. They were still picking up all this fish on the beach and all of a sudden that, that came up from the water and it walked into that house there and got that girl and they went into the water together. The girl's parents didn't know what was going on. Someone come up and told them that the fish took their daughter.

So they took her. The parents was crying, but they told them that any time that they didn't have anything to eat, there'd be food for them when they wake up down there. So it was arranged that way, and the parents kept thinking the daughter was not going to be able to stand being in the water and that maybe she'd come back. So the parents used to sit and watch the beach to see if the girl came back. Finally, the guys that hunts the whales got all the canoes. They went and s-e-a-r-c-h-e-d around the islands to see if they could find her, because they didn't think that she could live long enough in the water.

So they hunted for her around and around the islands. Finally they seen her up on the reef. The canoes went close to her to take her home, but she didn't want to go back with them. She fought. While she fought, her nose started bleeding, just gushing blood when they had her. She already changed. So they had to let her go. So they let her go.

This is supposed really true story; it happened so many years ago. This is one of the stories that was told from our great-great-great-grandfather. So they never tried to capture her after that. They just let her go. And, it was true, they didn't have to go out to get the seafood. It used to just come to them on the beach, because they made a deal. It can be better explained in our way in our language. You can really understand it in our language.

KEEPING YOUR SPIRIT STRONG

All them things I did as a young woman, when I had to pack the water and do it uphill, two buckets. It seems to keep you strong, keep you exercising doing all those things. Now, when they got nothing to do, just little bit of something, sweep the floor and something like that. No hard work like we used to have. Soon as they do some hard work like go out and split wood, they're all soring up already. I think to myself, the old ways is better than the way it is now. It keeps your body strong. It keeps your spirit strong. Nowadays maybe that's why there's so much suicide, because their spirit is so weak that they can't come out of their problems, and then they just shoot themselves.

When they used to do all that handwork, they live even if they're ninety. They still live from doing all that, all that work that had to be done there by hand.

Body and spirit work together. Get your body strong and your spirit gets strong too. When the spirit's working, you can feel it right here. In the middle, bottom of your ribs.

LOSING OUT ON OUR CULTURE

We're losing out on our culture too much, too much, and too fast. My daughters and my sons growed up in the residential school, and they got punished when they said their language. They completely lost the language on account of that. All the things that our young ones need, it's just going away. There's no more. Now the kids just run around and do what they want. I went by that really strict way, myself. It wasn't my mom; it was my dad that got on my back. As young as I was, I didn't understand, but it dawned after what he was trying to do. In those times there was no electricity or running water. You have to go pack your water up by the buckets. You have to split wood and make fire in the cookstove. All those things you had to do. And my dad used to be behind me all the time telling me this and telling me that. Not to be slow. I'm supposed to be fast when I'm doing things. And all that's lost with my grandchildren that I have coming up now.

We've lost out in all the things of the teachings from the old people to the young ones. We're supposed to prepare them for the future. As soon as they're old enough, eight or nine years old, we have to start teaching them how to take care of themselves. Make beds, sweep the floor, wash the dishes, and keep neat. None of that anymore.

Look what I had to do in the old days. Nowadays, they just open the tap and there's hot water. And still they have a hard time to do dishes. Look what I had to do. No washing machine. I had the scrub board and a big black pot.

BECOMING A WOMAN AT THIRTEEN

When a girl becomes thirteen, she's become of age. Different from young girl to a young woman. They used to get everybody down to the Big House to witness that girl who has become thirteen years old, and they used to use masked dances. But they don't do that with their girls anymore.

She sat in the middle with the blanket on. The family gave her everything. Blankets, dishes, and stuff. She can't choose herself which man she wants. The boy's parents will decide if they want her, and then they talk to her parents. She doesn't even know what he looks like.

That's the way it was with me. It worked out OK. That's why I got eight children!

So when they give her everything, the whole family, she goes and marries and she takes all what has been given to her. And she's ready for her own.

The young girls was spoken for even when they're small. They're spoken for by the parents of the boy saying, "She's going to be mine." Soon as she becomes of age, then they come and take her. But the boy's parents would have to wait out there until the girl's parents decide whether it's yes or no. If it's no, then they sent somebody out there and just say it's no. When it's a yes, everybody comes and they have a big get-together before they let the girl go.

When it was me, I was so very young. My parents were so strict, they never even let me off the island until I was thirteen. At that time my kids' father must have seen me. Must have fall in love with me or something like that.

My grandfather was in his eighties, and he must have told my dad, "The very first one that's going to come and speak for your daughter, we're going to have to let her go." So when they come over and spoke for me, it was a "yes" right there. I was about fourteen. They take me out there and sat me down by him. He was seven years older than me. He was twenty-one.

When I saw him, I like him. Next day he took me away from the camp, and we went. I just tried to kinda laugh and giggle at the things I used to do, being so young. Didn't know those things before that.

I was married so young that I growed up with my four daughters. People even ask me if this one is my sister. I was married for about two years before I had a baby.

By the time my daughter came of age, things had changed. My daughters just went and picked their own men, husbands.

It bothers me that our ways have changed so much.

THE REAL TRUE MEANING OF LIFE

The real true meaning of life is your family, the love that you have, the respect, the traditional ways, carrying on with them. You don't have to be rich to have these things; you can't buy them.

What is going to happen to all of us?! That's what worries me. It really worries me, because my grandchildren are not getting the things that I used to get. And they're not prepared for the future. They're not prepared for anything; for some but not for all. It really worries me.

Some people don't even have enough bread by the end of the month. Most today can't find jobs. They have to live on welfare, and the welfare they get is not even enough to go like one month. By the end of the month, they got no bread on the table. It gets harder and harder. I got three grandsons, and two of them that can't even find work even though they've graduated. I got one that found work in Victoria and he's doing pretty good. Maybe one out of ten make it.

They say they want our elders to put down what they got in them and to pass it on to our young ones. Well, why don't they give us a chance? They don't. They don't. That's why I say it's getting more and more difficult and getting more and more hard to teach our young ones.

What are we supposed to be about as Indians? Our way is vanishing.

KEEPING AN EYE on the clock as she laid out intimate details of the Big House's spiritual teachings, Ethel began to become edgy. To no one's surprise, Ethel had plans and those plans had to be kept. Only sickness could change her schedule. It was bingo time and she had to be going.

Ethel, without realizing it, had left Mary with much to consider. Mary now knew that in the initiation into the Big House there would be fasting—no drinks, no eating for four days and four nights—to purify the body so that she would be able to accept her song. Being "worked on" would come next, with appointed individuals blowing into the body's midsection to restore life. It would have to be done morning and evening—twice a day for the next four days.

Then, there would be the drums going with the hooves and the rattles as the "redoing" takes place. After four days a blindfold would be put on her to make her senses more aware of what's there around her. This is done, she was told, to sharpen up every part of her body as she was being born into the recognition of the spirit. Next would come the baths.

Returning home, Mary held her instructions close to her heart. She would have to go bathe daily in spring water before the sun comes up. Four times she would have to go under the water. If she did this in ritual she would be surrounded by a white light, so be prepared. This rite of cleansing herself of the material world would be her way of greeting the morning, facing the day and her creator cleansed. Having been warned that during the day the material world would chip away at her, she would have to cleanse herself each day to renew. After four years of disciplining herself in this manner, she was assured that she would be reborn a new person—an original person.

Knowing her following through would be for her benefit, her own well-being and spiritual transformation, she silently made her plans while the ferry seemingly floated back over the now still waters of the strait as the stars and the distant night-lights of Port Angeles merged. She was not just going home, she was home.

MOHAWK

Cecilia Mitchell ▾ *Akwesasne*

MIDNIGHT CLOAKED AKWASASNE under a dark veil. The sliver of the waxing moon, shimmering across the rolling current of the Saint Lawrence, yielded little relief from the blackness. Shades dimmed what few lights remained on in houses along the narrow waterfront street where I sat waiting in the driveway of her little bakery for the prearranged tea-leaf reading from Mohawk medicine woman Cecilia Mitchell. She had invited me to meet her at the time she usually fired the ovens and rolled the dough for the next day's pastries, donuts, and biscuits. Now there was no indication of movement at the bakery or within her tiny house next door.

Minutes of waiting turned into a long hour. My imagination soared. I felt a hundred hidden eyes peering out of the night at me from behind curtained windows. The cool August breeze abruptly turned clammy. Fear surged from the pit of my stomach and lodged in my throat as I became starkly conscious of my aloneness—an unaccompanied white parked on the reservation in a car with an out-of-state license in the dead of night. Aware of the violent confrontations between Mohawk political factions over the past few years, I seriously contemplated leaving and resetting my appointment for what I considered a safer daytime meeting.

Jolting my already fragile state of mind, steps, rapid-fire one after the other, echoed in the distance off the hollow asphalt and grew in intensity coming in my direction. As the rhythmic cadence approached, I started my car, believing I had made a mistake about the time and knowing that a person in a parked car may be perceived as being up to no good or worse—the FBI. Turning on the lights, I saw my "phantom"—only a child running down the street, probably heading home from a friend or relative's house. Relieved that it was only my imagination playing tricks on me, I jumped at the outline of a figure heading my way from the bank of the river. I recognized Cecilia's son, Tim, quizzically approaching my car. He was returning from an evening fishing trip, and his docking had slipped my notice.

Hearing my explanation, he disappeared back into the shadows. Soon lights came on in the house and a sleepy-eyed but ever buoyant Cecilia jubilantly emerged and motioned me toward the front door of her donut shop. Leaving the door ajar and waving her arms at the electrical switches, she soon had the bakery blazing in light. Turning, with the coffee pot already in hand for the preparation of a fresh brew, she asked laughingly with brown eyes dancing, "How long you been out there?"

Without waiting for an answer, she beamed, "I guess I got a little extra sleep. Get it when I can with my schedule. But, you should've knocked and got me up. Timmie shook me up saying there was some white guy out here waiting for me," and her hearty rafter-shaking chortle seemed to insinuate she had gotten one up on me. Cecilia knew me already. Without my being aware of it, my teachings had begun, with patience ostensibly being the first lesson.

Cecilia and I laughed and drank coffee, finishing one pot then starting another. Time passed. I relaxed. Sensing my skittishness over having my fortune told, she knew exactly what she was doing. Soon I would be ready, even eager, for what I had earlier considered the foreboding tea.

Cecilia paid close attention to the cup of coffee I was slowly sipping. When only a swallow remained and I was contemplating yet another refill, she slid a juice glass in front of me and filled it with milk. Reassuring me with a smile, she said, "Coffee can lay heavy on your stomach; the milk will help. Besides, we've got some tea to put down and some leaves to read. It's that time."

Quick-as-a-flash she set out a saucer and two clean cups. In one cup she had already put the tea leaves. After pouring in boiling water, she transferred the darkening liquid from one cup to the other. Back and forth it went. "This makes the tea stronger," she said. "Got to have it strong to make it work right."

Then, laughing, she added, "Want it to work right, don't you?" Gently pushing the now dark green tea in front of me, she told me, "Drink up! Drink it all down. To the last drop, if you can."

Hesitating for a moment, I put the cup to my lips.

"Let the tea leaves settle to the bottom between swallows," she said. "When you polish it all off, turn the cup upside down in the saucer."

She looked on carefully as I followed her instructions.

"We read the leaves left in the bottom of the cup," she explained, "not the ones that may fall into the saucer."

Three times during the reading, she repeated the process, filling the cup with water while using only the original leaves left in the cup after I had drunk the tea and turned it upside down on the saucer.

Cecilia talked on as if nothing out of the ordinary was taking place.

"A long time ago, in our Six Nations, if you talk to a lot of people, they'll tell you about our dream readers who we used to have. We don't have them anymore. So now we have sort of gone to tea-leaf readings. We have some who read tarot cards, some read the sky, and all kinds of stuff. The times change. People do different things. There are special gifts; doesn't matter what they use."

After a spell, as if just remembering, she took the cup, turned it over, put on her reading glasses, and studied the Rorschach-like remains glued to the bottom.

"We got news coming," she said. "It's coming in strong."

Seeing my alarm, she patted my arm. "It's OK. It's how you look at things that make them scary. None of this is going to be bad; just a little bit about you and your future and the future you can change if you really want to."

Taking her glasses off and giving me a "Are you ready for this?" glance, Cecilia looked back into the cup, turned it methodically, waited. Then, after what seemed an eternity, she said, "Believe it or not, you are being guided by people from beyond, in the spirit world. It could be your mother, your father, your grandmother, or somebody, people not from here. You're going to find it strange, but I do readings for Indian people and come across this quite a bit.

"We are guided by unknown factors and ... maybe you don't believe it ... but sometimes when you are going down the road and you know there's something wrong with your car, and, well, 'I know I will make it to the next gas station, but I am really running low on gas,' and sometimes by some freak accident or something you seem to be riding right on the fumes of your gasoline, and heavens behold, there happens to be a gas station right there. Well, Indian people are very psychic people, and they say, 'Well, somebody's helping me, somebody's up there looking out for me.'

"This is the case with you. You have unknown helpers helping you in things you do. Not only one person, but a family, a family of three. Somebody beyond; it could be friends or family. It's usually family, like a grandmother, a grandfather, an aunt. Somebody that left your environment at one time together. They left at the same time, and they are beaming down on you, looking out for you.

"Lots of things could have happened to you at one time or another, but they guided you to safety. Isn't that weird?

"I will show you why. You see this? They are very, very close to you right now. I see you standing right there, and I see these people. See, these people are not touching the ground. They are up in space. They are in another dimension. But there's three people I see there. I see an old man, an old lady, and a woman there. You are being guided by forces that you wouldn't understand. They're gone beyond. And these people will help you."

Sometime short of dawn, Cecilia finished reading my tea leaves. Instead of feeling sleepy, I was wide awake with all that she had deduced from the clumps of wet tea leaves left hanging in the bottom of my cup. I was ready for more, maybe not about my fortune, just more about the Mohawk way of life and Cecilia herself.

Cecilia began sharing events of her life and the ways of her people—the Mohawks.

AWAKENING TO THE VALUABLE CHILD

I learned medicine from different people, from my grandmother's sister. She awakened my mother to the valuable child she had. She said I was the seventh one. "Send her out and make her go get medicine."

My mother would say, "Get your ass out there and go get that stuff."

When I was maybe five years old, they told me to "Go and get that; get me a branch off the raspberry. Get me a branch off the chokecherry, the apple, the plums," and this and that. So I knew what that was. I went out and got it.

My father's people told my mother, they said, "Do you know that child is gifted and she can perform medicine?"

My mother said, "I know. All my children are special."

"No, you know what I mean. This one is the seventh one."

My mother just laughed. I was only like five or six years old, just baffled by what they were talking about. They were talking about me.

They told her to tell me to go get some medicine and show me what it was. "Check her out. See if she can do it."

So we used to go out walking up over the hill, down to the river, all over. They would tell me about these different plants, what they're good for. You know, I'm kicking sticks around and stones and listening to these old people.

So one day my father's aunt told my mother, "Mary, tell her, tell her to go get seven varieties of fruits."

And my mother says, "Come here."

I went over to her. She says, "I want you to go here and I want you to go there. I want you to bring me seven fruits and some branches of this certain tree."

So off I went. I had to get the branch off the chokecherry, and then the branch of crabapple tree. I had to get plums and cherries and several varieties of different fruit.

What happened at that time was my older sister had TB, and she had like three or four children. She had to be sent to sanatorium for a year and a half. My father's aunt came to my mother and told her, "That girl right there can help her. You tell her to go get these medicines and see what she can do. We can cure your older daughter within a week, reverse her TB. But we have to get this medicine done now."

So I went out. I was maybe six years old, but I remembered the trees they'd pointed out to me and different medicines. I went and got it and I got the right things, too.

So this old lady says, "See, I told you she can do it. She is gifted and you better start nurturing her."

When I was a little girl,

the older women knew the potential of every child that was on this reservation. What they could do and what they couldn't do. For some reason or another, they just knew. They knew. They had picked me to pick medicine.

They only had to show me once. I would always remember it. To this day, I know every piece and blade of medicine that these people had showed me. I never forgot.

See, this is why I say I am so fortunate. Fortunate that something must have gotten through. Because I was so bad when I was young. I quit school. I got the shit beat out of me so many times, it was funny. I can sit here and laugh about it now.

I'm glad I was born the way I was born. It seems so sad when I think about all the things I went through in my life, but I've learned so much from that. I can sew, plant a garden, make baskets. These are things I was forced to do 'cause my mother hated my father for leaving us so bad. She took it out on me, because I was

his baby. And she thought she was punishing me, but all the time she wasn't. She really hurt my sisters but she didn't hurt me. I grew from it.

I learned a lot. To me, everything was fun and games. My mother would say, "Don't you have anything to do?"

I'd say, "No, nothing; I got my work all done, mopped the floors, made the beds, did this, did that," which I did.

She'd say, "OK, go in the garden and weed it." So I'd pull the weeds out and look at the plants, and I'd say, "How come this plant got leaves, a leaf coming here.

Some come this way and then up here they go this way and that way." And I'd look at the plants, how some stems were square, some were round, some had sorta like hairs on it, some didn't. I learned a lot. I would keep weeding and I would study it. Then, I would pretend I was one of the little people, like in our culture we know of the little people who live in the woods, and would crawl under the weeds, and I'd look up, and I'd see the leaves. They're so pretty from the bottom. They're so different from the top.

I'm strange, huh? Strange! That was my great escape.

TRYING TO BREAK THE SPIRIT WITH BAD MAGIC

My mother really hated me 'cause I was so strong. There was a spirit in me that she couldn't break. She tried to. . . .

So one night, long after I was married, she says to me, "I want you to stay overnight 'cause tomorrow morning I need you to take me to Cornwall."

This is after I have children, I have a home, and a husband. But I says alright. So I told my family I'd be at Mom's and, "I got to stay overnight, and I got to take her to Cornwall first thing in the morning."

They says, "Alright."

So, she had a little house, not much bigger than this room. She had a fireplace and a bed and a bathroom and a kitchen. She had a cot there by the stove so she can wake up when it gets cold and put wood in there. So she says, "You can sleep here if you wanta and keep the fire going tonight." She says, "I'm going to lay there."

And I says, "Alright."

Make the story short, she was sitting at the end of my bed and I was laying there and I fell asleep. This was very unusual for me just to fall asleep. In my sleep, I woke up, supposingly I woke up, and looked at the window. On the windowsill there was a snake laying there. It had stripes—gray, brown, black, you know, regular snake. Then I felt my bed; I went like this on the folding cot, and my hand fell and I hit a snake. Touched the snake and the snake crawled around my fingers and came across my arm, and he slid over here and right across here, and he came right between my breasts and he looked at me. I says, "Holy shit." Then I looked around, and the snake, he's sitting right here and looking at me. I could, ah, notice his nose which was kinda square. His tongue was coming out with slime like on it. I says, "Holy shit." I knew if I showed fear he was going to bite me, touch me, and poison me. And he knew that. I don't know why I knew he was a man.

So I looked at him. I says, "If you're here to scare me, buddy, you're not scaring me at all. You can bite me if you wanta but you can't kill me," I says. "There's only three poisonous snakes, and I'm sorry, you're not one of them. 'Cause they don't exist in the cold weather." And I kept looking at him and I seen his eyes; they were brown and black and yellow. I kept looking at him, so I says, "Why don't you back off? You don't scare me."

He slid back and disappeared. Then I looked around the room. Snakes all over the house. I dreamt how there were polka-dot snakes, snakes with daisies, and some with a, like, coil. I looked and I looked and I looked and I looked and I thought, Now if I see that snake with orange and red and . . . like that coral snake, I know I've had it. I didn't see it, but I seen all these other kinda snakes. Geez, the snakes, round and gray snakes.

Finally, I shook my head and tried to move my feet, and I couldn't move my feet. I couldn't move my head. Finally I was just able to move my head a little bit and I woke up. My mother was sitting at the foot of the bed. She was sitting on my legs, holding my feet. They went numb.

She was trying to do bad medicine on me. My mother was. She was trying to give me a heart attack. She apparently did give me something to make me dream of all these snakes to scare me. You can get so frightened in your sleep that you have a heart attack.

WHERE THE SOUL GOES

I'm not educated. I don't claim to know a lot of things, but I have feelings.

And this is the way I feel. Don't you laugh at me. This little circle, here I'll draw it, is to me our world. That's where we live. That dot's where we are now. There's another circle out there, this circle around the little one. That's where the soul goes when it leaves the body. They say the minute the body dies, three or four ounces of your body disappears, like a puff of smoke. I really believed that when I heard that. Your soul leaves the body and it goes into this other dimension, and you hang around out there for forty days. Ten days after you die, there's a little ceremony like a feast or something. That's when the soul can be contacted. Ten days, in our tradition, ten days after we die we have a ceremony.

Let's say this is the tenth day. Ten days after you die you're still hanging around here. Ten days. You have a ceremony at the Longhouse, and you have chiefs coming in to talk and help you release this person. Like my mother, when she died … my mother was quite a woman. She was good but she was bad, too. You could take her either way.

When my mother died, they had this ten-day thing that they release the spirit of these people, let them go and rest. They didn't do that ceremony right, the people doing that ceremony didn't know what they were doing. I didn't know that. I had so much grief about my mother, sometimes I feel guilty about it. But then I think about it, and I'm not wrong; I'm right in the way I think. I'm not going to lose no sleep over it. My mother didn't do me justice, I mean by my sisters and me because of her problems.

So I contacted our traditional chiefs. I asked them about having a traditional feast for my mother to release her, because she had hang-ups about how she treated me and my sisters. I wanted to let her go. Not to keep her hanging around on account of that. Just let her rest in peace. I figured my mother had a reason why she did those things. There had to be. So I wanted to release her. I had been taught that treating your children bad is a mortal sin, and you will go to hell and burn forever. I didn't want my mother to do that. She's still my mother. I didn't want her to suffer, if there's any suffering to be done in the next life.

Without realizing … these people who had my mother did this ceremony, but they didn't do it right. My mother was not released. But then in the same spontaneous time, I was having another ceremony for her and she got released. There's a formal escape route for her.

I believe there's a spirit world here, and I've never had nightmares or nothing about my mother since my mother died. I've been sleeping very good.

There is her life. This is the world she's in now, and she's free. Forty days after she died I could have contacted her. But I chose not to; I was too busy. I think she is probably in another dimension now.

In white society, what do you do when somebody dies? Like say, if your wife died, she died and maybe you had problems, maybe you were unfaithful to your wife or something, and you knew it bothered her, and you never told her you were really sorry, never showed her that, she would hang around here. Come back in your life, haunt you. You never set her free with a ceremony. She's always going to be haunting, trying to get even with you or something like that. But, in our society, we release these people.

YOU HAVE TO PAY FOR EVERYTHING YOU'VE DONE

When you leave this earth, you have to pay for everything you've done. You pay for the road to your Maker. However you lived is the road you travel on.

If you've been bad, the road's going to be pretty rough to travel on. If you're a good person and try not to harm anybody and do what's right, the road that you travel to your Maker will be smooth.

I believe whatever you do on this earth, you're going to pay for it before you die. And you're going to pay heavily too. That's what happened to my mother. I hate to say that.

PEOPLE ARE AFRAID OF DYING

A lot of people are afraid of dying.

I'm not afraid of dying.

If my time came tomorrow, I'd be ready to go. And I'm not afraid.

I'm anxious to see what it's like beyond this life. And when I die, I'm not going to be dead. The things that I leave behind will live forever.

The things that I have instilled in my sons or grandsons or other people around me will live forever. That is me, what I leave behind. The knowledge. You don't ever die.

You are part of the sun; you are part of the universe.

You are part of it. You can understand the sun, the moon, the thunder, feeling, being, but death … Nobody can, nobody can understand that, and I'm really anxious to see what it's like. When I'm dead and gone, I'll know.

I'll show you a strange thing. See this tree right here? That tree right there. I used to stand here, do dishes, and I'd look up. I'd see this bird. It'd sit right up there on one spot. Oh, I'd say, it's just a bird. There's plenty of birds like that, I'd say. So next day, I come out, and that bird would fly and would sit there and just look in here. That went on for about two weeks. I started getting really eerie about it. So I told the girls working with me in my bakery, "Look at that. That bird's sitting up there again."

One day I went to Cornwall and a friend came in and said, "You know I came out here, and I was doing the dishes. I looked and that bird flew away. But the door was open and he flew in here. And he flew around in here. Went in the other room, and he flew around. Then he went on the floor and walked around and looked and went out the door." We never seen him again after that. That's the day my mother died. Of course, I've never been dead, so I don't know. But I believe in the spirit.

Just because we don't understand, doesn't mean it's not so.

With a lot of people, anything they don't understand or don't know, does not exist. I say a lot of things exist. Doesn't mean, if we don't know it, it doesn't exist.

It's just

we don't have the knowledge of that situation.

YOU HAVE A NEGATIVE AND A POSITIVE

Just like everything, you have a negative and a positive. Lot of times fire is very good for you, but fire can destroy you, too. Water's good for you, but too much water is bad. It can kill you. That's the way these things are. It's like day and night. During the day you have light, and at night you have darkness. Just like everything, and just like people. You have good people, you have bad.

Medicine's no different. It's a positive and a negative. There's medicine that's good; there's medicine that's bad. Just depends on the person that's practicing that.

It's the person that has the knowledge. It's up to how it's used. That's the way our society is.

I know this medicine that if I took a tablespoon of it and put it in the water tower, it would wipe out everyone on this reservation in a day. Then, that medicine is really good for people that have trouble with their body, but if it's not used right, it could wipe you out in three seconds. They'd never find any traces of it, either. So that's how strong medicine is. And it's even more potent at certain times of the year.

See, I had a problem one time. This young man came into my life. He told me about all the problems he had. This guy was on the verge of suicide. And I didn't know this, because I didn't know him. Apparently he was going to the psychic, and she was feeding him all kinds of garbage. He was so scared, and I read for him. I saw none of these things in his cup. I seen some negative things, and I saw some positive things that he could control. And, ah, he says, "You know, I can't believe it." He says, "I feel like there's been a big rock lifted off my shoulder."

I says, "Well, I'm only telling you what I see in the tea leaves," and I says, "You seen it."

"Yeah," he says, "but nothing like she told me. Man, I'm telling you, I was ready to blow my brains out."

He really was serious, and I couldn't believe anybody telling somebody things like that. This woman who read him, I think, was with playing cards. You can put anything in there you want to. But in tea leaves you see things. He's alright now; he's got his marbles back together.

He came in the other day; he was laughing. He says, "I can't believe I was so stupid to believe that." I says, "Well, sometimes when we're depressed and things are not working right, which is only normal," I says, "we let ourselves get depressed and get strange like that. You got to remember, life is not a bed of roses. You got rough roads to travel, and you got to make the most of everything. You can't give up. You got to get in there and work."

I Am Indian, I Know a Lot of Things

I am Indian; I am close to my people, and I belong in their traditional beliefs, and I know medicine. I know a lot of things. I am like two people.

There's a lot of things going on. People talk about the world, about sex, and man and woman. I can associate myself with that, too. I know how some people

tend to move to other people, and they can't open up their hearts to somebody. They think that people will laugh at them. I deal with a lot of people and a lot of problems, and I can relate to people that don't speak English or don't know nothing about the white society. I can relate to people that's lived with white people and how they lived, 'cause I've been there, too. I can associate myself with the white people, too, and their beliefs in their society.

I can relate to women with children and to women that have husbands and women that don't have husbands anymore and they have a broken marriage. I've been through all that. So I can relate to that.

I can relate to teenagers with their problems 'cause I was a teenager once, too. I can put myself into that state when I was fifteen and remember all things as they were. If I'm going to talk to a teenage girl, I put myself in there as a teenager and understand what she is thinking about. What she is going through as a teenager.

Lot of people live just for the time right now. I'm fifty-four years old, and this is not just my life at fifty-four. I had a life before, and I'll have a life in the future.

I STUDIED THE GOOD MEDICINE

I studied the good medicine. I could go for the bad, too, but I don't want to get into that because that is really bad. Some want to do that because they want to hurt people. Don't ask me why. And that's so sad. I think the reason for bad medicine and negative people and the world the way it is right now is because it's to

keep us on guard all the time. We're going to be tempted sometimes; sometimes we're not. The Creator gave us a mind to use, whichever side we want to be on.

SPOOK STORY AND THE OLD WITCH

Once, I lived in Syracuse and the Onondagas invited me to live on the reservation with them. Normally, the Onondagas hated the Mohawk. They don't come out and say it, but they do. Anyways, I was really impressed with them when they asked me to come and live in their village with them. Not because of me personally; it was because I studied medicine. They wanted me in their midst, so I could help them. So I did. Then this woman—she hates the Mohawk, she doesn't come out and say it, but she does—she said, "Get rid of that bitch; I got to get her off this reservation." So she says, "I know, I'm going to find out just how brave she is." She came to my house about eleven o'clock at night in the dead of winter, and she starts telling me about all these witches, and stuff like that, and how much power she had.

I says to myself, "I know what you're up to, you old witch; you ain't scaring me a little bit."

So she started telling me all these things. I says, "Yeah, really?" I let her go on and on. It was after two o'clock in the morning. Then she says, "Are you scared?"

I says, "No."

She says, "I'm getting scared, all the things we're talking about," and she says, "Ah, geez, I got to go home now."

So I says, "By the way, I better walk you home; it's kinda slippery out there."

She says, "You're not scared?"

I says, "No, that ain't nothing compared to what we got in Akwesasne."

I walked her home that night, and, man, when I took her home, man, did I ever run. I ran back like hell. I didn't even look back.

She did scare me, but I didn't let her know she did. She was trying to scare me. She couldn't do it though. I was stronger than she was. I've been through too many things for her to scare me.

THE MOON HAS POWER

The moon has power on the earth. I don't know if it's got more power on the women than it does on the men, but it certainly has a lot of power on the human beings. It produces women's periods. Because our body consists of, what, three-fourths of our body is liquid and the flow of it is a lot stronger in women because we have a release of blood supplies, we notice it more than men would.

So we are connected to the moon. That gives us a power, a connection to the earth and the moon, men don't know about.

Most women don't understand it, though.

THE MOON AND MEDICINE

The moon and medicine is affiliated, too. Medicine that grows on top of ground is to be picked when the moon is full and it is growing. Medicine that grows underground, like roots, should be picked when there's no moon, and medicine that should be picked for the winter use—something that would be kept—is picked after the fireflies come. That's probably in August, sometime after August it's picked, because that way the roots are more mature. You can pick any medicine you want when you want to, but anything to be preserved is picked after fireflies.

Of course, you can go into more depth with this. Now, certain medicines have to be picked at the harvest moon. When that is being picked, if it's growing above the water ... I mean in the water but above the ground in the water ... then you pick it on the darkest night at the harvest ... around the harvest moon. That would be in September or October, because you have to dive under water, and they say when you get a hold of that thing, it will vibrate. When you grab, it moves just like a snake. Did you ever get a hold of a snake? You can feel the movement in there, and the vibrations ... say when you get a hold of that thing, you better get a hold of it with both hands because it starts to move backwards … knock you right off your feet if you're not stable enough. You have to get that and pull it out.

THERE'S A TIME AND PLACE FOR EVERYTHING

Anyways, with medicine there's a time and a place for everything. It only comes around once. You have to get it at the right time.

Just like that special time a woman can get pregnant. And a special time when medicine can be gotten that it's got its full potential. Full power.

When you look at these roots in the water, they look just like snakes. And when you go under water, they really do feel like snakes. When you get a hold of that, man, I telling you, it's a rush. It's at a certain time, like the Indians have thirteen moons like the Japanese or one of them Orient people, and I think on that thirteenth moon is when you should go down and get those roots. That's when it's got the most potent magic.

It's called in your language a water lily, but there is a white and there is a yellow one. The one that I'm talking about is the white, and they do move just like a snake and they're long. When you get a hold of that and it seems like it pulls you, pulls you under water. It's because they have so many little roots; the roots have roots of their own.

The time you can get the most out of it would probably be in the fall between September and October. That's when that new moon hits. That's when the medicines have their most potential powers. Oh, my God, it's really something.

POWER OF INDIAN MEDICINE

Indian medicine goes right inside of your body to the area that needs to be cured, and then it works its way out. Modern doctors, they correct the outside.

They leave the bad stuff inside. Sooner or later it's going to emerge someplace else. So we have to use preventative medicine.

MEDICINE PEOPLE CANNOT TREAT THEMSELVES

Medicine people cannot treat themselves. It might sound foolish, but I think it has to do with caring and love. I think when somebody's sick, take for instance my dad, love has had a lot to do with his getting better. He knows I love him, and he trusts me to do what is right to help him.

US INDIANS ALL STICK TOGETHER

Us Indians all stick together and care about one another. That's why the medicine people stay with their people to help them.

I care about Indian people because there's so few of us left. You can take the map of the United States and take a pencil and put dots on it; that's where the reservations are. That's how few we are. So we do care a lot about each other, but with other cultures I don't know if they're that close to one another.

White people don't have that closeness. I think it's because they go by the governments and the states, and the laws try to homogenize them, and apparently white people homogenize very well. Us Indians don't. We keep our own culture.

HEALING MY FATHER

My father was a party man. He loved to dance and he loved to drink, but he wasn't a bad person. He just enjoyed life. He had blood sugar, diabetes, for twenty years. He was giving himself the needle. So, he says, "Well, honey, you're home. What you got to do every day, see this needle?"

Took his fat arm, stuck that needle in there. I said, "Oh God, Bubba," I says, "I ain't doing that. No way!" I says, "I don't do windows and I don't clean fish and I don't play bingo and I ain't doing that."

My toes, I swear to God, they went just like that. So, he'd laugh, you know, and he's so used to it. I says, "Tomorrow morning, Bubba, you get out in that boat and get it ready." I says, "We're going out and get some medicine."

So him and another old man down here I gathered and worked medicine with for twenty years, I told him, "We got to go get medicine. I'll be damned if I can do his needles like that. I'm not doing that."

He laughed, says, "That's your Bubba; you got to do it."

I says, "*No,* I'm not!" I says, "I ain't doing that."

So next morning we went out, started right out here. We got some medicine. We got seven varieties. I went home and I started administering that. Within four months I had that man completely cured of blood sugar. No traces of it whatsoever. It's going on seven years now.

Four months after I came home, he had a stroke because he was out of his medication. He hadn't been taking it, because he never took care of himself. He didn't know how to do that. So, anyways, he had a stroke and the doctor says, "Don't get your hopes up. Your father is eighty-three years old." At the time, he says, "There's nothing left; another year, six or seven months, he'll be done."

I said, "Don't tell me my dad's going to die, 'cause he ain't going to die."

Well, I went back and got some more medicine and, ah, these mustard bottles that hold a few ounces … I came home and made a big pot of that medicine, take it back to the hospital in those mustard jars. He couldn't talk; he just laid there. I'd get that straw or spoon or whatever I could get and started giving him that. Even in the hospital I made sure he had his medicine. But we cured him!

He had four strokes, but with Indian medicine he still lives. Still gets up. He walks. Goes to the bathroom. I have no trouble with him.

I told him, "Don't you die on me. I didn't come home to bury you. You get yourself together, make yourself well."

Most of Indian medicine is preventative medicine. In the white society they try to homogenize everybody. Everybody is not the same. You eat one type of food, I eat another type, she eats another type, even though we might live in the same geographical area. We all eat differently. Once you go to a doctor that says, "You can't eat that; it's got sugar. You can't eat that; it's white bread. You got to have whole grain." But you have to eat what your body is accustomed to.

Well, my stepmother told me that before she died, "Your father can't have white bread, and your father can't have red meat, and your dad can't have ... your father can't have wine, and he can't have liquor."

So I says to her, "Jesus Christ, excuse my language, Mary, what the hell does he eat? No wonder he's sick."

She fed him whatever the doctor told them. He was on nine different types of pills the doctor gave him. One was for gas, one was for nerves, one was to make him sleepy, one was to thin his blood, another was to whatever.

I looked at the medicine and I looked at the doctor and says, "Can you explain to me what these pills are for?"

So one by one he explained to me, and one by one I says, "He don't need this; he don't need that. What's this for? He don't need that."

He says, "You can't do that!"

I says, "You watch me. You're killing my father. I'm trying to save his life." He says, "Do you have any degrees to tell me what you can do and what you can't?"

I says, "You let me be responsible. I'll take care of my dad."

He has no gas now, he has no trouble with his blood, he has no trouble with sugar anymore. He has no problem sleeping either. And he has no problem going to the bathroom. He has a bowel movement every day. Many old people have only one or two a week.

My Dad eats ice cream, he eats cakes, he eats donuts, he has milk, and it's not that water milk—skim milk. My dad eats everything, and he has no problem with sugar.

I told him, "Don't you goddamned tell me my father's going to die, 'cause I ain't ready to let him die."

The doctor is dead; he died.

CASINOS AND MONEY

The things I do with the tea leaves is very minor things. To me it's not very important. But to some people it is. I come in contact with people on the side of gambling, like the warrior society. These people are so troubled. But when they come to me, I don't see a warrior in front of me. I see a person that is very troubled, that needs guidance.

The warriors, as they call themselves, they need help to understand the situation they are in. They need to see what is coming, what has happened. Tea-leaf readings helps them come to the conclusion where they should be. I am labeled as an "anti," because I am opposed to gambling and all these things going on like smuggling cigarettes. And here is a person in front of me that supports gambling and all that comes with it. The sad part is that the people believe that if we don't have gambling, we don't have money, and there's no progress. We don't need that, because with the gambling comes disruption of our lives. Therefore, inside their hearts, deep inside, they know it is dangerous. But they need money. They don't understand they don't need all that.

The more money you got, the more problems you got, too. Like this little shop; I don't make a lot of money, but I make enough to pay my bills and do what I want to do. If I want to close this afternoon, I just lock my doors and close. Some say I'll lose money. I say it's only money. I will make it tomorrow. I'm not going to die if I don't make that extra $30 or $40 this afternoon. I am going up in the mountains and pick sweet grass and enjoy the air and take my dad out. That's worth more than $30 to me. Me, I do what I want to do, and I thank the Peacemaker for it. It is important I go up into the mountains. I'm going to do it.

TROUBLE AT AKWESASNE

We had this trouble here with the gambling. Shouldn't have happened in the first place. Our governments, three governments for one people ... so divided.

There's a tribal council, there's the band, and there's the Longhouse. The Longhouse, these are the traditional people. The Canadian side, these are the band people, and the tribal people are the Americans. These all banded together, and they called the community in to give our input, and I told them, I says, "You know, this is your chance to be sovereign people. You have your Longhouse, you have your band council, and you have your tribal council. The tribal council called Cuomo and the troopers to come and help us. And they wouldn't help us. The band people can't help us; there's no way they can do it. Now we have just the traditional people here. We're the ones; I'm one of the traditional people, and I don't oblige what's going on. In time past when you had trouble with people like that, you cut their ear off and abolished them from this reservation. Just say to them, 'If you don't like the things the way they're done here and you're here hurting the people, then you're abolished.'"

WARRIORS

People are using the name *warrior*, and they shouldn't be. Warriors, true warriors, are picked by the clan mothers in time of need. They're picked to protect the family and the people. Today there are some radicals; some of them are very young. It's sickening to see them not be able to understand the ways of their own people. It is sickening that they call themselves warriors when they're self-appointed and they're not picked by the clan mothers. These people don't know what the true meaning of warrior is.

Some people are so troubled. Some are just now learning about their traditions which they never knew before. And they took up arms against their own people. Now it is starting to bother them. So I gave them a reading of what I saw in the cup, tea-leaf reading, and I told them they were on the wrong path. It was up to them to correct it soon, because according to our laws and regulations in the Longhouse, if you go off a fraction of an inch at the beginning, by the time you get

to where you're going, you'll be two miles apart from your real path.

Today at Akwesasne there's a group of about twenty kids from ten to thirteen or fourteen years old. They call themselves Dagger Warriors. They're such beautiful boys. They could be so important to the community, but they go around terrorizing people. Their parents must have money, because these boys have four-wheelers and three-wheelers. They usually carry three or four hundred dollars in their pockets, and they pick on others. They just fly through the community on these four-wheelers.

About two weeks ago one of these kids went up the road and picked up a friend and came back, flying through the community here at St. Regis, and they hit a car. One of the boys was killed immediately and the other is brain-dead. These are the same two that had terrorized me back when I was cooking for the blockaders who were trying to keep the casinos out. These guys came around and threatened to blow up the propane tank here at the bakery. I told them, "You're crazy! You blow this tank up, you'll blow yourselves up, too. You're stupid. You don't know what you're doing."

I felt so bad about those two boys. I kept wondering why I'm feeling so bad when some people in the community were saying, "Good, we don't have to put up with them anymore."

They were little shits. You wanted to slap them around, straighten them up. But, I would never wish them dead.

ON BEING AN INDIAN

Some people today are not going along with the traditions, but they're show people. They're stereotype people. They dress in elaborate Indian things and they put on the black sunglasses; they wear the long hair.

To me, if you're Indian, you're Indian. You don't have to put on your buckskin, beads, and feathers, and stuff like that. I always say when you see Indian people dressed like an Indian like that, it's because they're a stereotype. Well, I got buckskin, I got black sunglasses, I got long hair, I'm Indian. Of course, white people come around and look and say, "Where's the Indian? Oh, there's one, got buckskin, long hair, black glasses. That's the Indian."

And it's sad, because these people know a lot of things, but they hide behind the Tree of Peace. They use it for a cover, and that's too bad. But I think they started getting into drugs and stuff like that because they had such knowledge of being Indian and the Indian ways.

We got this saying, too. The sins that the parents commit, the children have to pay. But you see this every day, things that the parents do and the children somehow or another always have to pay for that. It's sad.

WOMEN'S STRENGTH IN THE CONFLICT

The Mohawk women are the strongest. We're the best. We're the backbone of our society. Here we're strong. If men can't do what we want them to do, we go out and do it. We're the warriors, the real warriors.

We couldn't get the state to come in and help us. We couldn't get the Quebec Provincial Police or QPPs to come in, couldn't get the Royal Canadian Mounted Police to come in. It was too much. We went around and our chiefs could not do it; it was just not there. When they couldn't carry out the order that we women had given to close the gambling casinos, we had to take matters in our own hands.

I said, "Nobody else's going to do it for us. Let's get up and fight."

So we did; we got up together and we went out and kicked ass. I don't know where that energy came from. But, boy, when we got that in motion, there was no stopping us.

I worked, sometimes, twenty-four hours a day cooking for the blockaders during the siege. I don't know where my energy comes from. I say it's the higher beings up there. The gods. They just take over my body. I don't know how I do it, either, myself. And I don't take no drugs, no medication, nothing. It's just something I can't understand.

People saw me and started asking, "What can I bring?" I said, "Give me some oranges or some apples," and all of a sudden food started coming in, money started coming in. I didn't have to spend my own money like I had been doing.

We cooked and cooked that food. Everybody was happy. From day one I cooked till the last day of the siege.

We closed those casinos.

WOMEN HAVE THE POWER OF GENERATIONS

Women. They have the power of generations. Women have the power to have children and not to have children.

If all the women

decided not to have children, you know how long this world would last. It would be wiped out.

You've heard the old saying, "Behind every successful man, there's a woman behind him pushing him all the way."

It's the way the Longhouse is run, too. We put the men in office and we can take them out. It's thought the chiefs have the power. No, they don't; they're just a tool. The women are the main spokes of this society. You have to bear the children; you have to make sure they're brought up right. And you have the clan mothers.

Women are the main source in anything. Without women, life would not exist.

I think what to you might sound crude, but in, ah, reality, you know, when men are going for training like boxing or wrestling, they abstain themselves from sex. And it's because, I don't know, there's ... I don't know how to explain it ... but, ah, when you have, ah, I can explain it so much easier in my language. But the thing is, when a man abstains himself in training or in sports, he's much more alert and he's much stronger.

In our culture, long time ago, when women were having their period, menstruation, when you're not allowed to mingle anywhere that people are, they had a cabin in the back. That's where they stayed. Well, let's say I had three or four daughters, and two of them were having a period; they couldn't come out here. They'd have to stay there till their period was over, because in our beliefs, when they had their period they attracted the men. That power sort of made the men's minds wander without the men knowing the power. It's just there.

When there are younger women around, like maybe virgin girls, men are ... seem to be more attracted to them than they are of women that have already had sex, without even knowing it, especially if they're having a period. They don't even know it. They, they really don't feel it, but it's some kind of magnet.

But more powerful were the women having a baby; they have the same effect. They were kept away from people ... kept right away ... because they pulled energies and were powerful. It's strange and it's hard to explain.

Pulls the power. That's just what it does. Any energy or power, that baby inside of her automatically pulls it. Have to keep away from it.

To me it's an everyday occurrence.

Because of our society, the women rule. The women have such a strong law in our society. There are many ceremonies that are just for the women. We never usually talk about these things; they are sacred.

WOMEN: BACKBONE OF THE HOME

Take your own self for instance. What would you have if it wasn't for your wife? Who would keep the home fires going while you're gone? Nothing; there would be nothing left. You go home and what do you have? Not a home, just a house. A house without a woman is not a home. When you were younger, when you were coming home from school, first thing you opened the door and you called out, "Ma!" If she wasn't there, you had that empty feeling in your heart.

Even in my home, the minute that door opens, before the door is shut tight, I hear them calling, "Ma-a!" It's like that in every home. You never hear anybody says, "Dad." It's always "Ma."

If there's not a mother, there's nothing.

A person has to be very strong to go without a woman. So I guess the basic foundation of our system is a woman. It's the backbone.

A woman without a family is nothing, because if a woman doesn't have children or a family, her life is very empty.

A woman in our culture married a man to bear children and to take care of them, to teach them and to watch how they grow, and see signs of what they're going to be and start nurturing that. Don't do that anymore. Four years old they ship 'em out to some stranger that won't know nothing about their child. Child grows up, and he's never been nurtured to what his capabilities are. The kid is lost, and before he's thirteen years old, he's on drugs because he's so confused. He's got all this energy blowing up inside of him and he don't know how to defuse it, so he poisons his mind.

THE TIME OF FREE SEX

Women used to abort their children when they wanted to. They would set medicine if they didn't want to have children. Sex played a very important role in

their lives, too, because there was a time when they had free sex, and there was a time when they didn't have it. There was a time when young boys needed to have sex or whatever, and they could only have it with older women who couldn't bear children. It's almost like, ah, it was almost like an orgy, a whole minischool. That custom was in the springtime. They had like an orgy where the young men were shown how to have sex, but not with the young girls. It was with older women that could not have any more children.

It stems back to the times when they used to sacrifice the virgins when the women would have gotten married but the families picked the husband. The girls had to be in pure form. Sex played so much in that, you could probably write a whole book about sex.

Nowadays, I don't care what culture you come from, it all stems back to the way you're brought up to, ah, how much you're being a part of your culture. To me, bearing children without the man you are married to is not right. I can still relate to that, and, ah, a lot of women they don't care. They don't care. Especially here, a lot of 'em have children because the government gives them money. The more children they have, and they don't give a damn where that kid comes from, that's more money in their pocket.

In the beginning of our time it was, it was very sacred thing to have children, to not give yourself to a man unless you're married to him. Now, in the Longhouse, it's almost the same thing.

SOME PEOPLE YOU DISLIKE INSTANTLY

Some people you dislike them instantly when you see them and you start finding faults, looking for things that you can slander them with. Even if they never done anything to you, you just want to hurt them. Then, some people can do so much harm and still you can't hate them. What is it? I don't know. Like this guy, he's got such a bad reputation; he's such a womanizer. Some say they should kick him out of the Longhouse. I says he don't hurt nobody. I says, after all, a woman can run faster with her skirt up than a man can with his pants down. Right?

THE CHILDREN ARE ALWAYS AROUND

In our society anything that we are doing, the children are always around; but go to the white society. With their children it is always, "Go outside and play."

When I married my husband, I moved into the white society. He was white, and these people would strike their children, and they didn't teach them anything.

It was different when I was growing up. There was no family gap. The children talked and played with the elders. The middle-age people would talk with the teenagers. Now you don't see that. Even the Indian people are not like that anymore like they used to be. I think that's why we have so much problem.

Got to nurture that good you got, and not to change it. See, this is one thing, I've never tried to change my children, never. I've never baptized my children. Their father was Catholic; I'm a traditionalist. I've never baptized my children for their father's sake. I've never taken my kids to the Longhouse. I want them to be whatever they want to be. I say, "You want to be a holy roller, then go be a holy roller, but be a good holy roller. You want to be a Catholic, then be a Catholic, be a good Christian. Don't become a Catholic because your father was Catholic and he wants you to be. I don't want you to become a Longhouse person because I'm one. If you want to become Longhouse, then you better really support. Better be what you want to be. If not, then just hang loose until you find out what you want to be."

OUR LAND IS LIKE OUR MOTHER

The amazing thing is our environment. As I get older, I tend to listen to the world, listen to our mother, like our mother the earth and the planets and the trees and the bugs and animals and everything all round me. I pay attention to what our environment says. The moon and the sun and even the wind affects us. And I says, "Look at the moon. The moon's going to be full tomorrow, and the energy in our universe is going to be stronger, and the mosquitoes will be out. You watch now. There's no mosquitoes now; they're going to come out because the energy is going to be in the full force around five o'clock."

Sure enough, it was like six o'clock that night. We were in here, and we were getting ready for tea-leaf reading. It was the full moon and a mosquito landed on my arm. Sure enough, I said, "See what I told you?"

Like us, us Indian people, our land is like a mother, because she gives us everything, like medicine. Anything we hold dear is sacred to us, like our land because that's where our medicine comes from.

You take care of the land, it takes care of you. That's why we call it Mother Earth.

SOMEDAY WE WON'T BE ABLE TO GO SWIMMING

Us Indian people care so much about our environment. Once, when I was a little girl, my grandfather would sit on the porch with his pipe and his legs crossed there and say, "Yep, my little baby, someday won't be able to go swimming, because the rivers will be polluted."

I used to look up at him and think, "How are they ever, how can they ever pollute all that water?"

Here's another thing he said, "There's going to be a time my granddaughter and her sisters won't be able to swim in that river anymore. It will be all polluted with all the airplanes and the factories in Cornwall dumping all their sewage in the rivers. And the medicines will be no good."

WHITES LOST THEIR CEREMONY

You whites lost your ceremony and that's the sad part. You used to have these things, but the government has homogenized the people so much that they lost their identity, and that's why you have so many problems in the world. 'Cause people don't have these things now. The Creator built you, made you. You had these things and you lost it. And it's not your fault, like lot of the people's fault nowadays. It's your forefathers' fault.

Whites do have a certain culture. Like when your man comes home from work after eight hours and flop down on the couch and watches TV; that's his culture.

Sunday morning, got to get dressed up and go to church. See who is the best dressed. In that case we all have our rituals we follow; everybody does.

Football teams, baseball teams.

See, with us ... like my son, Timmie, when my son was in Korea, overseas in the army, he wrote to me and he says, "Ma," he says, "it is so empty here. There's no meaning to anything here. I wish I was home with you right now, I know you are getting ready to pick sweet grass." And it was time. I got his letter and I read it and I said, "Ah, my kid is really paying attention to these things." He knows when sweet grass season is, and he said how hollow he felt.

Even now I don't really need to go pick sweet grass, 'cause I don't make baskets no more, but I still go up in the mountains to get the grass, 'cause that's what makes me go. I get back into the nature of things when I do this.

WE'RE JUST LIKE FLOWERS ON THE EARTH

It's so sad when people try to homogenize everybody. Everybody be the same. We're just like flowers on the earth. Would be so boring when we go out there and we see nothing but daisies, black-and-white daisies. Different people, different ideas, and different beliefs, makes life so much more interesting.

The people on reservations are Indian people, but a lot of these people are not Indians. They're more like white people. They believe in the Christianity, and therefore I don't consider them as Indian people because they're involved in the white man's beliefs and his laws and stuff.

EVERYTHING WAS SACRED WITH OUR PEOPLE

Everything was sacred with our people. How sacred everything was. How sacred it was to them when spring came and the new ground was being broken.

New things emerging from the ground, and all celebrated the strawberries and the beans and the corn and the coming of

the fall and the medicine and stuff. I says, "Geez, look at this. They're so pathetic; they call us savages." And I said, "They don't know. They don't really know. They don't have the pleasure of looking forward next week when you hear these green bugs that come; they got long legs, green … praying mantis. But anyways, the people would be doing their work, and all of a sudden they'd hear this chirp, and they would stop and they'd say, "Oh, wow, the corn is going to be ready to be checked because they'll start to ripen now." That's when them bugs come. Then, when the fireflies would start flying, we'd say, "Wow, we can get ready to pick the medicine."

And then we start seeing the grasshoppers coming and say, "Oh no, here they are again, them pesty things. We're going to have to be picking our sweet grass." If you don't, they're going to go and jump on the sweet grass, and wherever they land, they're going to put their tobacco on there, and that tobacco kills the grass. When the wind hits it, the grass breaks.

It's little things like that Indian people knew.

CATHOLIC CHURCH AND THE WAY OF THE CROSS

When the Jesuits settled here, they found that in order for them to exist and survive, they would have to coordinate our system and theirs. So they used to have what they called the Way of the Cross. Well, they used to have a procession that went around the village. This I'm talking back now, ah, fifty-four; yesterday was my birthday. I was about fourteen; I talking back maybe over forty years ago when the priests and the nuns and the people would get all dressed up in their Sunday best, and they'd have this guy with a great big thing there, and they'd carry it all over the reservation. And what they did was, they stopped at different places, and them places were where the Longhouse people were, where their clan houses were. I used to remember somebody saying, "Well, they're going to start at the wolf, where the Wolf Clan people were." That was up on the hill where my mother and father lived.

There was a little house there; so they built a little shack to represent that Longhouse that was there before. And they had a wolf symbol there. So they stopped and prayed there. Then there was one where there was a turtle. That was up the hill; that was downtown by my grandmother's house. And they make this shack like, like three walls, like a back wall and a side wall and a roof, and they'd thumbtack bed sheets on that, and they'd make flowers and stick them on there so when the priest and them came, they would stop there and pray.

So they coordinated that so they can draw all the people. See, the Christians were like that. They wanted to suck up anybody. If they didn't make you believe, they'd beat the shit out of you and make you believe. That's how it was.

I asked my mother, I says, "How come they stop here and they stop there and over there?"

She says, "That's where the clan people used to be."

I was very inquisitive as a little child. So I go down the river to this old crippled lady. She was bedridden. So I says, "What's the clan people?"

She says, "Oh, are you talking about this?" And then she'd tell me. I say, "Yeah."

She says, "At the beginning the Mohawk people that lived here was only three clans. The Wolf, Turtle, and Bear. That was the three main clans we had. And out of them three main clans, there was a station for them. And then there was another one. There was a Snipe. People that didn't have a clan, they gave them a Snipe clan." That was my dad, 'cause he came from Oklahoma and he was descended from white people. So there was a station for them, too.

But it was amazing how they coordinated the Christians with the Longhouse.

The priests don't come out and get cold and walk in processions anymore. But they used to do it a long time ago.

There was a time—it must have been when that things was going very strong—where the Catholics wanted to become one of the Six Nations of the Iroquois Confederacy. And we said, "No way, you have no place in our society."

They wanted to be one of the nations in the confederacy like Mohawks, Onondagas, Oneida, Cayuga, Seneca, Tuscarora. They wanted to become one of us, like a Christian tribe. We said, "Get out of here. You don't fit in our society."

And they got after this Mohawk station right here in Akwesasne. They got after them to try to get them to join, and we almost got kicked out of the confederacy on account of them Christians. That's how pushy they are, the Catholics. If I had my wampum belt, I could show you. There's a wampum belt where it tells about two people holding hands with two houses or one house and on the end of the wampum belt there's seven lines on there. Check that out, there's seven lines on it. Everything is symbolic with the wampum belt. When you look and see them seven lines on it, that's where the Catholics wanted to join. That's the seventh one. Each line represented a nation in the confederacy. The wampum tells what happened at that time, what had happened where they wanted to join.

If you study more into that time, it'll show you that the Mohawks were pressured into making a seat for the Christians, and as a result, we come very close to getting kicked out of the confederacy. They forced us to try to make them a seat, and the people wouldn't.

THE LONGHOUSE IS LIKE SACRED GROUND

Now, the Longhouse is a place where all the people meet. It's like a sacred ground. Because you hear people mention sacred grounds, and to me the best way to explain the Longhouse to a lot of people who don't know or don't understand, it's a place where people worship. They come in there for everything, just like other people do in their churches. But we don't consider it a church, because we hold our council meetings there, we have our social activities there, we have our Midwinter festivals there; you know, everything. It's like everything combined ... your political, your sacred things, everything, everything is there.

At one time people had homes where people of certain clans lived in one building. It was a Longhouse. Now we have only one Longhouse because everybody has a house now.

The Longhouse, it is very sacred to us, very sacred. It should be strictly just for the native people. It shouldn't be for the public. 'Cause a lot of the people are there just to observe and see what the Indians are doing. I think that time is very sacred for us.

LEAVING ALL THE BAD FEELINGS OUTSIDE

When we go to the Longhouse, we have to leave all the bad feelings and the bad thoughts and everything outside. We have to clean ourselves and get rid of that. I do that because my Maker and I talk, and I know that's the law of nature with us. Him and I know what I say, and when I talk to my Maker, that is between Him and me. It's not like the Catholic where you can confess your sins and you're forgiven and you can go out and do it again and go back to confession and confess your sins. With us, we don't do that. We leave it behind. When we clean ourselves, that's forever. You don't go out and do it again.

That's why in our society when you get married, you only get married once. It's not right for people to go out and get married and throw their wives or their husbands away and pick up another person. That's not right. You have to make sure you know what you're doing when you do get into things like that. That's the law of nature.

It's all within yourself. You got to always be very sincere. In other words, you have to be sincere in what you do.

Indian ways are so beautiful and people just don't never hear about it.

Most people don't even know what the true meaning of being Indian is. There are universal laws. Generally, the traditional people are following these ways and know what the meaning is. But so many of my own people don't know what the meaning is; they don't even know the meaning of their own ways. They have been misled and misdirected.

Once you have lost your way, it is harder to get back.

KEEPING THE LAND

Here's another thing, too. When you have land ... it's very hard for me to explain. I was raised and brought up as a Christian, and when I became fifteen, I couldn't understand many things. I started going to the Longhouse, and right there and then I started to understand a lot of things, and it was so-o-o right, and the things the Christians told me were too, so mixed up I couldn't understand.

They say when you have land you're not supposed to sell. You don't sell your land; you give to your family or somebody that needs it because if you sell land, that's like selling your mother. You don't do that. So when I got older and I got married and I bought this land in Potsdam, I never could find it in my heart to sell that piece of real estate up there. So I turned around and I gave it to my youngest boy, and I told him, "You don't sell land. You get land, you get property, you never sell. You take care of it. You pass it on to your children. If you don't have children, then you pass it on to somebody else. You have to take care of it just like you would take care of your mother, or your father, or your grandmother, but you don't sell it. You take care of it. But if you have no need for it, then a family member gets it." To me that's sacred. It's very sacred.

MIDWINTER IS LIKE OUR NEW YEAR'S

We have a Midwinter ceremony, Midwinter festival, and it starts sometime in January. It's like our New Year's. It's based on the moon and the stars. People come from all over, from all over the Six Nations. When we have this Midwinter festival it'll hit one week here and hit at another place like Onondaga, then Oneida. It goes around. No two nations have it at the same time.

The Longhouse is an independent place of worship. It's like a church, but it's not a church. It's a place where we all go, the traditional people go, like if we have to bury somebody, have a funeral or something, or when the time comes for our festivals. A lot of times they will not let non-Indians go in there, like when we have our festival, like our Midwinter. Other times they can't go in there, especially when the Hadoui are there. They're the medicine people. They have the False Face Society going on, so non-Indians are not permitted. In fact, when that's going on, once in, go in that building, you cannot come back out. You have to stay till it's over. It's really unbelievable; it's so beautiful. Like when the clan mothers, ah, starting about maybe ten o'clock at night, they start to do the dance. These old ladies, some of them are in their late seventies, they get up and they dance from ten o'clock till about 5:00 or 5:30 in the morning … nonstop. You can't experience anything more beautiful than that.

I first started going to the Longhouse when I was fifteen. My mother used to beat the hell out of me for going there. She used to say, "You're so bad." She says, "You know you're following the longhair people." She called the traditional people "longhair." And she used to put them down. I remember going into the Longhouse and these women with their babies would be in there. And you never hear a child cry in the Longhouse. Never!

The Longhouse never ceases to amaze me, all the things I see and learn in there. It's really something. Once you go there and you keep going there, I can't see anybody ever leaving it.

GRANDMOTHER MOON AND BROTHER SUN

In our society, we don't have a specific god we pay all our attention to, give all our prayers to. We have our grandmother as the moon, our brother is the sun, you know, and so forth and so forth and so forth. Just as in the Greek mythology there's a this and that. Same as in our society. We have the Four Winds. We have Thundermakers.

We also have the little people, too. They're just little people, like the Irish have their leprechauns.

In our society we give thanks to the corn from Mother Earth. We give thanks to Mother Earth for sending us the corn to feed us and to nurture us. And then we give thanks to the beans, too, and the squash. And then we give thanks to the strawberry. The strawberry is a great medicine for women to clean themselves, to cleanse the body.

The non-Indian people believe in God, but we believe in the universe as a god.

Like the sun is our brother. He gives us energy; he gives us life. Then, you have the moon is your grandmother. The earth is your mother. The Indian prayer explains everything. A man should give the prayer. There's legends handed down that says wherever you go where there's Indian people, there's sweet grass growing because that's the hair of the Mother Earth. That's Mother Earth's hair. The sweet grass.

Lorraine Canoe ▾ *Brooklyn*

THE WALLS OF THE MOHAWK LONGHOUSE at Akwesasne in Upstate New York on the U.S.-Canadian border creaked, old rafters swayed, and aging hardwood floors vibrated like the taut skin of a drum as hundreds of feet rose and fell in unison to the ancient rhythmic beats of traditional turtle rattles. Chanting and pounding out the intonations of the Great Feather Dance, seasoned singers repeatedly struck the rattles on the primitive wooden bench in the middle of the great hall. With the shy bride leading the women and the groom proudly guiding the men, the joyful dancers moved with deliberate reverence around the circle, participating in the sacred rite honoring the Creator, assuring His presence, and sanctioning the couple's marriage.

Sitting in the place of the Wolves with other members of her clan, Lorraine Canoe watched intently as the bride and groom moved from one to another, feeding each person in the Longhouse pieces of the wedding cake made of corn bread and strawberries.

At the beginning of the dance, the last rite of the wedding ceremony, the outspoken traditionalist, who lives in Brooklyn, teaches at New York City's Hunter College and sells green vegetables in Manhattan but returns to her house at Akwesasne for summers and ceremonies, became alarmed—non-Indians, without knowing the meaning of the hallowed ritual, had joined the circle of dancers. Lorraine held her peace.

Only an hour earlier Katsi'tsiahawi had turned heads and stirred whispers in the packed-to-capacity white frame Longhouse as she timidly entered through the women's door. Dazzling in her tasseled white buckskin wedding dress, she glowed with the brilliance of a full moon in a clear star-studded night sky. Slowly, with all eyes following her, she demurely made her way through the crowd, meeting her soon-to-be-husband halfway, and with wedding baskets in hand, the two took their seats beside their mothers in front of the assembled chiefs and faithkeepers.

Unhurried, the chiefs' preselected speaker rose and waited patiently for the excitement to settle. Without fanfare and in a gentle voice, barely above a murmur, he acknowledged and greeted all gathered, thanking them for coming. Then, in the ages-old manner of beginning every occasion, he recited from a deep-rooted memory the ancestral Opening Prayer or Thanksgiving Address. After reminding everyone of the beauty and duties of all living things in creation, the presiding elder proclaimed that the marriage ceremony, the oldest continuous instructions from the Creator, was officially opened.

Solemnly he admonished the attentive couple that they made their pledges to one another and to the Creator. Chiefs did not have the power to marry them; they only carried the instructions from the Creator. If they did not follow through on their vows, they would be cheating themselves and the Creator.

The couple exchanged wedding baskets. In the bride's basket were items of clothing signifying her devotion to caring for her husband and children by mending and keeping clean their clothes.

In giving his basket containing the wedding cake, the groom promised his bride he would, for the duration of his life, provide food for her.

Then the speaker placed the wampum, representing the Mohawk nation's sacred fire, first in the hands of the bride, then in the groom's as a symbol of their pledge to the Creator that they had embraced all the instructions and responsibilities of marriage.

BACK IN NEW YORK CITY, Lorraine Canoe's cheerful voice rises above the Saturday blare of customers and other vendors at Union Square's fruit and vegetable market. Smiling broadly, with hands cupped in front of her face and nose puckered to sniff, she explodes, "Arugula! When you pick it up in a bunch and hold it and go like this on your hands and you smell, it's like Chanel Number Five."

In a commanding guttural voice for emphasis, she proclaims, "I'd rather smell arugula than Chanel Number Five."

Having left home as a young woman, much to her mother's displeasure, Lorraine headed away from the security of family to heed the call of adventure beckoning from within and to find much-needed work not available on the reservation. When she landed, drawn by the allure of big city lights, she was in Brooklyn—married and a mother, raising a family with two daughters—where she has been ever since.

THE DANCE IS NOT FOR EVERYBODY

When I saw non-Indian people get up and do that dance, the meaning went out of it. The dance after the wedding is not for everybody, and when I saw white people get up, for me, the meaning went out of it.

I have two daughters. Should they ever get married in the Longhouse, I have friends all over this country—non-Indians, Jewish friends, I have black friends—and they're not coming into the Longhouse at all. No white people, no black people, in the Longhouse. They're not going to sit there to be curious, to learn something to help themselves, no. Because they understand who I am and where I'm coming from and out of respect, they would accept it without getting their feelings hurt. That's what makes them my friends.

Every reservation in this country has a state road going through it, and there's no sign that says everybody's welcome. It's not that everybody's not welcome; everybody has their own way. It's hard, very hard for us to maintain our way if everyone can just come in.

Sometimes when I tell that to non-Indians, it hurts them. Sometimes I can see the water welling up in the eyes. It hurts; it's very painful to them. Some really

want to be a part, but they can't. They have to find their own heritage.

In social dance, the turtle rattles aren't used. Never! So my thought is that if you take out the turtle rattle and sit it on a bench, white people should never be there. Where are we lax in permitting them? I don't like to say anything, because I don't live at Akwesasne twelve months a year, and who the hell is Lorraine Canoe to say anything?

But … I will *never* compromise my tradition, my way of life, my ceremonies for *anyone, nobody,* if I have to die for it. I have to let it be known where I stand.

I will do everything I can to protect the Longhouse from outsiders, and Akwesasne from gamblers, from the Mafia, from influential people that are going to come here and think they can buy anything … our young women, and people who bring drugs for our young people. Now they're going to bring in gambling, and I'm going to sit in my house and hide because of fear? I think of five hundred years of fear of what my people have gone through being displaced from Deerfield, Massachusetts, which is the end of the Mohawk Trail, and to be pushed all the way to the St. Lawrence River, and I'm going to compromise my position, my belief so that we can have some kind of economic development from gambling casinos? *No way in this life* will I permit that to happen to me! Not to my children. And when they tell us in the Great Law to think of our children for seven generations, how can I think of my seven generations in the future if I don't take care of it now or do something that's going to take care of it? I could never compromise it.

If it wasn't enough to be constantly hit by the outside world, some Mohawks are helping to bring disruptions to our way of life. They don't know what they're doing because their mind is so assimilated to the point of, what do they need? Fancy cars? They want to be like those people out there? Well, then, go put casinos out there! A lot of traditional people have gone that way, and it pains me.

IT'S EASY TO GET THINGS TWISTED

It's easy to get things twisted up. The place where I was born, Caughnawaga, has three Longhouses, meaning three factions of Longhouse people. All believing the Great Law. That's twisted. This Great Law is better than the way you do it. So that kind of mentality did not come from within; it came from the outside. The more assimilation, the more divisions. There are still a lot of traditional people among the Mohawks, but where are they?

The reason I left Caughnawaga was political disagreements. Three Longhouses! If I went to this one, those are going to get mad. If I go to that one, those over there are mad. Why have three Longhouses when there's the same Creator, the same Great Law, the same everything? Why have three? They were following what's happening on the outside rather than paying attention to what we're really about.

I said, "I can't live here. How do I practice my traditions? I can't."

Oh, my God. And it's still continuing there. It's not hard to see it.

I miss Caughnawaga. These past couple years, oh, how much I miss Caughnawaga. With all the turmoil, with all the underlying bullshit, I miss it. I miss the people I grew up with, their children. I miss that community,

but I am not the type to side with someone's political ideology to satisfy my needs. I will not compromise. I can't compromise.

When you compromise and you look at yourself in the mirror, you're not going to like what you see.

I went to Akwesasne fourteen years ago. Everybody was pleasant. Kind. Akwesasne was just what I needed. Then what happens? Turmoil. Traditional Mohawks went over the fence! Why did they go over the fence? Gambling! Money!

I Won't Compromise My Tradition

I won't compromise my tradition. A friend of mine's daughter got married four years ago. I didn't see her at all before this wedding. Her mother was a clan mother; why she is not anymore I can't say. I parked outside the Catholic church, and when she got out of the car, I went over and took her wrist, and I pulled her aside. And I said to her, "You're wearing a white dress; you look beautiful; don't go in this building knowing what you know. You have time to change your mind, because once you go in, when are you going to turn around to come back?" She cried, but she went in.

I will not go in the Catholic church. I will not participate in something that destroys our culture. Most of us are baptized, but I renounced the religion, renounced two governments, Canada and the United States, renounced all the teachings of how to conduct my life in those systems.

If we have a Good Mind, a complete Good Mind that we are taught in our instructions, that's what we should live with daily, but other religions want to impose another system on us.

The other religions don't teach us to use the Good Mind; they teach us to adhere to their doctrines. Where's the Good Mind when we get up in the morning? Do we give thanks that we see daylight? Some of us don't.

Do we say, "Damn that rain"? That's not what we are supposed to say. Every day is a good day no matter the weather. There's a reason for thunderstorms. There's a reason for a blizzard. There's no lousy day.

My husband bought me a Sony Walkman. I listen to the water drum on the subway. That's how I keep in touch with my own. I take three subway trains to get from Brooklyn to Hunter College where I teach. When I get into the street, I begin my opening ritual. I give thanks to the people, all the people everywhere, of what they're contributing for this earth to continue, give thanks to the earth, and go on. I finish it on the subway.

Then, at night after my supper, after I do my dishes and cleaning, I do the closing of the day or just say, "I give thanks for having a great day today."

Other religions want to convert and control. We had to live through that. Now it's time to use the Good Mind.

THERE'S A BIG WORLD HERE

Sovereignty. Great word! On a reservation if there are two governments, one tribal elected system and the other traditional, there's no sovereignty. Sovereignty is

when the people agree. All the people. When the three Mohawk clans agree on a decision, that's sovereignty.

When two people disagree, the sovereignty is gone. If you take a team of horses and one horse goes this way and the other that way, you split it, and you can't afford to split. If a person does something that's not correct, you try to raise his consciousness that he shouldn't do this.

When you make a decision, it is not only for yourself but for the people who are connected to you. If you want to disconnect yourself, well, you know, there's a big world here.

You can go off and running, running on your own.

Our duty is to maintain that government that was given to us by that Great Law, to maintain that Great Law.

A WOMAN NEEDS TO BE INDEPENDENT

Growing up I was taught independence. That's a little bit different than sovereignty. My mother brought me up to be independent; then, when I grew up and I wanted to do this, she couldn't say no because of the way she brought me up. So she caught herself in her own web.

A woman on the reservation needs to be independent. She needs to know how to change a tire, how to change the oil, how to do a lot of manual labor, because the men have to travel to find work. Sometimes they're gone a month at a time. Mohawk women have to be mother and father to these children, because there's just no work on reservations. To get jobs, the men have to go someplace else.

Sometimes they don't come back. In the old days if a child came along to a single mother, with no father, that child was absorbed into the family. It had tons of mothers, tons of fathers. Everyone watched out for that child.

KEEPING THE OLD WAY

You never turn your back on your people, never! My grandmother said, "If you go away from here and you work outside, you never buy a house somewhere else, because if you do, you'll never come back. So, never buy a house outside. And don't ever, ever marry a man with white skin."

If one of my daughters goes with a white man, she knows the consequences. Even if she has children, she knows she is exempting them from the heritage of the Hotinonshonni.

And you don't marry within your own clan. You can marry into any other clan, but not your own. When my daughter was fifteen she went to meet somebody in Akwesasne. The first thing I did was ask whether his mother was Wolf. If she was, I told my daughter, "You can't go with him no more."

"Why?"

"He's Wolf. His mother is Wolf Clan. You can't go with him, because if you get involved emotionally, it's a no-no. You cannot marry within your own clan."

As children grow up, you try to give them both systems—the traditional system, the Great Law, the ceremonies, and also you teach them the outside system. They need to know that, too, to survive. All you can do is you guide them. That's what parents are for. There's no way in the world I'm going to let my daughter go just because she's twenty-one. When I let go is when I die. I can't do otherwise. I'm very hard.

SUBMIT TO THE MISSIONARIES

Submit to the missionaries and assimilate us to Christianity was what the church did to us. Still Indian people, all of us, lived traditional lives. The only thing different was they went to church on Sunday. They didn't go to the Longhouse because if you did, you were a pagan, and, ah, it was a shame to dance for religion. What's the shame?! When you dance in ceremony the women dance a shuffle and that shuffle tickles Mother Earth. That's shameful?

Well, I live my traditions, and as loose as some people might think it is with my living in New York, I go to Onondaga for ceremonies. It's my duty. I tell them at school that I'm taking my two children for ten days to go to Midwinter. I tell them, "Christmas is not our holiday; New Year is not our holiday. Ours is in January. If there's anything you can do to help my children catch up with their schoolwork for the ten days, great. But we're going!"

MOTHER WAS A DEVOUT CATHOLIC

My mother was a devout Catholic. I could never change her mind, yet she said to me, "This is the life you choose. This Longhouse. Then, you do it."

I said, "But Ma, we've been living it all our lives. The only difference is that we don't go to our ceremonies."

We talked about the Longhouse before she died. I said jokingly, "And you'd die on taking me to the Longhouse?"

She snapped back, "Don't you dare." She must have been thinking I would take her there for her funeral. So she gave me instructions. I followed them to a T. I paid for five years to have anniversary masses. I did what she told me to do. After five years, it was finished. In our society, we do it differently. Ten days after a death, there's a feast and it's over. It's over. Who does that anymore? We don't even do that much anymore.

WE DON'T HAVE A WORD FOR AUNTS OR UNCLES

My father left us. He couldn't handle it. So my grandmother took charge and told my mother you're coming home. You can't raise children by yourself. You need to have more people to help you. We went back to my grandmother's and her mother was there—my grandmother's mother and my mother and me. Four generations of women under one roof.

And all those other women ... you don't call them aunts ... we don't have a word for aunts or uncle. They're all mothers. And the men are all fathers.

GOING TO THE OUTHOUSE WITH GREAT-GRANDMOTHER

I remember going to the outhouse with my great-grandmother. Two seats are made in the outhouse. One for children, one for adults. So the two of us are sitting there, and the stories she told me! She was born in 1880, so she goes before 1880 with the knowledge handed down from the elders before her. Even the outhouse was for teaching!

We'd sit in that outhouse for a long time. The door is open. There's nobody around. We'd finish. She says, "Now go and run back and bring a washrag; we're going to clean our hands and we're going to pick chokecherries."

I haven't seen a chokecherry tree in forty years. They're gone. You know a bunch of grapes, well this one has little berries on it, not on a stem but a short vine covered with berries no bigger than a green pea, and it has a pit. You put the whole thing in your mouth and close your teeth and pull the stem out. Then you chew it and spit out the pits. Delicious! That's the only kind of grapes I knew as a kid.

We were made to be conscious of all the wonderful things around us, and we were taught to take care of our environment. Take the well where we got our water. The well that my grandmother and her husband built by hand. All of us were raised on that water. Every three years when the water is very low, one of my grandmother's nephews would come, take all the water out, use the brush and clean the stones. Even use an old towel to clean the rocks. And when that water starts to come again, my gosh, you've never tasted ice cold water like that, and we're not in the mountains; it's flat in Caughnawaga. Those are the memories.

USING THE GOOD MIND

How can you teach your children something when you're blowing your mind with alcohol? That's not using a good mind. The children know it. They could be two years old and they're smelling it and they're going to get high too.

Just like we were told, "Don't let no one hold your child who smells of alcohol. Because that child is going to smell it, it's going to go into the stomach. Don't let people come to your home with liquor, with alcohol on their breath. Make a nice excuse. Say, 'I'm going out; I don't have time.'

"Next time they come in the same condition you tell them the same thing. It's got to hit home sometime."

Now there's no alcohol in my house. Many, many people have come to stay with me. Many like wine and would bring it as a gift. I would not allow it to enter my home.

One of my daughter's friends came to pick her up to go somewhere. I looked in the backseat of the car and there was a case of beer. So, I told him, "Back out of this driveway and don't ever come back with any beer, any wine, any alcohol; I don't want it here. If you had a case of soda, I would be skeptical, because what are you going to mix your sodas with? My daughters are not going with you."

INSTRUCTIONS CAN COME FROM DREAMS

Instructions can come from dreams.

Instructions can come from when you're hit with something, maybe like your father's death, losing your job, losing … you know, when you come to that crossroad and you don't know which way to go?

Sometimes that's when you find out where your Instructions are and which path to take.

Then, you step back ten steps and look at the whole picture. That's when you say, "Ah, this is where I'm going, and this is what I'm going to do."

PRACTICING FREEDOM OF SPEECH

Walking into Hunter College and walking into the room with the students already in there frightened the hell out of me, but before I went out from my home … I do my own ceremony in the house that nothing out there's going to conquer me. Nothing! Absolutely nothing! Each semester that finishes I stand at the door and I shake hands with all of them. And this last spring semester a student came to me and she said, "Could I say what I want?"

I said, "From day one, I told you about freedom of speech. You can say whatever the hell you want here."

She says, "You're a real bitch."

But, see, she asked permission to speak freely, and that's what she said to me. Then she says, "But I have never met anyone to be as fair as you are."

That was the best compliment anybody could give me.

WHEN THE PEACEMAKER'S WORK WAS FINISHED

My friend's uncle told us this story of our Peacemaker.

When the Peacemaker's work was finished throughout the confederacy, his closest friend was Ayawentha; in the poem he's called Hiawatha. He said, "I'm going to leave now."

Ayawentha said, "I don't want you to leave. Why don't you stay here? There's so much we both can do."

He says, "No, we've done it all; my work is finished."

"Where're you going?"

"I'm going east."

"Where east?"

"Very far east."

"Can I come with you?"

He said, "No. Your place is here."

This is all oral history.

He said, "When I get where I'm going …"

"Are you ever going to come back?"

The Peacemaker said, "No. But where I'm going, you're going to know when I die."

He says, "How will I know?"

He said, "The tree! When you cut this tree and it bleeds, you know I'm dead."

How many times have people cut maple trees and there's blood coming from the trees? When he went over there, they killed him. They will never, ever live in peace. That's the way we rationalize it. But they will never live in peace.

The Europeans go to every continent to look for what their needs are; they still haven't found it. They should go back and repair what they did. Then they'll find it.

TAKING THE CHILD TO THE RED WILLOW BUSH

We talk about discipline. Traditionally, you go with the child to the bush that grows ... the red willow. Now let's see how much discipline the child has. They cut their own willow branch for the punishment. Take all the leaves off, and it's maybe three feet long, gives it to the parent, and you hit the child three times—no more 'cause any more would be to intentionally hurt the child—and then bring the

willow into the house and put it somewhere, kind of it's there, it's there. And every time they look at it, they know it's there 'cause they cut it; they watch their p's and q's.

One Sunday a little boy was in the Longhouse. When the dance was finished, he's coming back to his mother and running. He's about two and a half. He bumped into someone and fell. His anger was unbearable. He was so angry. His mother took him outside. I don't know where she got the glass of water, but when he wouldn't stop, she threw the glass of water in his face. That's traditional punishment in my culture. He wouldn't stop. She got the second glass of water. That's when I got there. I saw her throw the glass of water. His clothes were sopping wet. She had him by the wrist. I told her, "Let him go."

When she let him go, he carried on, but he's in his own power now. He's doing it by himself. He's on his own now. He's on his own two feet, and he wants to go near her. When he would push his body near her, she pushed him. She heard what I said when I said let him go. She understood it meant to let him work it out. I didn't have to say anything. When that didn't work, he hit her. She grabbed his wrist and smacked his hand. He must have hit her about six times. The clan mother came out and gave her water. She says, "I already hit him twice."

The clan mother said, "Well, a third won't hurt." And she let him have it with the water ... the clan mother.

Then, I said to the boy, "Do you want some more?"

And he stood near the Longhouse crying. He was doing a dance he was so angry. But he didn't have one blessed tear, not one tear. So after we talked, he calmed down.

I asked his mother, I said, "How often does he do that?"

She says, "He's only doing it for a month."

I said, "Where did he get it from? Who did he see do that? What you need to do is go back to where that happened, if you could remember. And when you get there, you talk to him how that person behaves is not the way for you to behave. And it's going to register because what you have in the back of your head is a computer. It's going to register. It may not be conscious for that minute, but it's there, three months, three years."

The thing with children is to remind them of things that are past so they don't forget. There's so much coming at them from every direction—books, the telephone, television, the CDs. Their heads are so full with so much bullshit, they don't think of what it is to live like a human being.

Our Language Honors Women

In Indian the words are female; the words are honoring women; *it's a female language.*

The Spanish language, all the o's are men. It's not like that in our language. The language is female. It's light, it's not harsh, it's not hard. You could scold, in the language, and it doesn't hurt as much. I scold my children in Mohawk because it doesn't sound as hard. In English, it's hard. So what I have learned to do, what I have taught myself, think Indian and come out English.

Think of the Earth and Woman as One and the Same

If I'm pregnant, my husband is pregnant. When I bring that baby home, it's not only me. It's him too. How he treats me is how that baby's going to react.

The men who are brought up to respect women, the men who are brought up to respect the earth as woman, think of the earth and the woman as one and the same, are the real men.

Everything that gives birth is female. When men begin to understand the relationships of the universe that women have always known, the world will begin to change for the better.

Teachings come from the women, all the teachings. All the teachings come from the woman. The devastation of all these governments and all these countries is because they put women down. Put the women down, your place is not going to work. When you honor women, it's going to work. The Bible says honor your mother, right? And how many people believe in the Bible and don't honor their mother?

There's no way I could live with a man who's going to be out there and I don't know what he's doing. By the same token, he knows where I am, what I'm doing, how long I'm going to be doing it, and he doesn't need to call to make sure I'm there. My word is my bond. And the same with him.

I Don't Have to Prove What I Am

I thought it was an accusation the first time I heard that I'm a feminist. No. I don't need to prove to a man how strong I am. I don't need to prove to anybody what I'm capable of. I don't have to prove what I am.

From a little girl, when I was registered for school, my name is Lorraine Canoe. That's my father's name, Canoe, his Anglo name. Good name! I like it! There's no way I'm going to change it. I'm going to die with that. Some women get married and they can't wait to change their name. I don't understand that. I don't

understand women changing their name. I think it's taught. People learn that. They learn that when they get married that they're now Mrs.

Kanaratitake. That's the only thing I want in front of my name, because the name was chosen for me before birth. Nobody else in the Mohawk Nation has this name.

EVERYBODY HAS A ROLE

I did a woman's work at six years old. My brother was only three and my mother went to work, a second job. I took care of my brother. I made sure that we had a snack before we went to bed at eight o'clock, like we were supposed to. Make sure his hands were clean and tend to his needs. I took over her role.

The role of the woman is to take care of children, whether they're yours or they're not. The men provides the food that comes in, the hard labor. But the one pulling the strings is the matriarch of the family. It works. Sometimes you don't like it, but you keep quiet.

We all have what we're supposed to do. It goes way, way back to everyone's roots. Indian and non-Indian. Everybody has a role. When you go and do two roles, the man's role and the woman's role, then you're a dynamite super person.

Women don't need to go to work. If you're going to have a baby, you're pregnant for nine months. The baby's born. The baby's three weeks old, six weeks old, that baby needs you whether you're breast-feeding it or not. That baby needs that mother. That baby needs you until it's five years old. If you're going to deal with that child when it's ten and fifteen, and if you didn't prepare it between birth and five years old, forget it.

If anyone's going to raise my child, it's me. I think Sarah was six and Monica was eight when I went back to work. I budgeted. I went without. But I did it. They're not less for it. I haven't changed. I'm still the strong obnoxious person that I've always been. Stubborn!

LIFE AFTER DEATH

Life after death! I know there is! If I sew with a needle and thread by hand, I'm seeing my grandmother's hands in mine.

When I wash the dishes or do cleaning, I see my mother's hands.

I know what my mother did for me. I see her when I am doing the same things for my daughters.

I didn't cry when my mother died. There was too much to do because we had to go to Montreal to the hospital. I didn't have time and I didn't want to show my children that, that kind of experience to see me cry. The only thing that I said to them was, "My mother is now resting. There's no one that's ever going to upset her, make her angry, hurt ..."

It was over; it was done. But I reserved my crying to when I got back to Brooklyn. And I was really hurting. My husband said, "Lorraine, get your stuff together, go to Caughnawaga; go back in the house and stay there until you get over this. You can't stay like this."

That's when it hurt ... when I got back to Brooklyn ... because there's no way I could pick up the phone and call her. So I went back to Caughnawaga by myself, and I had boarded the windows, you know. I kept the wooden boards on the windows while I was inside. My friend Eleanor said to me, "Why are you staying there? Come and stay here."

HEARING THE DIRT HIT THE CASKET

I'm having a hard time now. My great-grandmother died in January in the dead of cold. Buried through the Catholic Church. Leaving the church, going to the cemetery and standing there, the coffin is lowered, and the men picking up this dirt that had froze and hearing that hit the casket was devastating to me. But that's all the process we go through, including Longhouse; it's not only Catholic. We came

home and ate and drank something hot, and my brother and I used to sit on the top of the stairs to be out of the way of the adults as they talked and we're hearing this. So him and I are up there having a conversation; we're the oldest of the grandchildren. My uncle used to go to Montreal to bring back *Life* magazine and the pages at that time; fifty years ago I'm talking about, that's when Gandhi died, and it showed how they built this altar type. Put his body on the top, and a member of his family lit the fire to be cremated. I knew how to read. And we decided at my great-grandmother's funeral in January that we're going to be cremated. That we're never going to be buried because it was so devastating to us—ice hitting the coffin hard.

My brother never went to the Longhouse. When he died, his instruction was to be cremated. He was cremated. His wife had his ashes. She told me she puts his ashes on the chair and has coffee with him in the morning.

I said, "You made a contract when you married him in the church. Until death do you part. Well, death parted you. He's my next of kin. I want his ashes back in the dirt."

I called my cousin and I said, "Go help her." They got a sweet-grass basket. I said, "Take the cloth from the cupboard, clean dishrag, anything, put it inside the sweet-grass basket, open that can, and pour his ashes in there." They made a hole in my mother's grave and they buried it there. I didn't want his ashes to be having coffee.

So now, this promise I made to my brother about fifty years ago, I'm having trouble now. Will I be cremated if I die in New York? Because if I die here, they're still going to put stuff in my veins … embalmed. So if I'm going to be embalmed, doesn't matter where the hell I am. How are they going to ship me from New York to Akwesasne or Caughnawaga to be buried with my people when my people are supposed to be on consecrated ground? I can't go there. The ground to me is all the same, yes. What am I going to do with my life after death? I'm having trouble with that.

MUSIC

If you want to hear music, the only way you can hear music that's done by man is the water drum, or the turtle rattle. Now, there's other ways to listen to music. Sit outside and listen to the birds sing, argue. They argue, birds argue, and as long as you listen to that you don't need a psychiatrist. You don't need a therapist; you don't need anybody if you listen to the birds.

The other thing you listen to is you sit near the water and listen to the river, 'cause it talks to you. Or listen to the trees. The sound of the leaves and the branches when the wind hits hard and it c-r-a-c-k-s and it comes back. That's music.

THE EARTH IS TELLING US SOMETHING

Maybe the earth is telling us something. How much have we learned from processing uranium and what they use uranium for and how water tables are destroyed to get uranium from the ground? They didn't only do it on this continent. They did it in Africa … to get uranium. It's a destruction.

How well do you respect your environment? The spirit of the water, the air, and all those things is what you need to live … the life that supports you.

The stuff that's leaking into the St. Lawrence River from the Alcoa plant, the river is trying to fix itself. The fishes who go on the bottom to clean it, they're coming up with their bodies upside down, the belly is up. With that kind of sign, they still miss the point of how bad the pollution is. How can these big ships go through here? … I'm afraid to eat the fish; I won't eat the fish from that river. I won't eat seafood, because most of them are scavengers, and what are they eating on the bottom and I'm going to put that in my body? No!

HE TOOK THE COW'S SHIT, PUT IT ON MY FEET

I was playing in the barn and jumped off and I stepped on a rusty nail. It went right through my loafers. That man took a pliers and pulled it out. So, he went and got the water, poured water on my feet, and there was cows in the barn. The cow had just taken a shit. He took some kind of spatula, took the cow's shit, put it on my feet, took his handkerchief and bound my feet, and carried me home. "Don't take that off."

Next morning the hole in my foot was as clean as white paper. It pulled everything out. Everything! Healed in three days. You think kids today would permit that?

The same thing with moss if you get a cut. I remember my mother getting a cut, went to the shed where we keep the wood and found all the cobwebs. Take all the cobwebs, make a little ball, put it on the cut, and bind it. It stops the bleeding instantly. So don't kill the spiders! The web is all medicine. Any spider.

GIFT OF THE WOLVES

I am Wolf. All the Wolf Clan people are speakers. Most Wolf Clan people are talkers.

I did a talk in Rhyne, New York. Afterward I got together with the women. They asked me if there's a chance I could come back and talk to women only. I said, "Sure, I'll come back. Saturday's a good day because everybody don't work."

I proposed we do a talking circle. Only with women. You open it by giving a thanks; then the women decide if it's going to be closed or if it's going to be open—

meaning that when it's finished they can't leave and go talk about it. Now, they decided it was going to be closed. So now, here's women who are going to trust that what they're going to say is going to stay there. And one of the things you have, what I have, is a stick this long and it has four eagle feathers. It was given to me on the Longest Walk. I took that, use it as a Talking Stick. When I'm finished giving instructions, I burn sage. Now, there's no smoking in that room but I burn sage. And then gave it to the one to my right, which means it goes counterclockwise. One of the participants was a nun who was seventy-five years old who has retired. What she talked about … something pertaining to her life. When it was finished, she told me, "Where were you forty years ago when I needed you?"

There was a grandmother, her daughter, and two grandchildren, because I told them it's not limited to just married women; all women. The youngest person in that group was twelve years old. She made everybody cry … the things that she said. Her sister was sobbing.

Many of them wanted to talk but were holding back. I know they were holding back. I could see it in their faces.

The talking circle goes way way back. And AA meetings come from that. That's where it comes from. Sometimes those circles amongst Indian people takes days, because if you end the day … say five o'clock and you're not finished, you resume the next day. It could go on for days.

Non-Indians worry about the time. Indians have the time.

What I found is that women want to talk. It is time for the woman. It is time to talk and set things right, for women to stand up. And when the world honors women, the mothers, and Mother Earth, everyone will be better off.

TIME TO GO PICK BERRIES

My grandmother was the matriarch in our home. She told us, "If you do something and I think it could be better or easier, I'm going to tell, because if I don't, how are you going to learn common sense?"

My grandmother couldn't speak English; my mother was the first generation to speak English; and who's going to label my grandmother illiterate? When I hear somebody say that word *illiterate*, I want to burn 'em. *That makes me so mad*, that English word *illiterate*. My grandmother wasn't illiterate. She was smarter than a Ph.D. person. Much smarter.

So my grandmother would say, "When you get to that point that you don't know where to go, what do you do?"

My grandmother's therapy was she gets the pail, everything ready, makes us go to bed early, and she wakes up at five-thirty in the morning and she says,

"We're going to pick berries."